WHY, WHEN AND HOW TO GO PUBLIC

WHY,

WHEN

AND HOW

TO GO PUBLIC

EDITED BY

G. Scott Hutchison

SENIOR ASSOCIATE EDITOR

HARVARD BUSINESS REVIEW

PRESIDENTS PUBLISHING HOUSE, INC.

NEW YORK, NEW YORK · 1970

Library of Congress Catalog Card No. 70-107393

Copyright 1970 by Presidents Publishing House, Inc.
Printed in the United States of America by
Van Rees Book Composition Company, New York, New York

FIRST PRINTING

Design by Sidney Feinberg

Preface

Many traditional owner-managers of profitable closely held corporations are motivated to "go public." It is the "in" thing to do, and in many cases it can be the right thing to do.

Nevertheless, few areas of decision making offer such owner-managers a greater challenge than doing a first public offering. Requiring as it does a high degree of expertise in planning, evaluation, and coordination, *Why, When and How to Go Public* is an undertaking that encompasses all facets of corporate life, any one of which can be critical to the success or failure of the underwriting.

The purpose of this book is to focus on the important considerations which owner-managers and their staffs must know in order to make an effective transition from private to publicly held corporation. Within these pages, experts in the finance and security markets, legal and accounting professions, and financial public relations cover the essential steps in the going-public process.

From their experience in handling numerous public offerings of corporate securities, these practitioners stake out the advantages, disadvantages, and costs of going public; they consider alternative sources of capital; and they fix the individual roles of what the team of lawyers, accountants, public relations people, and investment bankers can and should do for the private owner-manager who wants to go public. In addition, these experts discuss how the strategy and timing behind an initial security offering can determine its success or failure.

The publication of this book comes at a time when an increasing number of private companies are considering first public offerings of their common stock. Not since a decade ago have so many new equity offerings been registered with the Securities and Exchange Commission in Washington, D.C.

Moreover, the stock market's reaction has been largely favorable. During this time, the bid prices have been consistently higher than the initial offering price. Thus excellent opportunities exist for the owner-managers and major stockholders of closely held corporations that now want to consider going public.

Why, When and How to Go Public is intended to be a guide for the insiders most affected—the owner-managers, major stockholders, directors, legal counselors, and accountants. It discusses weighty policy issues that must be considered by private companies which have the immediate or near-term intention to go public.

The seventeen chapters comprising this volume are based on material presented in a series of informal lectures at executive workshop programs on "Why, When and How to Go Public" held during 1969 by Corporate Seminars, Inc.

Although this book purports to be neither a complete treatment of the complex subject, nor a reflection of the entire content of the particular seminar workshops, it represents today's finest management thinking on some of the more critical and broader aspects of the strategies and techniques of a first public offering.

Corporate Seminars, with headquarters in New York City, is a management education organization which since 1966 has served the executive community by offering in-depth analyses of problem areas of vital interest to corporate policy makers.

I wish to thank Editor Edward C. Bursk of *Harvard Business Review* and Editor Raymond Brady of *Dun's Review* for permission to reproduce articles first published in their magazines. Chapter I, "Public Offerings for Smaller Companies," appeared in the September-October 1968 issue of *Harvard Business Review*, and Chapter 14, "Private Placement: The 'New' Money Game," ran in the February 1969 issue of *Dun's Review*.

I am particularly indebted to Miss Catherine E. Ferrick, who typed the entire manuscript during an extremely busy time, and to Mrs. Diana Lees Tamoshunas, who assisted in the checking of galleys and page proofs.

G. Scott Hutchison
November 1969

Contents

Contents

Contents

WHY, WHEN AND HOW TO GO PUBLIC

Public Offerings for Smaller Companies

In recent years, stockholders of small, closely held companies have increasingly chosen to sell their interests to larger, publicly held companies in order to get a more liquid holding. This has resulted in a fast-paced merger and acquisition momentum that is unparalleled in the history of the United States.

A public offering of part of the stock can often be a better solution, because it permits the owners to retain control of their company and reap the benefits of an increasingly more valuable equity position if the company continues to grow. Moreover, "going public" can sometimes result in getting a higher long-term price than does selling out to a single buyer.

In this chapter, I shall discuss the pros and cons of going public, and also offer some suggestions on establishing a public market and selecting an underwriter for the consideration of

Mr. Sears is President of Sears, Sucsy & Company, Chicago, and formerly Vice President of Glore Forgan, Wm. R. Staats, Inc.

stockholders of privately owned companies who wish to create more liquidity for their investment.

Not Every Firm a Good Bet

There are three main reasons why owners of companies sell their interests to a publicly held corporation or make an offering of a portion of their stock to the public:

1. They desire to diversify and take some of their eggs out of one basket.

2. High federal estate and income taxes force the owners to alter the foundation of their estates so that they can leave their heirs with maximum assets.

3. Because of expanding markets and new technology, many small companies suffer acute growing pains, and need infusions of capital beyond their own resources and the credit available from financial institutions.

The need for working capital was by far the most important motive for a public offering given by 209 presidents of small companies in one survey.[1] The results are shown in *Exhibit I.* A need for operating cash was the impetus behind one third of the stock issues of these companies.

Half the presidents gave corporate financial needs, including working capital, as the primary reasons for their public issues. This is not surprising; we are a technology-oriented society and, as long as one or a very few men can together push the state of the art in any technology, small companies will be formed to capitalize on this ability. Their growth can be rapid, creating acute cash needs.

----

[1] Cited in Solomon J. Flink, *Equity Financing for Small Business* (New York, Simmons-Boardman Publishing Corporation, 1962), p. 87.

2

Exhibit I. Reasons for Going Public Given by 209 Small-Company Presidents

	Percent of Total
To meet company objectives—	
Financial needs:	
Working capital	36.0%
Fixed capital	9.5
Research and development funds	5.7
Investment activity:	
Establish market for later offering by shareholders	9.5
Probable purchase of another firm	3.8
Contemplated merger	2.4
To meet owners' personal considerations—	
Minimize estate taxes	13.4
Resolve personal conflicts	2.4
Provide "nest egg"	4.8
Diversify investments	4.8
Take advantage of a bull market	3.8
Other reasons	3.8

Corporate Criteria

Whatever the motives for making a public offering, success in doing it is limited to companies that meet certain criteria. I shall list three criteria and describe what happens after the offering to a company that fails to meet each one.

The company should have a growth rate higher than its industry if it is to attract investors. Consider the small company that staggers on from year to year showing below-average growth. Since the stock market is mainly a vehicle for capital gains—few investors nowadays buy equities for dividends—the slow-growth or no-growth company soon falls into that vast wasteland of "lost" public issues.

Financing becomes difficult to obtain. Because the company's price/earnings ratio is very low, a great amount of stock would be needed in a subsequent offering to raise even a moderate amount of cash. And when the market price of the stock

3

falls near or below book value, debt financing can be impaired as well. The result is that the company has few of the advantages of the public market.

Owner-managers, accustomed to answering to no one in running their businesses, must be able to adjust to operating in the sometimes uncomfortable spotlight of attention. The creation of a public market brings with it the "financial crowd" of brokers, analysts, auditors, and stockholders. They feel they have a right to be given certain information about the company, and some of them place no reasonable limit on this right. Management can find itself in the annoying position of fielding myriad requests for explanations about actions that previously have gone unquestioned.

When the company's performance is good, management can bask in the applause. But it may not be easy for onetime entrepreneurs to handle critical questions on operations, on executive salaries, or on stock option plans, not to mention explaining a downturn in the business. Often they react to such questions as if they were personal reflections on them. If management is uncomfortable in the spotlight, the result can be strained relationships with the financial community which can cause more harm than the public market does good.

The effect of public disclosure must not be to compromise the company's business. In a case where concealment of profit margins, share of market, and so on, is essential for competitive survival, the required disclosure of these facts by a company issuing a prospectus can spell disaster. This is particularly true for a one-product business. Even with a multiproduct company, however, disclosure of sales by product or by product group—increasingly demanded by government agencies and investors—can affect the company's competitive position.

A public offering is not appropriate for a small company with slow growth, a company whose owner-manager is a prima donna, or a company dependent on a single major, nonproprietary product with a high profit margin and large share of the market.

The proceeds from a public issue of stock can flow to either the company or the selling shareholders, or both. With some investors, there remains a lingering suspicion of an initial offering that mainly benefits the selling shareholders. This stems largely from the "bail out" theory—the idea that management has information on a future downturn for the business. Though this occurrence is rare indeed, the suspicion lingers. A wise management will think twice about proceeding with an initial offering if it will benefit only the principal shareholders' personal interests.

Advantages of Going Public

The advantages of a public offering are not always clear. Small-company owner-managers who are considering selling their interests, or a part of them, generally hold certain beliefs about selling to another company which in my view are erroneous. Let us use the case of "Mr. Jones" who sells his company to "Big, Inc.," a publicly held corporation, to illustrate these largely unfounded beliefs.

Jones believes he should get a price based on as high an earnings multiple as he would have obtained if his company had gone public. But Big, Inc. recognizes that if comparable publicly held companies are selling at 10 times earnings, Jones's lack of a public market should knock down the price a few multiples to 8 or 9 times earnings. In short, Big, Inc. will avoid "giving away" the many expenses it incurs as a publicly owned company, maintaining a market liquid enough to attract Jones. As a rule, the more liquid the buyer's stock, the greater the

5

discount the seller must accept from the buyer's price/earnings multiple.

Jones's contemplated position with Big, Inc., either as an executive or as a consultant, gives him a security that often turns out to be false. Big, Inc. has control after the sale, and Jones's position continues only at the company's pleasure.

Jones's only certain stream of income is from the investments he makes with the cash proceeds of the sale. But if Jones takes Big, Inc. stock in exchange for his with the idea that he will have a "management-free" investment in a marketable stock, he will have traded the uncertainties of running a small business for the vagaries of the market.

Jones may have elected for a private sale because it is supposed to be quicker than a public offering. While the preparation for a new public issue can take as long as a year, a private sale seldom takes less time and can take longer. The initial contact, evaluation, research, investigation, and negotiation all precede a sale. A small company seeking the best deal often goes through this procedure from two to six times before it concludes a satisfactory sale. The duration of the courtship with each prospect is seldom less than three months and often is five or six months, meanwhile draining enormous amounts of top-management time.

On the other hand, entrepreneurs like Jones can find in a public offering a potentially profitable alternative to outright sale of the company. The success of the offering depends on creation of a liquid public market, which takes time and good management of the new issue and the all-important after-market. The time factor poses a greater risk for the company than is present in an outright sale, but the reward can outweigh the risk.

Rising Market Values

In the last few years, the demand for equities has made the public market increasingly attractive to smaller companies. Institutions are putting more of their portfolio resources into seasoned equities, creating a market shortage of them that spurs investing in less-tested issues; mutual funds, feeling an urgency to show "performance," are looking harder for stocks with high growth potential; the sales forces of brokerage firms have grown substantially in size, resulting in pressure to build greater retail volume; and the long economic boom, coupled with inflation, has stirred investor interest in common stocks (which, in bull markets, has caused rampant speculative fever).

That small companies have taken advantage of these conditions is evident from a look at the over-the-counter (OTC) market. Some 10,050 issues were quoted in the National Quotation Bureau's daily listed services as of early last year. This figure compares with 7,930 as of early 1959. That is an average annual growth rate of 3%. But a 1966 study for the National Association of Securities Dealers (NASD) showed that unlisted stocks have declined rapidly in both volume of trading and dollar value compared with volume and total values on the stock exchange.[2] This indicates that the OTC market has become one of the smaller publicly owned companies.

A sample of OTC companies by market value and assets, taken from the Securities and Exchange Commission's study of the securities markets in 1963, supports that conclusion.[3] The results are shown in *Exhibit II*. The companies whose assets totaled less than $1 million, for instance, comprised 23% of the

----

[2] Booz, Allen & Hamilton Inc., *Over the Counter Market Study* (August, 1966).

[3] *Report of the Special Study of the Securities Markets*, 88th Congress, First Session, House Document 95.

Exhibit II. Sample of Issuers of Over-the-Counter Stocks, Classified by Market Value of Outstanding Stock and Amount of Assets

Market Value and Total Assets [in thousands of dollars]	Number and Percent of Issuers		Market Value Cumulative Percent	Number and Percent of Issuers		Amount of Assets Cumulative Percent
	Number	Percent		Number	Percent	
$1-$249	238	14.6%	14.6%	105	6.5%	6.5%
$250-$499	153	9.4	24.0	111	6.9	13.4
$500-$999	229	14.2	38.2	161	10.0	23.4
$1,000-$4,999	449	27.8	66.0	483	29.9	53.3
$5,000-$9,999	166	10.3	76.3	245	15.1	68.4
$10,000 and over	308	19.1	95.4	504	31.1	99.5
Not reported	75	4.6	100.0	9	0.5	100.0
	1,618	100.0%		1,618	100.0%	

total, while those companies whose stock had a market value of less than $1 million made up 38% of the total.

By-Products of a Public Market

Once a small company's stock is in the public domain, and if the company's growth continues at the same rate, the company derives some benefits other than the rising market value of the stock.

Since the advent of stock option plans and high personal income taxes, privately held companies have been at a competitive disadvantage in compensating management, as all executives know. Beyond a certain level, higher cash compensation enriches the tax collector more than the recipient. Because of this, managerial talent has tended to migrate toward companies that offer less heavily taxed compensation through stock option plans. To net an executive the same after-tax income as the option-compensated officer of the publicly held company, the privately held firm must pay him almost twice the amount of cash.

Cash salaries come out of company earnings, while stock option gains are "paid for" by the rising market value. The exercise of options may have a slight effect on earnings per share but none on aggregate earnings. Moreover, one of the better ways to encourage good performance is to make the rewards to an extent depend on how valuable management makes the stock.

Obviously, a company can sell additional stock more easily in an already established market. Another source of financing growth is the increased borrowing capacity which is a result of the public market.

The company has increased its borrowing ability to the extent that lenders use a debt/equity ratio as a guideline. The sale of stock increases paid-in capital and therefore net worth, or book value. Thus, if lenders use book value as a yardstick, borrowing capacity has been enhanced. If the company's stock enjoys a high price/earnings multiple, lenders using market equity value as a guideline will be even more receptive to meeting the company's capital needs.

Moreover, the strict reporting requirements for publicly owned companies give lenders more confidence in their financial statements, resulting in a better reception for their managements. Finally, in addition to having a greater borrowing capacity, management can be more flexible in its borrowing, using the public debt market for both straight and convertible debt. Convertibles, in particular, can help to free management from the shackles of tight money.

Because of the tax laws, sellers are more interested in a tax-free exchange of stock than in a taxable cash transaction. The acquisition business is intensely competitive—a seller's market. So the ability to compete is enhanced by having a marketable stock.

Smaller public companies may even have a certain advantage over large ones in this competition, since they are generally interested in acquisition of smaller companies ignored by many large corporations. I am not making the suggestion that every small private company should go public and then set out to build another Litton empire. But frustration at seeing their suppliers, competitors, and customers acquired has led many small company owners to "sell out" themselves. Creating a public market and using the stock for growth through acquisition can combat this trend.

Even if a small company plans an eventual sale of the assets after it has gone public, the market value of the stock can provide a base for negotiations by establishing a minimum price that the buyer must pay. In that event, assuming that the initial offering and after-market have been handled competently, the final net price to the selling shareholders can be considerably higher than if the stock had been disposed of in some other way.

The first time a company goes to the equity market, great interest is created in it. Customers, suppliers, and competitors treat the company, its products, and its services with a new respect. The reputation of being substantial, which most publicly held companies enjoy, also may enhance consumer acceptance of their products. While it is difficult to tie increased sales to the publicity arising from the market, it seems to do the recipients of this attention no harm.

Broker and Underwriter

In considering whether to go public, and in order to understand better the mechanics of the market, the owner of a small company should be familiar with how the over-the-counter market functions and with the role of the underwriter.

The Float

The buyer of a security wants the market for that security to have sufficient depth and liquidity. He must feel assured that he can buy the desired amount of stock at a price he is willing to pay; and when and if he decides to sell his shares, he will want assurance that he can find a buyer with little delay and sell to him at a fair price. Brokers, of course, make markets in OTC stocks to facilitate these transactions, adding a markup to the price in lieu of a commission.

The market must be capable of handling a volume large enough to cause little or no change in price in each transaction. This is ideal liquidity. Between the ideal and the inability to trade at all are an infinite number of shades of liquidity. In its Special Study of the Securities Markets, the SEC reported on a sampling of the National Quotation Bureau's daily price quotations of OTC stocks (known as "the sheets"), from which it tried to determine what proportion had a liquid market. Over a 10-day period, two or more dealers entered quotations on 161 of the 300 stocks sampled, or less than 54%. By this measure, only about one half of the OTC securities have a reasonably liquid market, since one measure of liquidity is both a bid and an offer on a firm basis from two or more dealers in the sheets. (Since the sheets quote stocks with a degree of national investor interest, there is no telling the extent of liquidity of the thousands of issues traded only locally over the counter, nearly all of which are small companies' securities.)

The liquidity of a small OTC issue depends directly on the amount of stock changing hands—"the float." This is the stock held by short-term investors or speculators that comes into the market regularly (obviously, the stock held by long-term investors seldom comes into the market). The ratio of the float to the total shares outstanding depends on such factors as the type of company the issuer is, its growth potential, and so on.

To understand better the nature of competition in the OTC market, it is helpful to look at the market from the dealer's standpoint. He advertises his willingness to buy and sell for his own account by placing a bid or an offer in the sheets. In doing this, he is in direct competition with other dealers who are in the sheets in the same stock and in potential competition with all dealers who may decide to make a market in that stock.

If the dealer has no competition, he will make the spread between his bid and offer wider, in order to compensate for possible losses from inventory and make his profit equal to what he is gaining from more liquid stock. He will probably also keep his inventory very low, which, with the wide spread, can result in poor liquidity. If the float should increase, more dealers would be attracted to make a market in the stock.

To enable two or more dealers to make a competitive market, the float should be a minimum of 50,000 shares. This is not an absolute figure, but it is difficult to maintain a market if the amount of float declines below that figure. It is a general rule of small OTC markets that the annual trading volume is about three times the float. So, assuming that two dealers are equally sharing a 50,000-share float market, each will trade about 75,000 shares a year and will probably have an average spread of about one fourth to one half of 1% (25 to 50 cents per share). This would be a trading gross profit of $18,750 to $37,500, before expenses and inventory losses, for each.

Selecting an Underwriter

Until about 50 years ago, the underwriting function was the principal source of income for the securities industry. Since that time, firms for which underwriting is a principal source of income have declined to only 1.7% of the total broker-dealer community, according to the 1966 OTC market study for the NASD. The principal activity of 80% of the 2,483 firms reporting was selling existing securities; firms retailing listed and OTC stocks accounted for 45.6%, while 34.4% dealt primarily in mutual funds.

Substantially all the underwriters in this 1.7% are large organizations; it is difficult to name more than a handful of small underwriting firms. So there are very few bases of performance comparison between large and small. *Exhibit III* shows the percentage of new issues that were at or below the offering price one month after the offering, broken down by size of the underwriting firm. It indicates some tendency for a more favorable after-market performance as the size of the underwriting firm increases, but not enough to make a direct correlation between market performance and size.

Exhibit III. Percent of New Issues at or Below Offering Price One Month Later, by Size of Underwriters

Adjusted Net Capital of Underwriters [in thousands of dollars]	Percent
$0-$9.9	33.8%
$10-$24.9	40.9
$25-$49.9	35.3
$50-$99.9	22.7
$100-$499.9	31.2
$500 or more	30.5

Source: Securities and Exchange Commission, Report of the Special Study of the Securities Markets, 88th Congress, First Session, House Document 95.

The typical national underwriting house requires a company to have had at least $750,000 to $1,000,000 in net earnings before it will consider a public offering of the company's stock. A regional house with underwriting capability will generally scale the minimum down to $500,000 or $400,000. This income may be either for the fiscal year completed just prior to the contemplated offering or for the year ending immediately thereafter. In the latter case, it is assumed that there has been a record of earnings growth in previous years.

Many large underwriting firms have a continuing financial advisory relationship with their large clients, but this is not as common in the case of smaller firms. The NASD study attempted to classify these relationships by size of firm. Large firms indicated that they have been the underwriters, if not managing underwriters, of about one third of the issues in which they maintained active trading markets. The firms were asked about other traditional relationships—a directorship, a financial adviser, and past underwriters for the same issuer. Less than 8% of the small firm market makers had had any one

14

of these three relationships, compared with 14% of the medium-sized firms and 43% of the large firms.

Selecting an underwriter is not an easy job. Not only must the issuer make a decision as to the underwriter's technical ability, but he should also try to find an underwriter who is familiar with and understands the issuer's industry. In addition, the underwriter should have the ability, either alone or through correspondent relationships, to distribute the stock in a geographic pattern that closely follows the geography of interest in the stock.

There are very few other business relationships which reflect as much deep mutual understanding as that of the issuer and the underwriter. The Special Study included a statement by one underwriter that expresses well the nature of this relationship:

"We are frequently asked to help new issuers with general problems of a company going public for a first time, such as advising them on the basis of our experience on handling stockholder relations, meetings with the investment community. . . . Related to this, we are a sounding board as to how the financial community and the public generally might react to proposed corporate actions. . . . We advise the company on a broad range of their financial problems, including such matters as the need for new financing, the methods of obtaining new financing, either publicly or privately, dividend policy, the desirability of mergers, acquisitions. . . . We feel a responsibility for seeing to it that an orderly after-market in the security is maintained so that persons who have purchased the issue will be able to liquidate or increase their investments if they desire."

Underwriting remains a very personal business. The "personality" of a firm is directly attributable to the one or two key people in the organization who decide underwriting policy. So

15

a firm's policy on the size, industry, and other criteria of companies which it is willing to underwrite can change as fast as the makeup of the top echelon changes.

Often there are not enough comparable publicly held companies to arrive at a clear-cut determination of the public's interest, the issuer's industry, and an estimate of his potential for growth. Nevertheless, the underwriter must make a judgment. The judgment about public reception is an area where reasonable men can differ. This is particularly the case with small new issues, where public receptivity to the issuer's industry is crucial.

An underwriter may have managed one or more public offerings in the issuer's industry, so he would be a likely prospect. But the underwriter might be precluded from managing another offering in that industry because of conflict of interest. Because of the constantly shifting underwriting marketplace, the best course of action for a small company is to rely on the advice of its auditor, banker, and lawyer in suggesting two or three underwriters. After interviewing them, the company will select one as the managing underwriter.

Preparing the Offering

Making an initial public offering of stock is a complex process. The Appendix at the end of this chapter lists the major functions of an underwriter in preparing for the offering. Some of them are entirely the underwriter's responsibility; in others, he works with lawyers or auditors; and, in this example, the firm is managing the offering in association with other underwriters. If the offering is more involved than the relatively simple one illustrated in the Appendix—presenting tax considerations, for instance—the 40 steps could easily be increased to

100.[4] It has often been said that the underwriter must know his business and understand the issuer's. From this list, some appreciation can be gained of the technical complexity of the underwriting business.

Many questions about the offering naturally will occur to the company's management. For instance, if the underwriting is done by a syndicate, how should the stock be distributed to its members for sale? What is a reasonable gross spread or underwriting commission? How much information should be included in the prospectus? Should the managing underwriter be represented on the board of directors? What part should the company play in determining if the underwriter and other market makers are inventorying enough stock?

Any one of these questions requires far too much detailed analysis to be addressed within the scope of this chapter. Company managers, however, should keep certain points in mind.

The underwriter takes the same civil and criminal risks as the company for the representations made in the prospectus. So he will be careful to make adequate and truthful disclosure. (And in an important recent federal court case, lawyers, outside auditors, and company directors have also been held liable for false information in the prospectus.[5])

The prospectus is by law the underwriter's only permitted selling document. Therefore he will make sure it is well done.

While the terms of an underwriting will vary widely according to the size and industry of the issuer, any aspect of an offering has enough published prior practice so that the underwriter should be able to show why he is making a particular recommendation. Whenever company executives are uneasy

----

[4] For a discussion of the complex subject of taxes, see James R. Wimmer, "Tax Effect of the Privately Held Corporation 'Going Public.'" *TAXES—The Tax Magazine,* December 1967, p. 932.

[5] *Escott v. Barchris Construction Corp.,* 283 F. Supp. 643.

17

on a point, the underwriter should be able and willing to show them sufficient evidence of prior practice for companies of comparable size in the same industry. Enough information is available in any situation so that reasonable men should not differ.

Perhaps the most severe test of the underwriter-issuer relationship comes at the time of pricing the new issue. Although it is not always immediately obvious, the goals of the underwriter and the issuer are the same. Both are concerned that the offering price be sustained in the intermediate and long-term market. But since the long-term market is very difficult to forecast, the responsible underwriter is usually most concerned with pricing for the foreseeable future.

The pricing decision is largely based on comparability. The underwriter is strongly influenced by the price/earnings ratios at which comparable companies are selling in the public market. An issuer can obtain a range of his probable P/E ratio by doing this analysis himself. It should encompass at least 6, but preferably as many as 12 comparable companies; and it should include information on their growth rates, balance sheets, cash flow to earnings ratios, proprietary products, and depth of management. A comparison of this type will show why companies sell at significantly different P/E multiples. It will also show the issuer's management where the company stands relative to its industry.

This comparative "spread" is one of the major tools any underwriter uses for pricing. Since no two companies are alike and no company is exactly like an average, however, the final decision on the P/E ratio must depend on the underwriter's judgment.

Concluding Note

The public market gives the smaller company an opportunity to expand with its own resources.

Not every such company, however, meets the growth, management, and product requirements for success in that market. For the company that does not, a public offering can have a devastating boomerang effect. For those that do, it can bring substantial long-term capital gains. When a small company meets the criteria for a public offering, an outright sale of the stock to another company can be equivalent to selling the horse for the money to buy its feed.

The underwriting fraternity is increasingly recognizing that its customary reluctance to take on small-company public offerings needs reevaluation. Smaller companies will always be more vulnerable than large ones. But the demand for equities, as well as a lack of other suitable vehicles to enable investors to participate in the exploitation of new technology, is lowering the size minimums.

Appendix: Managing Underwriter's Selected Steps in Preparing a New Issue

1. Review SEC rules regarding public statements with company.
2. Decide on financial data to be included.
3. Prepare underwriters' memorandum.
4. If offering to employees or other special persons, determine price, liability for unsubscribed stock, time schedule, subscription and confirmation mechanics.
5. Prepare S-1 registration statement.
6. Decide on form of stock certificate.
7. Obtain indemnity insurance policy, if appropriate.
8. Prepare prospectus.
9. Prepare agreement among underwriters (AAU).
10. Prepare underwriting agreement (UA).

11. Prepare underwriters' questionnaire to make sure they have not recommended the stock.
12. Prepare blue-sky memorandum (preliminary).
13. File registration statement with SEC.
14. Clear proposed underwriters' comfort letter with company's auditors.
15. Advise as to the number of copies of preliminary prospectus ("red herring") necessary.
16. Clear with NASD.
17. Issue invitational letters to prospective underwriters.
18. Determine makeup of underwriting group.
19. Coordinate with syndicate department for any directed sales to officers, other employees, stockholders, or creditors.
20. Compile summary report of the distribution of the red herring and amendments thereto.
21. Furnish own accounting department (for closing) with tentative time schedule, copies of prospectus, AAU, UA, and other pertinent documents.
22. Arrange "due diligence" meetings with company and underwriters.
23. Arrange (with underwriters, company, auditors, sellers, and counsel for underwriters) inspection of company's facilities, time of signings of underwriting agreement, and requested effective date of SEC registration.
24. Prepare memorandum to salesmen.
25. Prepare copy of published announcements and schedule of publications and tentative dates.
26. Determine where offering will be advertised.
27. Clear deficiencies with SEC and revise documents.
28. Send red herring distribution list to SEC.
29. Request SEC acceleration.
30. Establish final terms.
31. Prepare sets of AAU and UA and sign with underwriters and with company (and with selling stockholders, if any).
32. Recheck final prospectus.
33. Release offering for sale on telegraphed receipt of SEC clearance and after confirmation of good standing from state of incorporation of company.

34. Send copies of prospectus to underwriters, selected dealers, financial services, publications, and others.
35. Send copies of agreements to underwriters who gave power of attorney.
36. Decide on closing date with counsel, auditors, transfer agent, and registrars.
37. Advise underwriters and own accounting department as to closing arrangements and stabilization of stock in after-market.
38. Send legal opinions, comfort letter, and other closing papers to underwriters.
39. Take steps to get new issue quoted in newspapers and listed in stock guides.
40. Advise company of its responsibilities after offering.

The Advantages, Disadvantages, and Costs of 'Going Public'

How large should a company be to do an initial public offering of its common stock? What are the advantages and disadvantages of "going public"? What does it cost? What is my company's stock worth? These are the most commonly raised questions by officers, directors, and major stockholders of closely held companies that are considering going public.

The Requirements

There are two fundamental aspects to initial public offerings. One is to raise cash. The other is to create a readily mar-

Mr. Shad is in charge of the Corporate Finance Department of E. F. Hutton & Company Inc., a leading national investment banking and brokerage firm. He is a graduate of the University of Southern California, the Harvard Business School, and the New York University Law School. He has assisted over 50 companies in public and private financings and mergers, and serves a number as a Director.

ketable security—a security which the investing public can buy or sell in reasonable quantity over a reasonable period of time without materially disrupting the market, and which the issuing company can use to raise additional funds and to acquire able executives and physical assets, just as readily as with cash—and often on better terms than with cash. Such a security must enjoy a representative public market—one that is sufficiently broad and active that the price fairly reflects the investment merits of the security relative to comparable investment opportunities.

Therefore, the company must have a sufficient following among stockbrokers and the investing public at large so that if the market price of the security falls below comparable investment opportunities it will attract buyers and be brought back into line.

As a general rule, the minimum size initial offering necessary to establish a representative market is $2 million—typically 200,000 shares at $10 per share. Such an offering might of course only represent a small portion of the issuing company's total shares outstanding following the offering. The balance would continue to be held by the original stockholders. While a small offering, a $2 million issue should result in over 1,000 public stockholders.

National and leading regional underwriting firms should participate with the managing underwriter in the offering in order to assure a broad distribution and the continuing support and sponsorship of the securities by an important segment of the financial community. The offering should not be concentrated in the issuing company's "backyard," for it will not result in a representative market. Further, as the result of the activities of local security dealers and investors, the tendency is for stock to gravitate back to the area where the company is best known. This desirable after-issue market buying support should not be dissipated by saturating the local market on the initial offering.

In order for a company to do a $2 million initial public offering, it must generally have an established position within its industry, clearly defined future prospects, capable management in reasonable depth, and sufficient size and financial resources to assure its continued successful operations in the face of possible economic adversities, competitive pressures, and the normal vicissitudes of business. While there are no arbitrary mathematical standards, such companies will generally have net income after taxes of over $500,000 and a favorable operating experience of at least five years. Of course, the larger and more successful a company, the more suitable it is for public finance; and the larger the offering, the broader the distribution and the more active and representative the after-issue market.

If a company is not large enough to permit a national distribution of its shares, it would be well advised to exhaust alternative sources of finance, rather than do a limited public offering.

Premature public offerings do not result in a representative market, and the high effective costs (typically in excess of 25% of the funds raised) seriously limit the benefits to be derived by the issuer from the offering. Desirable alternative sources of capital may include the sale and leaseback of fixed assets; loans from banks, insurance companies, pension funds, and others; investments by business associates and venture capital groups; and mergers with related operations or companies which are already publicly owned.

Leading investment banking firms assist both large and small companies in raising capital on a private placement basis and in mergers.

Major Advantages

A public offering might consist of:

1. Authorized but unissued shares, for the purpose of providing the company with funds to expand its operations or retire senior obligations.

2. Shares held by the company's existing stockholders, in which case the proceeds would go to such stockholders and not to the company.

3. A combination of both unissued and selling stockholders' shares.

To the Corporation

There are a number of advantages which accrue to a company itself (and therefore to its stockholders) from a public offering and the establishment of a broad public market in the stock.

Additional capital is obtained with which to expand the business or retire senior obligations.

By thus broadening its equity base, a company can generally increase its bank lines of credit and obtain substantial additional funds from other institutional lenders in the form of 10- to 20-year loans—and on better terms than would otherwise be the case. It can also generally obtain better terms on leases, installment purchases, and similar contracts.

Once a representative public market has been established in the common stock of a company which does well over the years, substantial additional capital can generally be raised from the public and institutional investors on increasingly favorable terms, not only in the form of common stock, but also through issuance of bonds, debentures, preferred stocks, and

25

convertible securities. Thus a marketable common stock substantially increases management's financing alternatives—in
terms of both the needs of the business and the class of security
which currently enjoys the most favorable market.

A marketable common stock can also be used directly to
acquire able executives and physical assets just as readily as
with cash—and often on better terms than with cash.

Promising top management candidates can be attracted and
held with qualified stock options. While few medium-size
companies can compete with the nation's largest corporations
on a straight salary basis for able executives and promising top
management candidates, they can compete with qualified stock
options. The profits realized on such options are only subject
to the capital gains tax, rather than the much higher personal
income tax. They provide considerable incentive and afford
one of the most practical means for an executive to build an
estate. An able executive can have a dramatic impact on the
profits of a medium-size company, and as a result, the market value of its stock and his options—whereas such an individual is not likely to have as dramatic an effect on the
profits or market value of a substantially larger corporation.

A company's growth can be materially accelerated through
corporate acquisitions. Other companies can be acquired with
a marketable security through a tax-free exchange of shares.
Few company owners are willing to merge into closely held
companies and accept a nonmarketable minority interest, but
they seldom object to becoming minority stockholders of publicly owned companies.

Going public is also a major step in the corporate growth
process. It enhances a company's prestige and public following.

A company's stock is often purchased by its customers, suppliers, officers, employees, friends, and by business associates
of the management. The interest of these important groups in

a company's profits, products, and continued success is thus significantly stimulated. Public stockholders are also an important element in supporting or opposing legislative and other measures affecting a company.

A public offering permits a company to do a broad national public relations job with important segments of the economy—those dealing with the company directly and indirectly, the financial community, institutional investors, and the investing public at large. Several thousand copies of the company's prospectus are distributed to such individuals and organizations throughout the nation.

A well-prepared prospectus effectively projects a company's image in well-documented facts. It becomes the basic reference document on the company. Statements it contains are incorporated in reports and write-ups on the company by investment firms, financial manuals (*Moody's, Standard & Poor's, Dun & Bradstreet,* etc.), the financial and trade press, and others.

The ready availability of information on publicly owned companies generally results in greater exposure to business opportunities and better press relations and coverage.

To the Stockholders

The advantages to a closely held company's stockholders of a public offering and the establishment of a broad public market in the stock are clear cut.

Many contend that it is not prudent for the owner-managers of a company to have both their capital (as represented by their ownership of the company) and their employment income largely, if not entirely, dependent on the fortunes of a single business. It often makes sense for them to sell a portion of their stock to the public and to invest the proceeds in a widely diversified portfolio of high quality stocks and bonds.

A public market minimizes estate-tax problems on the untimely death of a principal. Such taxes can be met from the proceeds of a prior offering or the sale of a portion of the decedent's shares to the investing public at large, without withdrawing any funds from the business itself.

A public market simplifies appraisal problems in connection with gift and inheritance taxes, mergers, and consolidations.

A public market permits the existing stockholders to sell their shares at the most opportune times in terms of their personal needs, taxes, market conditions, and other considerations.

A public market alleviates minority stockholder problems. When a company is closely held, minority stockholders may at times demand an inordinately high price for their shares and otherwise harass management. Since such negotiations, and sometimes litigation, divert management's time from directing a company's profitable operations, both groups generally benefit from the establishment of a public market in which the minority shareholders can readily sell their shares.

All other things being equal, the mere conversion of a nonmarketable interest into a marketable interest materially enhances its value.

Principal Disadvantages

The major drawbacks of becoming a publicly owned company are likewise quite clear.

Through family trusts, partnerships, multiple corporate and other arrangements, it is sometimes possible for the owner-managers of closely held companies to minimize their personal and corporate income taxes. However, careful analysis often discloses that such measures merely result in temporary deferment, rather than permanent avoidance of taxes. Consequently, this is an area in which owner-managers should proceed with caution so as not to work themselves into unextricable positions which preclude the greater long-term advantages to themselves, members of their families, and their companies of public finance.

Whether closely held or public, a company's management is accountable to its stockholders. If the stockholders of a publicly owned company are dissatisfied, the vast majority merely sell their shares. However, if there is evidence of so-called insider dealings or conflicts of interest, dissident stockholders can bring derivative suits against a company's management. When such actions are brought, they make headlines in the financial press. When they are won by management a year or two later, they are hardly noted by the press, and unfortunately, by then, the damage has been done to the company's public image and investors' confidence. For these reasons all interests of the owner-managers and members of their families which are related to the company's operations must generally be consolidated into the prospective public company prior to the offering.

Publicly owned companies, their officers, directors, and major stockholders become subject to certain reporting, proxy, trading, and other regulations. For example, "controlling" stockholders (within the meaning of the Securities Act) are limited as to the number of shares they can sell on the open market at a given time without registering them with the Securities and Exchange Commission. Also, officers, directors, and individuals who own more than 10% of the outstanding shares of listed companies are required to report their purchases and sales of the stock to the exchange, and they can be required to turn over to the company so-called "short swing profits" (i.e., profits realized through the purchase and sale of the stock within a six-month period).

Closely held companies can be informally directed, whereas

public ownership entails more formal board and stockholder meetings, and annual and interim reports.

Financial and other data must be made public; however, a publicly owned company is not generally required to disclose information which could be used prejudicially against it by its competitors or others.

If over half of a company's shares are sold to the public, the original owners could lose control. However, initial public offerings seldom result in the public holding over half of a company's outstanding common stock; and even if such were the case, the shares sold to the public would be very broadly distributed in small amounts. Many publicly owned companies are effectively controlled by managements which hold a negligible number of the outstanding shares.

A public offering reduces the original stockholders' interest in the company; however, they receive the fair cash value of the shares sold, which can of course be invested in other securities which may enjoy even greater future appreciation in value than the shares sold. Further, a well-conceived public offering should result in the original stockholders retaining a smaller but more marketable interest in a company, with improved prospects. The original stockholders' total net worth should thus be enhanced in value.

The Cost and Offering Price

Generally, the larger an underwriting, the lower the cost when expressed as a percentage of the principal amount of the offering. In the case of initial public offerings of $2 million to $20 million, the discount to the underwriters will generally range between 5% and 10%, depending on the size and nature of the offering, the issuing company's operating record and capital structure, market conditions, and other considerations.

The issuer also incurs legal, printing, and other expenses which vary with the size and nature of the offering. As a general rule, the total expenses to be borne by the issuer, including the underwriting discount, will be from 7% to 12% of the principal amount of such an offering.

The question: *What is my company's stock worth?* is sometimes asked of the investment banker in the course of initial conversations. It can be a bit like asking a doctor for his recommended treatment after he has done little more than take the patient's pulse. Responsible bankers are reluctant to give ill-considered price opinions concerning companies of which they have limited knowledge, for they are alert to the multiple considerations and changing market conditions which determine price, and they do not wish to mislead the issuer by providing too high or low a preliminary indication. However, they will spend considerable time and incur significant expenses carefully appraising a company and its industry in the light of current market conditions in order to provide a considered opinion as to the fair market value of the company's shares.

Corporate Appraisals

Information typically requested in connection with such appraisals includes the history of the business; copies of all available long-form audits; interim financial statements, loan agreements, and other material contracts; the Charter and By-Laws; projections of the balance sheets and operating statements as of the end of the current and following fiscal years; current and historical backlog data; breakdowns of the sales and profits by major product and customer categories; descriptions of the company's major customers, suppliers, and competitors; research and product development programs; expansion, acquisition, and diversification plans; major operating

31

divisions and policies; physical facilities; intercorporate and other material transactions; management compensation, bonus, and profit-sharing arrangements; employee relations and wage scales; contingent liabilities, guarantees, and warranties; the intended application of the proceeds of the financing; and brief biographical sketches on each officer, director, and middle management executive. While all of the foregoing need not be disclosed in the prospectus, it is essentially the information required to prepare the Registration Statement which must be reviewed by the Securities and Exchange Commission before the securities can be offered to the public.

The investment banking firm digests this information, studies the immediate and long-term prospects for the company's industry, visits its plants, interviews its management, makes trade checks, and prepares Comparative Pricing Schedules which include pertinent financial and other data on the issuer and the most comparable publicly owned companies. Key considerations include the relative quality of the various companies' earnings and assets, historical and projected sales and earnings, profit margins, return on invested capital, fixed charges (i.e., debt service and rent) ahead of the common stock, debt-equity relationships, net working capital, net worth and book value per share, and the price/earnings ratios and yields at which comparable securities are currently selling. Such appraisals typically take 30 days. Just as a doctor's advice and treatment are no better than the diagnosis on which they are based, so it is with the investment banker. In the absence of such an appraisal, it is evident that he would not be in a position to propose a sound financing program.

A new issue must compete with existing investment opportunities in a free auction market. In order to assure a successful offering and a favorable after-issue market, initial offerings are priced at a modest discount from the current market prices of the most comparable securities which already enjoy seasoned public markets.

Overpricing Dangers

The market value of a security is a product of investor confidence. Once abused, it is exceedingly difficult to rebuild investor confidence.

In his offering-price discussions with the investment banker, the issuer is in the final analysis "negotiating" the price to be paid, not by the investment banker, but by the company's future stockholders.

If an initial offering is overpriced, it sets in motion a combination of compound factors which have serious long-term consequences and a much more adverse effect on the market's future valuation of the stock than merely the amount by which it was overpriced on the offering.

Depending on market conditions and other considerations, 10% to 20% of the shares purchased on initial offerings are typically sold within a matter of weeks. If the market is not sufficiently broad and strong to absorb such selling at or above the issue price, the stock will go to a discount. This attracts additional selling from individuals who would otherwise have been long-term investors. Further, if the stock is selling much below the issue price as the year-end approaches, it attracts still greater selling from individuals who wish to establish tax losses to offset gains. Initial tax-loss selling attracts additional tax-loss selling.

Finally, when and if the stock recovers to the issue price level, many of the individuals who have held on become sellers when they see the opportunity to get out even. Consequently, there is a considerable supply of stock at the issue-price level which has to be absorbed before the stock can move higher.

33

As a consequence of such progressive selling and the supply at the issue-price level, the stock will establish a low market valuation (i.e., price/earnings ratio), relative to comparable investment opportunities, during its crucial seasoning period—the year following the offering. Once a stock has established a low relative valuation, it takes years of above-average performance by the company to improve its relative valuation. Consequently, the lower prices realized by the company in the event of mergers or subsequent offerings, and by the original stockholders when they sell a portion of their retained shares, can offset many times over the advantage gained by overpricing the stock on the initial offering.

This is not to say a new issue must go up, for security markets are of course subject to fluctuation, but if the financing was soundly conceived and executed, the stock will not go down more than comparable investment opportunities.

The foregoing merely assumes the issue was overpriced on its merits. If it develops following the offering that material adverse considerations were not adequately disclosed or that the company strained to report maximum earnings in the prospectus in order to obtain the highest possible price on the offering, the reaction in the price of the stock and demoralization of the after-market will be even more severe—not to mention exposure of the issuer to suits by the Securities and Exchange Commission and recision suits by stockholders.

After-Market Support

As indicated earlier, up to 20% of the shares purchased on initial offerings are typically sold within a matter of weeks. If it appears that the market may not be sufficiently broad and strong to absorb such selling at or above the issue price, responsible managing underwriters will attempt to establish a short position on the offering. For example, if the offering consists of 400,000 shares, the underwriters may attempt to sell 420,000 shares, with a view to buying back the extra 20,000 shares in the after-market. Ideally, the underwriters expect to incur a modest loss on the short position, for this will mean the issue was neither significantly underpriced nor overpriced on the offering.

Further, if the stock is traded over the counter following the offering, responsible managing underwriters will continue to make the primary market in the stock until it is listed on an exchange. Their objective is to maintain an orderly market. Therefore, if the buy or sell orders from the public do not pair off at any given moment, they will buy or sell stock for their own account and gradually raise or lower the bid and asked prices to a level at which the public's orders are in equilibrium.

The managing underwriter should also keep the financial community and investing public informed of a company's progress through research reports and releases. This does not mean indiscriminately recommending purchase of the stock regardless of its merits, but it does mean appraising current developments in the light of the price of the stock and recommending its purchase if it is more reasonably priced than comparable investment opportunities.

Continuing Relationship

Leading investment banking firms would not be interested in handling a company's initial public offering but for the prospect of establishing a continuing relationship with the issuer. However, they do not request the right of first refusal to handle a company's subsequent public offerings, for the essence of their relationship with corporate clients is mutual confidence.

A contractual relationship will not suffice in the absence of such confidence.

Investment bankers are in a position to make both an immediate and a continuing contribution to their corporate clients, particularly in such areas as after-issue market support and sponsorship, financial planning, mergers, corporate acquisitions, expansion and diversification plans, dividend, stock option and pension plans, Board and top management candidates, annual and interim reports to stockholders, bank and term loans, and listing the stock on a national securities exchange.

With able management direction and sound financial planning, one material variable in the business equation—that of the availability of increasing quantities of capital on attractive terms—can be significantly reduced.

Floor Discussion

Question: Going back to your $2 million net worth example and, say, perhaps $500,000 annual earnings after taxes, what would be typical as to the amount underwritten? What would happen to the original owners' stock? And what might be expected in the after-market?

Shad: You mention $500,000 after taxes. Let's assume that it's a company in an industry that is selling in the area of 15 times earnings. That would be placing a value on this business of $7.5 million. We recommend holding that initial public offering to a minimum because it should be—this is a sort of reverse way to say it—the most expensive financing that company ever does. If the company does well thereafter, the stock should become more and more valuable. As a consequence, fewer shares could be sold for the same dollar amounts as time went on.

Since the after-market is a direct function of the size of the offering and the nature of the business, initial public offerings rarely go above 40% of the shares to be outstanding following the offer. Thus, in our company example, 40% of $7.5 million would be a $3 million initial public offering. At this point, the owners of the business would receive the net proceeds less cost, say, of roughly 10% or 11% including printing, legal fees, and so forth, and still retain 60% of the business.

Question: What part does the net worth play in the price of the stock?

Shad: Net worth does enter into the picture, but it is a secondary consideration in the pricing of a new issue. Analysts and underwriters do look at the net worth as an area of possible downside protection in pricing the security. In today's market, few securities sell at or below book value—that is, net worth per share. More often, companies come to market at 3, 4, or 5 times their book values per share, depending on the circumstances.

So even though the pricing of new issues is heavily weighted on the price/earnings multiple, it would be a rare situation in which a company would go public, say, at 10 times its book value. It would be quite extraordinary that it was earning such a high rate of return on such modest equity capital that you would get up to that kind of a multiple relative to the book value. Nevertheless, net worth is a secondary consideration.

Question: The public investors will be buying on the basis of what they think the business will do, but the owners are selling on the basis of what it has done in the past. Doesn't it then become a reflection of how much their own individual net worth has increased?

Shad: In closely held companies, the book value is often regarded as the hard value or the accumulated worth of the business. But rarely will it correspond, for instance, with replacement value, liquidation value, or market value. A security seldom sells at book value. It will generally sell either above or below, and most do sell above.

Question: Is that based on the multiple used for that particular industry at the time of the offering?

Shad: Yes, it is. Ideally, it is related to companies of the same size and comparable records in the same industry, but rarely do you find identically comparable situations. Every company is different, unfortunately.

Question: Isn't there always some stipulation put on the owners as to when they can sell their stock after it has been issued?

Shad: As a general rule, the managing underwriter will rarely insist on a limitation on the marketability or on the interest of the people who own the business. The reason is that the SEC does it. For example, if the owners wanted to sell any appreciable amount of the 60% outside of the 1% rule, they would have to fully register, and again fully disclose. Naturally, the market is going to react to it, especially if the implication is very strong that the people who know the business best feel this is the time to be liquidating their interests.

Question: Just how much of a disadvantage is it to have outstanding stock options in a closely held corporation considering going public?

Shad: It's not a serious disadvantage. As a rule of thumb, we don't like to see in a prospectus—whether it's an initial public offering or an existing company—options equal to or greater than 10% of the shares to be outstanding following the offering.

This is, in fact, a high percentage. Studies show that publicly owned companies, have significantly less than 10%. But we can run into situations in companies in the $350,000 to $500,000 after-tax bracket where there is an unusually large number of options out. You try to trade them off by recapitalization and get them down to a little under 10%.

38

Question: You say less than 10% would be a good rule of thumb. Is that of a new structure or an old one?

Shad: If it is a primary offering where the company is selling additional shares, include 10% of those to be outstanding, as well as the shares already outstanding.

Question: What has been the effect on labor negotiations where the information on profit, salaries, and so forth, has been publicized?

Shad: I have personally had no direct experience with it, but it has been very emphatically pointed out to us in some conversations that the unions are tough enough to deal with, and in going public you are handing them a prospectus with all of your intimate financial details. However, in my experience of having done about 50 public offerings, I can't recall a single one that precluded our doing a public offering because the company said, "Gee, it's just too big a problem."

We have had problems where the public offerings have had to be delayed because of renegotiations of contracts in process right then—which might result in a strike or in a substantial increase in labor costs—until those uncertainties were resolved.

Question: What are the disadvantages or the hazards of a premature public offering?

Shad: The most important one is not getting what you pay for—and by that I mean not getting a representative after-market because of the small size. Moreover, the cost to get an underwriter to do a distribution is usually 20% or more of the principal amount of the offering, as opposed to less than half of that being characteristic of appropriate offerings.

In addition, there are all kinds of conditions hanging on the situation—rights of first refusal, board representation, consulting fees, cheap stock, options, and warrants—which, if you were to figure out the effective cost of them, would just be prohibitive. You are really giving away far too much to go public prematurely.

Question: In your opinion do you feel that regional offerings initially would be detrimental to doing a national public offering at a later date?

Shad: In this general area of premature public offerings, which would include regional offerings, it can be a very serious inhibitor. There are always exceptions when you start to generalize. There are real risks in doing offerings that do not result in a representative after-market.

For instance, let us assume in a regional offering that there is a lot of enthusiasm for this company within the community and, then, a year or two later the company does want to do a much broader distribution of its shares and go national.

The problem, if the stock is selling at a high price relative to competitive investment opportunities, is it can't be brought out because its market value is overvalued relative to the nationally owned securities.

As a consequence, those people who have been buying the stock at, let's say, $30 a share will be very unhappy if the company does a national offering at $20 a share.

The other side of the risk in this area of premature regional type offerings is that if your stock is selling low, you can seldom go public at a higher price than the latest trading in your stock. This can really inhibit your ability to get fair value.

Many of the regional offerings are essentially done by one or two firms, and you are totally dependent on their making a market in the stock.

Question: What is the minimum percentage that should be offered in either a primary or secondary offering?

Shad: The answer is there is no minimum.

Question: What is the recommended minimum?

Shad: There is no recommended minimum. If a company

were of sufficient size to permit it to go public with only the distribution of a 1% interest, we would then recommend liquidity. The kind of sponsorship and the size of the underwriting group that is going to continue to put out research reports and bulletins, and to keep the public informed about a company, happen to be a direct product of the size and nature of the offering. And so every dollar you increase the size of the offering by, the better is your distribution and the more representative is your after-market.

Question: Since there is such a variety of considerations in determining what a stock is worth, do you, as an investment banker, rate these various considerations on some kind of a system, or is it a sixth sense that you use in pulling these all together?

Shad: I have never heard of anyone who tried to reduce this to a formula. By far the greatest weight that is placed in valuing a security is on the growth of company earnings.

The next area, then, is the multiple you put on those earnings, and all other things being equal—which they never are, of course—the higher the growth rate on relatively competitive investment opportunities, the higher the multiple.

Another fundamental consideration in trying to put a price on a security is the projection. This, naturally, is getting into the future and involves a great deal of uncertainty the further out you go. In some businesses, you can have a high degree of confidence in the projections; in others, the nature of the business is very speculative.

Question: How long a period are you talking about when you say that you put a lot of weight on the growth of earnings? Are you suggesting that possibly you need the entire history of the company?

Shad: You do look at the whole history because of the cyclical aspect of the business, and the overall growth and

41

profitability. But the tendency is to put the greatest weight on the most recent years. In other words, greater weight on the latest year, and diminish it as you go further back.

There is one qualification: if you see a relatively flat growth record, say the company has been running along at a 5% or 10% compound annual growth rate, and the year in which you are going public it is up 50%. That is quite a red flag. It looks like all the seams have been let out.

Question: When you say "growth rate," what if you have a company that is tied to a commodity so that the company may be growing in sales but the national commodity drops down and earnings go down for a year's time. What impression does the public get from this?

Shad: It would command a much lower multiple than a company that wasn't as dependent on such things. That is the risk of the business.

Question: Would you then recommend that the company back off at the moment?

Shad: When you get down to the wire, let's assume the company is simply not willing to go ahead with the offering at the price that it appears will be necessary in order to have a successful offering and a favorable after-market. In this case, there are essentially three alternatives:

First is obviously to reduce the price, but to lower the price may not be acceptable.

Second is to reduce the size of the offering, but that is usually undesirable because it's interpreted as a serious sign of weakness.

Third is to delay the offering itself. You can wait for market conditions to improve to a point where the price will satisfy both the underwriter and the issuer.

However, a delay for very long can be a problem, because if it gets much beyond a couple of weeks the indications of orders your brokers have will start to fade. Their clients will begin to invest their money in other opportunities. Rewarming the deal once it has come up to the wire and then cooled off is such a difficult job. You might as well just withdraw it, pull back for a matter of a few months, and then update your financials and come back in again.

How Investment Bankers
Appraise Corporations

In helping a corporation in the planning process that leads to an initial public offering, it is vital for us to have a complete understanding of that particular business. By "us," I mean the investment banker or the investment banking community. You might wonder why we need to have that kind of information or understanding. There are certain fundamental reasons.

First, we have to make a decision as to whether or not the security of the company we contemplate underwriting is one that we can recommend to our clients as an attractive purchase which meets our own high standards. In this role, we are performing, if you will, the same kind of function that an analyst performs in writing a basic research report on a company.

Second, we have to know the company and its intimate details well in order to make a judgment on the price of the

---

Mr. Symington is Partner and head of the Corporate Underwriting Group for the investment banking firm of G. H. Walker & Co.

security. The price is determined by company factors on the one hand, and by market factors on the other.

Any investment banker worth his salt does a lot more than just handle the public offering, sell it, and forget the company. He is in the business of financial planning. He works with the owners on a consulting basis for a continuous period of time, advising them on alternative sources of capital before they go public, and advising them on mergers, acquisitions, private placements, and so on, once they are public. He is continually exposed, for example, to opportunities for deals after they have gone public, and he has to know what the owners are interested in if he is going to be of much help to them in this endeavor.

Finally, we are charged with the legal responsibility of exercising what is known as "due diligence" with respect to disclosure of information that might tend to affect the price of a publicly marketed security. If we have not exercised due diligence, any purchaser of the stock at the offering or later, in relying on the prospectus, has a claim against us for recision of his sale.

A recent law suit gives an example of the extent of the inquiry an underwriter must make to satisfy this legal requirement. This is the so-called *Barchris* case, involving a company that had a convertible bond offering in the spring of 1962, just before the stock market took a disastrous decline and the new issue market really evaporated.

The bonds were offered at $100; they traded at a very modest premium, and then, subsequently, traded as low as $30 or $35 a bond.

One of the bondholders of the new issue brought a class action for all purchasers alleging material misrepresentations in the prospectus. He advertised in the newspaper that anybody who had bought this bond could join in the lawsuit, and a substantial number of the purchasers of the offering did.

The underwriters, accountants, lawyers, and the company officers and directors were held not to have exercised due diligence in that issue. One of the examples given in the case of lack of due diligence by the underwriters involved the perusal of the minute books by the underwriters' attorney.

He went carefully through the minute books, which is not the most exciting job in the world, and noted that the minutes of one meeting held early in 1962, just before the company went public, were missing. He was told that they were in the process of being prepared, and that as soon as they were available he would have them. However, in the pressure of putting the convertible bond offering together, he forgot to follow up on that request.

When the judge read those particular minutes later, he stated that they would have led to a line of inquiry which would have shown that Barchris's customers were having credit problems. Accordingly, the judge ruled that the attorney's failure to follow up on his request, and thus the underwriters' failure to ask the subsequent questions, was an example of their failure to exercise due diligence.

Essential Steps

Perhaps the best way to illustrate how we get to know a company well is to describe the steps we take once we have started to talk to a company about the possibility of going public.

Exploratory Meeting

The first thing that normally happens is an exploratory session in which representatives of both parties trade information.

On the one hand, the managers will basically describe their company's history, products, growth, and philosophy of doing business. They will also discuss, very roughly, their financial figures—both in the immediate past and what they think they will be doing over the next couple of years.

On the other hand, and I cannot emphasize this strongly enough, the managers should have no reluctance in asking the investment banker's representatives a lot of questions about their operations. It gives me qualms a lot of times. We meet with the company managers, and they have obviously built a terrific business. We are sitting down with them, and after about ten minutes we are getting into the most intimate details possible.

The purpose of this meeting is to determine whether the company is the type that could be of interest to the underwriter and to allow the company to judge the capability of the people it is dealing with in the underwriting firm.

After this meeting, there is an agreement in principle as to whether the company representatives want us to work with them further in deciding whether we can do an offering; and, if we can, the price at which we should do it. We will ask them either to send to us, or to leave with us, audited statements for the past five years, or whatever statements they have such as balance sheets, income figures, product brochures, and company history.

In regard to audited statements, we are often asked whether it is important for a company going public for the first time to have one of the leading national firms as its public accountant to certify the financial statements in the registration.

There is no question that, all things being equal, it is better —but not mandatory—if the accounting firm is one of the so-called "big eight." There are several valid reasons for this.

First, an accounting statement is, after all, an opinion. People are more likely to rely on, and to have confidence in, the opinions of people they know.

Second, it is generally true that a large accounting firm has had more experience in handling a public offering. Believe me, there is nothing more frustrating than working on a registration statement with an accountant who has never done one before. It is time-consuming, and therefore expensive both for the company and for the underwriters.

Third, the company is much more likely to have an easier time in attracting higher quality underwriting firms if it has a leading accounting firm as the auditor of its statements. Again, there is no blanket rule that says the company should have a member of the "big eight." But, all things being equal, it is better.

Executive Discussions

After the initial exploratory session with the company representatives, we will review the corporate material left with us. Then we will visit the company for one or two days. The first session is normally with the chief executive, and we will try to get from him a good understanding of the framework of his organization.

For example, what does he want to do with the company? Has he really thought through a five-year growth plan? If he has not done this, does he still have a real feeling as to the different factors affecting his industry? Is he doing the new things that are required for his company to get ahead in his industry? What are his thoughts in terms of his employees and middle managers? How important does he view them? What kind of incentive system has he set up in order to keep them motivated in doing the best possible job for him and the company?

48

We will then spend the better part of the day with the chief financial officer, getting a thorough understanding of the way the auditors keep the books. Do they compute their inventories on a LIFO basis? Do they utilize accelerated depreciation? What is their philosophy on capitalizing expenses? We ask all kinds of questions like this so that later, when we are making a comparative analysis with other companies, we will have a feel for the quality of this company's earnings.

Of course, one thing we want to make absolutely certain of is that the income is stated on a consistent basis for each period throughout the five-year period we are investigating. If there has been a change in the way the company accounts for depreciation, for example, we want to understand the reasons for it.

Sometimes we work on a company and we see that it has earned 60¢ a share, 50¢ a share, 63¢ a share, and then 85¢ a share. We want to make sure that the 85¢ a share has been computed on the same kind of basis as the earnings for the prior periods, and that the auditors did not hold back some expenses or artificially increase shipments.

We will take a very careful look at the company's margin of profit. If it is too high, I think that some of us tend to worry about it more than if it is too low.

Is it going to tend to attract competition? Are the owners holding back on research and development? Do they have flexibility in pricing their goods?

It goes without saying that at the time of the preparation of the prospectus these kinds of facts have to be disclosed.

The area of financial control is very important, especially in the kind of market environment that we are operating in now. There is so much emphasis on growth, and all managers want their particular business to expand. It is a very meaningful part of the evaluation of a company to determine whether or not management can retain control over it as expansion continues. For example, if the owners are in the retail business, are they possibly going to lose control of inventory on their existing stores as they open new ones?

Middle Management Interviews

We will want to talk with the key department heads in the company. Particularly important will be the sales people. We will investigate carefully how they do their selling. Do they use manufacturers' representatives? Do they have their own sales force? If they sell through manufacturers' representatives, how do they keep them motivated to handle just their company's products? How do they motivate their own salesmen? What is the average age of the salesmen? What are their average earnings?

In talking with the production people, we will try to get a real understanding as to whether unique production capabilities or facilities are required. If so, do they have them? Do they depend on raw materials that are hard to get?

We will spend time with the younger management of a company, especially in a smaller company going public for the first time. What is this second layer of management like? Do the managers have a stake in the company? Would they stay if the company were to go public?

A most difficult thing to appraise, especially in an era like the one we are in today, is a company's research and development capability. This is getting more and more important in trying to evaluate so many so-called promotional offerings. Really, the only thing that distinguishes one company in this area from another is the strength of its technological research capabilities.

We will go into the labor situation in some detail. If the

company is not unionized, we will want to know why, and whether the managers think unionization is a possibility. Is there a chance that this is an area where costs will be going up? If you can show me one where labor costs are going to go down, I think you will see a pretty good multiple.

Another area becoming more and more sensitive is that of projections, talking about the future. We will spend a lot of time talking with the president, the financial people, and the younger management about this to make sure that they are all keyed into the same kind of growth plan. We will not only want to know their thinking in terms of growth of sales and earnings, but to understand in depth the basis for their thinking.

They understand, as well as we do, that those figures cannot be used in selling the security, although we can discuss them with potential underwriters when inviting them to participate in the syndicate.

From the point of view of the managing underwriter, it is critical for him to have a thorough understanding of what the owners think they are going to be doing in the future. This is a very important aspect of what we have to know about the company that is planning to go public.

Along these lines, I recall one company we were working with in planning a public offering that was represented by a special counsel who had formerly been associated with the Securities and Exchange Commission. When we brought up the subject of the company's growth plans, he told us that under no circumstances could the company talk to anybody—not even the managing underwriter—about those projections. We patiently explained how we were used to handling such inside information, and the mechanics we had within our shop for making certain we did not violate the rules of the *Texas Gulf* case or the more recent *Merrill Lynch* case. But he still would not allow the owners to talk about them with us. Because of this position we had to terminate further discussions.

Insider Relationships

We will also look carefully into the question of a company's insider relationships. This is important, not necessarily from the point of view of having to alter all of them, but certainly the underwriter has to know them thoroughly since they have to be fully disclosed in the prospectus. All things being equal, it is best to get rid of them if possible.

Certainly, the owner-managers have to get rid of all things in the area of personal expenses that have been paid for by the company: fishing yachts, cars, vacations in Europe, etc.

On the other hand, if there is a longstanding relationship with an entity that happens to be owned by the management of the company, at a cost comparable with what the company could secure elsewhere, we would often not insist on terminating the relationship before the company goes public.

There are many companies that have relationships between the officers or employees and the company that cannot be continued after going public. For example, we have often found that, particularly in smaller companies, the stockholders have guaranteed loans to banks. This kind of thing must be changed, because a publicly owned company has to stand on its own feet. Similarly, in many private companies there are loans for a variety of reasons from the company to the top officers. This, of course, also has to be stopped.

Trade Checks

The last essential step of our appraisal consists of the so-called trade checks. We will work out an arrangement with the owner-managers on exactly how this should best be handled. In other words, we would never call up the company's principal supplier and say, "Company X is thinking of going public. They have talked to us about being their managing underwriter. What do you think of them?"

Trade checks are done on a much more subtle and sophisticated basis. The people who are contacted never know why they are being questioned about a certain company, and they often do not know that an investment banker is looking for information. By the way, one of the best sources of a company's reputation in its industry is the competition.

Key Questions

You might be interested in my description of what have been some key questions, as far as we were concerned, in appraising corporations.

In one case, we did an offering for a leading national toy manufacturer in which we spent a great deal of time evaluating how much of the company's sales came from so-called stable items such as games, as distinguished from new toys that could be a fad such as a hula hoop. We tried to find out what percentage of their sales came from stable items, and whether that was a growing percentage. This, to us, was a very important part of the question of exactly how even-keeled this company's business was.

Whenever you are dealing with a family-owned company, you are in the very ticklish area of evaluating the capabilities of the second generation. Are the owner-managers really interested in the future growth of their company? If they are, do they have the management skills to carry it through? If the second generation is not up to managing the company, has the company faced up to this problem by bringing along professional help?

In rapidly expanding discount chains, a key question has to be whether management has kept control over the existing business as new stores are opened. It is human nature to spend more time with the new things you are doing. We have to make sure that systems are set up so people have control over what has been so successful in the past. They will have to know which stores are profitable and which ones are growing.

In service companies, quite often the key question is whether the people who are utilizing the company's services are loyal to the company, or whether they are loyal to the particular salesman.

If the salesman left, would he take the business with him? This, then, leads to the question of how likely is the salesman to leave. And that, in turn, gets into the question of judgment of his compensation and fringe-benefit program.

My basic theme in this process of appraising companies is that the figures are only a starting point. They are the basis for asking questions to be sure we have as good an understanding as possible of the company and its industry. If we do not have an in-depth understanding, we cannot give the continued service expected of us.

Floor Discussion

Question: A great deal of stress has been laid on the necessity of having a well-known accounting firm give a certified audit. Would you care to comment on the need for having financial connections with well-known banking-financial institutions as well?

Symington: Are you referring to commercial banking relationships, as opposed to investment banking relationships?

Question: That is right. Is that any factor?

Symington: The answer to your question is that you should be very careful about these relationships and deal with the highest quality people you can. But, obviously, a company is going to deal with bankers in its own area. For example, there is no reason for the owners of a Chicago company to feel they have to deal with a well-known bank in New York City. There are extremely good local bankers, and there is no real problem if you have established a good relationship with them.

Question: You spoke about insider relationships and the complete disclosure that is necessary. Could you give us an example or two of what you mean by "insider relationships"?

Symington: I would say the most prevalent one is where a company leases a building from a corporation owned by the management of the company, or actually owned by the individuals of the company.

Oftentimes, you will have companies that will work out sale-leaseback arrangements with people who are affiliated with the company.

Question: How close is the relationship between the competitive underwriters?

Symington: It is not all that close. There is no more competitive business than our business. I think we tend to know our competitors a little better than is true in some other businesses.

We are all very careful in terms of how we handle inside information. We also have been, from a professional point of view, very strict; and that responsibility has I think been strengthened by recent legal cases.

We, for example—and all the investment banking firms that we do business with—have put in not only strict rules, but procedures to assure that those rules are followed out in the handling of intimate information about companies.

Pricing the Company's New Issue

There has been in the last year or two a market with a rich appetite for new equity issues with no prior public market. As a result, there has been a backlog of registrations filed with the Securities and Exchange Commission, a tendency toward high initial offering prices and, in many cases, significant after-market premiums.

I think you should realize that the frequent development of an after-market premium is not necessarily indicative of the price at which the offering could have been sold initially. There is a tendency for the stock to appreciate in the after-market because fewer and fewer shares are actually being traded, and the interest that has developed frequently provides support for the stock.

Mr. Calhoun is Vice President of Smith, Barney & Co. Incorporated, a leading investment banking firm. He specializes in finance and in acquisitions and mergers.

Pricing Variables

In setting the price of a company's new issue, I believe the investment banker is obligated to make a fair and equitable evaluation of the company; accordingly, he must concern himself with a number of variables, especially the size of the company, its history, and its expected future, both short- and long-term. Of great importance are the quarterly earnings record and projections between one year and the next.

In this connection, I recall a case where the representatives of a commercial bank took us to visit the owner-managers of a certain company. The corporate lawyers and accountants had prepared an excellent description of the company, its problems, and the offering schedule. Then, in the last paragraph of the description was the statement, "We have to do this offering in 1967 because our earnings are going to be terrible in 1968."

Needless to say, that company is still privately owned.

Industry Comparison and Financial Data

As underwriters, we often have people walk in and say, "I won't give you my figures, but tell me what my price/earnings ratio should be."

This attitude is quite understandable. Management is obviously curious about the investment banker's evaluation of its business. It is also quite understandable that the underwriter wants to accumulate as much information about the company as possible before committing himself even on an informal basis.

I think the attitude of the managing underwriter should be—although this is obviously not the attitude of the eventual buyer of the stock—that financial statements do not answer questions but merely provide an opportunity to ask them. This information is merely a prelude to our effort to become fully acquainted with the business. Then, in practically all instances, we develop an abbreviated but comprehensive statistical comparison. Such data provide us with a picture of the company relative to other companies of various sizes within the industry and indicate the evaluation the market is placing on similar companies. In particular, we place our emphasis on the trends in earnings per share and the price/earnings ratios of such companies.

We always do our thinking and make our evaluation on these types of data. However, we have all been familiar with small glamour companies where the pricing has not appeared to be quite so rational. I imagine that some of these are priced on current sales levels; others, possibly on the company's need; and then there are those in which the ingredients of pricing policy escape me completely. My guess is that such a company shops its offering around until it finds an underwriter who evaluates the company more generously than management does itself.

Now, what happens when we have the opposite kind of company—one without great growth or glamour? In this case, we would make our evaluation from the earnings per share and our estimates of the future earnings per share. We tend to look at yield value, and possibly even the book value.

The book value might affect future internal expansion or future cash acquisitions, either of which might turn this pedestrian company into one that is more exciting.

In doing a comparison, we sometimes discover that a company is unique and that it is hard to find a similar size firm in the same industry. In that case, we will try to find another company that is comparable in size and type, even though it is not in the same kind of business.

During the 1930's, the debt/equity ratio used to be an important analytical tool. However, people are not so afraid of debt today as they were then; as a result, emphasis on the debt/equity ratio has been reduced considerably, particularly in our dealings with companies that have some aspects of glamour.

Similarly, we do not emphasize profit margins unless, of course, the company's margins are significantly at variance with comparable companies. Clearly, if a company has $100 million in sales and only $1 million in earnings, it is working on a pretty narrow margin; we worry about it. Our attitude is largely the same concerning return on invested capital.

Use of Proceeds

The company's intended use of the proceeds from a new stock issue is an important consideration for the underwriter when he considers the price/earnings ratio. Let us say that the company's use of proceeds is for an exciting development, such as the construction of a new plant or the launching of a new product. Such an application gives the underwriter more confidence in the company's future earnings potential and obviously can affect the price/earnings ratio level based on current or recent earnings.

However, if the intended use of proceeds is just to raise working capital, say, to maintain the existing volume of sales, obviously such an application is relatively unexciting.

The use of proceeds also affects the way in which the managing underwriter looks at the diluting effect of any new shares. The critical question is how soon the fresh money from the new issue is going to be put to work.

For example, late in 1968 we were involved in a difficult new security offering because—while the planned use of proceeds was exciting—the projected lead time in building a new company facility was well over a year. This meant that we were going to have the diluting effect of the new shares in 1969, but not have the earnings benefit until 1970.

This delay obviously had an effect on our evaluation of the approximate multiple of the company's 1968 earnings. We knew the new facility would be a worthwhile expenditure, and we were aware of the company's profit potential in 1970. However, in 1969 there would be no additional profits, but only an increase in the number of new shares outstanding.

Adjustment of Earnings

Although really an accounting matter, I think I ought to touch on the adjustment of earnings. In several cases with which I have been associated there has been no problem in saying, "This owner, who has been drawing $200,000 a year, is now going to take only $50,000 or $75,000 a year. We can add back an adjustment and restate the earnings to cover that."

One time we went back and took an airplane out; another time, a luxury hotel. However, if the managing underwriter places too much emphasis on these changes, he can possibly complicate the owner's personal tax returns. But it is an area of concern to the underwriter if the owner's earlier tax return is still in doubt. The owner also wants to have confidence that the underwriter is not going to run into some objective factor —such as readjustment of taxes—that will depress the company's historic earnings.

Importance of Intangibles

After we look at the comparison of a company against its industry, we generally will determine a price range of, say,

15 to 18 times earnings, or possibly 20 to 23 times earnings. How then, does the investment banker know whether to go to the top, the middle, or the bottom of the range?

Here we look at the intangibles, such as the breadth and competence of management. We must have complete confidence in management's ability to run its business within a competitive environment and to plan for its markets of the future. The owner-managers' plans for informing the financial community is another important intangible. We want them to keep working on their relations with the financial community, so that the stock will have an informed after-market. This can be accomplished either through the use of a financial public relations firm or through the development of internal expertise. Unsophisticated managers and directors can potentially cause trouble, particularly because the government is continually defining and redefining their obligations in such areas as dissemination of information.

Then there are the surprises. Is the owner likely to surprise you in the future, either by making predictions to the financial community, or by not being careful in his representations with the financial community? Is he likely to do things without consulting you first? Some thinking in this area affects how much you are willing to pursue the company's business.

The quality and availability of labor is going to become, I think, an increasingly more important consideration. I recently spent a week visiting five scattered plants of a conglomerate. In each case, the first complaint of the divisional manager was about labor—the scarcity, chronic absenteeism, high rate of turnover, and so on.

Management went into the depressed areas where there were thousands of unemployed. They tried to recruit by advertising in newspapers and on radio, and even by setting up recruitment offices. In one case, in the South, where 3,500 people

61

in a small area were on welfare, only 20 eventually applied.

Thus I think future labor relations and the company's development of the labor resource and labor-saving capabilities are going to be increasingly important intangibles.

The prestige of the company can also be an ingredient in the investment banker's thinking on the price/earnings ratio. Perhaps if the company's name is a household word, the underwriter may be willing to price the security more generously as a result of the reputation of the client's product line and strong market franchise.

Another intangible is the appearance and adequacy of a company's facilities. Accordingly, when it comes time for the managing underwriter to tour the company's facilities during the registration period, he will frankly be more impressed with a new, modern, spacious, one-story plant than with a turn-of-the-century factory.

Still another intangible is the acquisition policy of the company, and whether there exists the management capability to implement that policy. Many companies, including some of America's largest corporations, have great acquisition policies and little or no implementation ability.

A sound and well-carried out acquisition policy can provide an important additive component to the internal earnings developments in the future. This type of program can create glamour in the stock and help to raise the price/earnings ratio.

There are many other intangibles for the investment banker to consider when he thinks about the price/earnings ratio. I shall run through some of these quickly. Consider:

• The ease of entering an industry. Frankly, we normally do not prefer industries where entry is easy.

• Whether it is a single-product company and thus more vulnerable to competition, change or obsolescence.

• The duration and extent of the company's patent protection.

• The quality of both the company's accounting firm and its commercial bank.

Other factors

The size of the issue can be an important variable that also affects the pricing. Some investment bankers, ourselves included, believe that the issue must be of a sufficient size, in both number of shares and dollar value, to generate an adequate after-market. In contrast, some new issues have been richly priced as a result of the scarcity factor—that is, the relatively small number of shares in the offering. It is obviously a lot easier to sell $1,000 of a product than it is to sell $10,000 of the same product. However, the shallow after-market may result in wider fluctuations in price.

All other things being equal, a higher price/earnings ratio would normally be attained on a stock selling at $5 a share in small amounts than on a security selling at $50 a share in large amounts. However, such pricing really does not reflect the true value of the security. It is our belief that pricing should reflect the intrinsics of the company's operations rather than the work of the market place.

Although it has been practice in my firm to make discrete decisions concerning underwriting spread and price/earnings ratio, these two factors may be interrelated in the judgment of some bankers. For example, a large spread may result in a higher net price/earnings ratio, especially if a more generous incentive can be given to the salesmen.

Also, if some managing underwriters can operate with a large spread, they may be more inclined to go short. For example, in a 200,000-share offering, the underwriting syndicate may sell 210,000 or 220,000 shares to the public, leaving the syndicate in a short position. Then, the underwriters in the syndicate would have to repurchase the stock in the after-market in order to cover their short position.

Frankly, I think that some underwriters may actually consider the potential future business with the company. Because this can occur, I shall elaborate on their thinking. If the offering is going to be a one-time secondary, with the likelihood that the company, because of the nature of its business, will never need any further financing, and the shareholders will have no desire to sell again for many years, the underwriter may believe he has to make his profit on this one offering. Obviously, this situation would be different from that of a growth company, such as a computer-leasing organization, where the underwriter could envision a recurring demand for financing.

Establishing the Price

Using the types of information and data we have discussed above, we arrive at a range of prices where similar companies are selling today.

Obviously, to sell a large block of stock some discount from the price level at which seasoned comparable equities sell is required. We believe it is important that after an offering, the price should rise to a moderate premium to ensure a satisfactory after-market. Hopefully, if we have correctly judged the market, the premium will not be excessive. It is not worthwhile to issue common stock at $20 a share and have it open at $40. Such a significant premium makes it obvious that the initial pricing was not a fair evaluation. It also makes the stock vulnerable in the after-market since there are a lot of short-term profit-minded sellers.

We prefer to price an issue to yield a 10% to 15% premium

64

in the after-market. A good example of such pricing occurred when we underwrote the security of a service company. While it had only a modest rise immediately, the security rose to a substantial premium long after the initial offering date. But this rise occurred during a year in which we educated the financial community about the unique characteristics of this company.

Dangers of Overpricing

There was a statement about a man, not long ago, who sold securities in a company he had founded only two years earlier. He said that he considered an underwriting to be a one-time opportunity and unless he received the top price the first time, he would be losing money irrevocably. Because there was a favorable supply-demand balance for the issue, he could have priced it at any figure and received a premium, temporarily at least.

The dangers of a somewhat less glamorous company are that, if the first offering is overpriced, the reputation of the company, the confidence in the company, and the charisma surrounding the company can be destroyed. Once an underwriting fails to take off, it becomes increasingly difficult to stimulate market interest and a downward propensity sets in.

Price/Earnings Spreads

Within the high-low range of the price/earnings ratio, we use the intangibles to influence us one way or the other. As soon as possible after we talk with a potential client, we normally mention the range so that he can be guided by our thinking on the issue.

The waiting period while the company's registration is at the Securities and Exchange Commission is also the marketing period. It is during this time that the syndicate department of the managing investment banking firm will be receiving indications of interest from the underwriters who have been invited to join in the syndicate and from their own salesmen in the firm's branch offices.

Since investment bankers are in the marketing business just as much as supermarkets are in the marketing business, we tend to move up or down on the range—depending on demand.

The day before the offering, we sit down and discuss where the price should fall within the range. If the indications of interest show there is a good demand for the security, if the market tone is good, if other new offerings are being well received, and if the Dow-Jones averages are doing well, then we tend to go to the top of the range.

But if, on the other hand, we are having a poor reception—indications of interest are modest or poor—we tend to gravitate toward the bottom end of the range.

How does the syndicate know our price thinking?

When we file the registration statement with the SEC, we enter a maximum filing price. Let us say that the company earned $1 per share, and we are thinking of an offering at 15 to 18 times earnings. Thus we may file a $19 or $20 maximum price.

On the basis of the maximum filing price, say, two or three years ago, the underwriters in the syndicate could pretty well assume that the security would have a 15% to 20% premium after the offering. In some cases in those boom days, even at 30 times earnings, we knew we were underpricing the issue and we would have to go back and revise the maximum filing price upward, because the demand was so great. Thus we would raise it to perhaps 35 times earnings during the period of syndication.

The maximum filing price is the basis on which the syndicate members judge whether our price thinking is too high. We do not get into the same detailed discussions with them that we have held internally.

Mathematical Methods

Now the foregoing may perhaps appear to be a very unscientific method of valuing an issue with earnings. I shall give you a number of other methods that have the benefit of being mathematically quite simple.

One is called the Conservative Growth Approach in which the managing underwriter takes 8½ times what he considers to be the basic earnings of the particular company. Then, he takes two times the company's compound annual growth rate, and adds the sum of these two. Let us say, for example, that the compound annual growth rate is 5%. Two times that is 10; plus 8½ equals 18½.

Another method is called the Stedman Approach, named after a man who was the great pundit of the pre-1962 market decline. He took the estimated number of years that a company's earnings required to double, and divided that into 100 to get the price/earnings ratio. Thus, if the company's earnings were going to double every year, the price/earnings ratio would be 100; if the earnings were going to double in four years, the price/earnings ratio would be 25.

Of course, his method was more sophisticated than that; he included a probability factor and various other data, but the principle holds true.

It is an interesting concept because if you had bought IBM ten years ago at 40 times earnings, today you would be getting a 6% yield on your investment, and your stock would be selling at five times earnings. This reasoning is why people were unafraid of these high price/earnings ratios and why

67

Stedman had so much success with his mathematical concept.

I have heard of several other pricing methods such as: "Let's see how this company's earnings compare to the Dow-Jones average," and "Let's see the price/earnings ratio in the Dow-Jones average and adjust it to this company."

I have also heard of people using *Standard & Poor's* 200 fastest growing companies as a criterion: "If this company went public, would it be one of the 200 fastest growing? If so, what would be its price/earnings ratio?"

These are great theoretical tools, but I personally have never seen any of them actually used. The most practical tool is the statistical comparison, adjusted upward or downward within the framework of the industry, by the weight the investment banker gives to the intangibles. The foundation for the intangibles, of course, is your estimates of future earnings per share, in many cases on a quarter-by-quarter basis. Of particular importance is the first quarter after the underwriting: it should be better than the previous year; if not, it should be explained in the prospectus that some adverse factors may be developing.

Concluding Note

In effect, pricing for the large company is a relatively easy job, because there are usually quite a few comparable companies that are already publicly owned. They probably tend to sell within a fairly narrow range of one another.

It is the smaller and the newer company that is harder to price. Here, in many cases, I think the beauty is in the eye of the beholder. And it really calls for artful negotiating between the company and the underwriter.

There is probably little doubt that when an owner-manager's little boy wanted a hula hoop at the height of the craze, that hula hoop was worth $1.50. But when the craze was over two months later, and hula hoops were selling for $.25, the satisfaction value to the child was only $.25.

We have had certain similar fads in types of securities. One example is franchising, and chicken franchising seems to be the most egregious example. Here it is not the underwriters who have been setting the price, but rather, it has been the public who has been putting the value on this type of security.

Floor Discussion

Question: Do you encourage the sale of new shares in order to create a use-of-proceeds section?

Calhoun: There is no question that some offerings by certain investment banking firms have been supplemented with new shares in order to get a large enough new issue to go public. Perhaps there wasn't any immediate need by the company. One clue is that the company isn't borrowing any money and this may be indicative of an unnecessary sale of shares. If there is an immediate need, fine. But we stay away from padding an offering to build it up to size, because unless the company can put the proceeds from the sale to productive use, it is going to have to live with those shares outstanding and suffer from their diluting effect.

Question: In other words, you have no objection to the proceeds from the offering going solely to the selling stockholders?

Calhoun: No, there are a lot of secondaries. Of course, in many growing companies, the problem is that management wants a public market for use in making acquisitions, but nobody wants to sell. They have to coerce each other to come up with enough stock to create a decent market.

Question: At what time in your discussions with the offering managers do you or they first mention the price range?

Calhoun: Usually, the owner-managers are asking us every quarter on the quarter-hour.

The point at which we give our price thinking to the prospect depends on the particular company, how difficult that company is to evaluate, and how many other comparable publicly held companies there are. For example, if it is an auto parts company, there are literally dozens and dozens of comparable public companies. Also, they sell within a very low pedestrian range; so the underwriter ought to have an immediate opinion, subject to adjustments. If the underwriter is not certain, he will compromise by discussing a wider price/earnings range until he is able to learn more about the company.

Here is another example, which happens to be a pretty good one because the privately held company is controlled by one of our Wall Street competitors. Our competitor chose not to do the underwriting, and came to us. Thus we were here dealing with not only an owner, but also with a neighboring Wall Street firm.

The company is in the leisure field which, of course, is an exciting area. Interestingly enough, as the leisure field gets more exciting, as is so often the case, the definition of leisure companies becomes less circumscribed because people are looking for more and more on which to place the leisure tag. In fact, all sorts of companies now are leisure companies.

We started talking in the winter of 1967, and quickly learned that the client had a heavy debt structure. Earlier, I said 15 to 18 times earnings, but in this case we were talking about 15. The owners came back in the summer of 1968 and we went up to 20.

Right about this time, another company called Leisure Group was in the market selling at 70 times earnings, so the owners came back to see us in the fall of 1968. We moved up to 25, and all along they were being very understanding.

Just before Christmas of 1968, they returned and said that even 25 didn't appear to be rich enough. Up to this point, they had always agreed with us, but now they were sitting back and watching Leisure Group.

This is a case of two professional groups seeing how the market was undergoing a change over a period of time. Moreover, the change was not only taking place in leisure securities multiples, but in what could also be defined as a leisure company. And both changes were of benefit to this company.

Question: Using your price/earnings ratio, what do you apply it against? The last complete fiscal or calendar year? The last twelve months? Or the estimated earnings for the current year?

Calhoun: That is a very good question because oftentimes we know that any conflict is really not going to be over the price/earnings ratio, but against which period to apply that ratio. For example, in a rapidly growing company, 30 times last year's earnings may be less attractive than 18 times this year's.

When you are working toward an offering, say, during the summer, that year's earnings should begin to become clear. Of course, it is more difficult if the seasonality is in the fourth quarter, because then we can't determine the earnings accurately; accordingly, the argument becomes "Which period's earnings or which earnings are we talking about?"

This can be more important than the actual price/earnings ratio. It is obviously a blend and a lot depends on the seasonality of the business.

Question: Suppose the primary reason for a closely held company going public would be to establish an estate value through the marketability of the issue. Would this be wrong?

Calhoun: I think establishing the value for estate purposes

71

is not a one-way street. Suppose the company has a small offering for $5 a share and the stock then goes to $100, but the owner knows it is only worth $20. Then he dies. In the event of sudden death in the owner-manager structure, the subsequent disposal of the stock may create problems more significant than those of estate taxes.

In my experience, particularly after the builder of a company has died, people think it is very logical and easy for the family to do an offering, and have everything run smoothly. Boy, it isn't! Money runs thicker than blood.

A privately held company can get away with a lower estate tax than a publicly held company with shareholders; thus it is a common request within my industry to perform an evaluation for estate purposes.

Question: It appears that a due-diligence meeting would be very helpful to the underwriter in determining if the price per share is acceptable. Would you touch on due-diligence meetings briefly and tell us if they have affected the price of shares?

Calhoun: The so-called due-diligence meeting is always held in New York, if the managing underwriter is located in New York. In order to generate interest in other cities, additional meetings may be held in Chicago, San Francisco, Los Angeles, or Boston so that members of the underwriting syndicate and their salesmen may be given the opportunity to hear the company's officers tell their story.

In prior years, a due-diligence meeting enabled the company to talk about matters that were not in the prospectus. Increasingly, the company's counsel and underwriters' counsel have limited the company and its management to matters that appear in the prospectus. So I would say that the due-diligence meeting is a less important factor.

However, I do think that, in companies which are highly technical, it may be of more value, because it gives people a chance to see the product and related exhibits and to see to what extent management is informed.

Question: At what point is the investment banker committed to go through with the underwriting or the raising of the money?

Calhoun: It is the day the offering becomes effective. This is the end of the road, so to speak, and generally it is a week before the closing.

Question: Up to that point either the investment banker or the corporation can back down and decide not to go through with it. Correct?

Calhoun: That is right, and for any reason whatsoever.

Question: What percentage of the total shares ownership should be available for public use?

Calhoun: I think this is a function of having enough shares out—dollar value—to make a decent after-market.

Yet we dislike seeing the insider group selling as much as, say, 45% or 50% on the first go-around. It then gives the appearance of what we call a bail-out. This is not to say that an insider sale of a full 50% the first time would preclude a successful offering; however, the underwriters may have trouble getting strong syndicates on such offerings.

Question: A lot has been said about not having too high or too low an issue price. Is the underwriting company legally responsible for errors in judgment?

Calhoun: I don't know what "errors in judgment" is. I know a number of managing underwriting firms have been sued, so certainly an error was made somewhere. But I don't think it was necessarily an error in judgment. It's similar to the medical profession and lawsuits that occur there—who knows?

The Comparative Pricing Schedule

An investment banker bases the price of a specific security on three sets of considerations: theoretical analysis, practical statistical work, and a determination of how much stock he can actually sell at certain prices.

From a theoretical point of view, the return on a stock purchaser's investment can be obtained in a number of different ways, and the nature of this return materially affects the method of valuing the security.

For instance, if the company is an investment company, or an SBIC, book value per share may be very material: there may be a possibility of the company being liquidated and stockholders receiving their proportionate share of the net assets, although that would be very unusual. Book value is occasionally relevant for a promotional company where the stock may initially sell at book value, or in the relatively rare liq-

Mr. Joseph is Vice President of E. F. Hutton & Company, Inc. He is actively engaged in the firm's Corporate Finance Division on public offerings, acquisitions and mergers.

uidation situation where book value per share may reflect appraised values and provide "downside protection." The investment banker may feel that in a specific industry, when a company's market price falls to 50% of book value, someone might take over the company, believing he can do a better job in employing the assets.

A company's stock may sell as an income security if people are buying it for the dividend income. Dividends are often considered as another form of downside protection. If a security is selling at a 4% yield and the stock falls 50%, the yield rises to 8%. At some point, the rising yield will prevent the security from falling further. In such situations, the evaluation is to determine the current yield of the security—or, if confident of the rate of increasing dividends, the *discounted present value* of the future stream of dividends—and to compare this return to alternative securities with high yields or fixed incomes.

The most important way of valuing a security is based on capital gains potential, which is usually a reflection of anticipated increases or decreases in earnings per share. Thus the crucial valuation relationship is that of earnings to the price of the stock (i.e., the price/earnings relationship).

The method of determining the appropriate P/E relationship is quite complex. Some theoretical analysis using discounted cash flows may be helpful to determine the outside parameters.

Coal Industry Example

Actual practical analysis and pricing uses a comparative pricing schedule, the most important statistical tool used by investment bankers to establish the price of a new stock issue.

The comparative pricing schedule shown as *Exhibit I* is typical of those used by an investment banker when analyzing a company. It shows many of the major statistical variables considered. (*See* pp. 84-86).

In this case, we were reviewing a medium-sized coal company (not shown in the exhibit) that had about $35 million of annual sales and an acceptable record of growth in recent years. The comparative pricing schedule shown in this exhibit is a greatly abbreviated version of the one actually used in this situation.

Establishing the Relationships

The comparative pricing schedule is used to try to determine those relationships important to comparable companies and to relate the price of the stock to be valued to earnings, book value, or dividend yield. It is apparent that the company doing a new issue is competing with many other securities for the investor's money, and that the investing public (especially the professional analyst, who is increasingly important) is going to compare this company to the most comparable publicly owned securities.

The investment banker tries to create order by looking initially at each company's size as shown by sales, net income, net worth, total assets, and shares outstanding. Company size can be very important in some industries when trying to determine the comparability of a particular company to others.

In examining the comparative pricing schedule, one usually finds that the price/earnings relationship determines the price of the securities. Thus earnings per share must be carefully compared. Next year's estimate of earnings per share is crucial. The five-year historical record is studied as an indication of the company's growth record and prospects for growth. (Five years is used because it is the period to be shown in the prospectus.)

This schedule excludes a comparison of the quality of the earnings. Often adjustments will be made to attempt to equate factors which affect the quality of earnings, such as different tax rates, the importance and treatment of investment credits, methods of depreciation, and methods of valuing inventory. In some instances, analysts will make standard adjustments to the earnings (for instance, insurance companies have heavy front-end expenses if they add substantial new business to their books, and analysts will adjust life insurance company earnings based on certain dollar values per $1,000 of new insurance).

The quality of earnings per share is also affected by the number of shares outstanding. Should an analyst use the number of shares outstanding at year end? Or should he use the average number of shares outstanding during the year?

Accountants are still arguing the treatment of shares to be issued on conversion of convertible securities, the exercise of warrants, and on acquisitions that are contingent on future earnings. Often the pricing schedule will show earnings per share "as reported," plus earnings per share "fully diluted."

The preliminary work that the investment banker does in appraising a corporation plays back into the comparative pricing schedule, especially in estimating earnings for next year. He will talk with the company management and with the analysts in his firm who follow the industry closely in order to come up with the best possible estimate of earnings per share for the following year for his client and for the other comparable companies.

The book value per share can be affected both by potential dilution and by adjustments to book value. In insurance companies, again as an example, the book value of the company's securities is also adjusted as new business is added.

If it appears that dividends will be critical in the examination, the comparative schedule may show some indication of the company's five-year historical pattern of dividend payouts.

The book values are interesting in the *Exhibit I* spread sheet because only two companies sell above 1.2 times book value. One is Coal Company A, which had a price/earnings ratio of 11.6 in 1968. Moreover, A's compound annual rate of growth in earnings is the highest of any company on this schedule, and its record of earnings growth is the most consistent. Perhaps this company's security should be selling at the highest multiple of book, depending on the rate of return being obtained on its common equity, which is second highest of all the companies listed.

As discussed, the investment banker considers the dividend yield either to discover if the companies are selling on an income basis, or to determine where the downside support on a yield basis will be. These coal companies, with yields ranging from nil to 3.8%, are obviously not selling on a yield basis; the yield is not crucial to pricing a coal company's common stock.

The remaining information on this comparative pricing schedule is less than normal. It is designed as a red-flag analysis to determine how the client compares or differs from others in its industry. How does its sales and income growth compare with others? At this point, an analysis may be made of margins and trends.

The balance sheet items examined include the current ratio, debt/equity relationships, return on common equity, return on total capitalization (including long-term debt), and return on invested capital (including capitalized lease obligations).

Depending on the type of company, the analyst will study different parameters in this part of the schedule. (If the client were, for example, a credit jeweler, we would spend a great deal of time analyzing receivables—receivable turnover, past due receivables, and bad debt losses.)

For coal companies, the percentage of sales and prices fixed on long-term contract basis to major utilities are important and should be examined closely.

Analyzing the Reasons

After doing the statistical work and looking at the comparative pricing exhibit, the investment banker tries to determine the reasons why the comparable companies are selling at their current price/earnings ratios.

Company E is easy—but irrelevant. At the time this schedule was prepared, it had agreed to be acquired by a larger company, and the merger had a favorable impact on the multiple. Therefore, it is not indicative of the proper stock price for coal companies.

But if you look at the others, you will note that they go all the way down to D Coal and Coke, which did not have a price/earnings relationship, but represented a special situation as the result of merger conversations then in process. The other companies' P/E ratios range from 9.9 to 16.5 times estimated 1968 earnings. This is not terribly useful in determining the price of our hypothetical medium-sized coal company.

Company C was selling at 16.5 times earnings; but despite its size, based on the company's rate of growth, book value, and indicated yield, there is no apparent reason that it should have had the highest price/earnings relationship. An industry analyst pointed out that the company had just obtained a long-term contract with a major utility to deliver over 2.5 million tons of coal a year at a high price. This is an excellent example of how such comparative statistical tools can point out exceptions for the investment banker.

Coal Company A appeared to be attractively priced. It had the best growth rate and a satisfactory price/earnings relationship. However, the company had suffered losses in the early 1960's and apparently had not yet regained full investor confidence.

Company D seemed to be quite typical. It had a lower price/earnings ratio than the others, but it had not had to pay any taxes. Also, it had an erratic record of earnings per share, and it was the only company that showed no growth in coal production and shipments. As the exhibit reveals, it was not quite as attractive a company as others in its industry; therefore, it should have a lower price/earnings ratio.

Thus, in this illustrative example of a comparative pricing schedule, we begin to narrow in on the fact that a coal company with a good record, but without any extraordinary potential, probably would sell at 11 or 12 times its estimated 1968 earnings.

Setting the Price

After the banker completes the statistical work and knows the current market for comparable securities, he is prepared to discuss the maximum price, which must be filed with the SEC.

Briefly, the company will normally file its S-1 registration statement and prospectus with the SEC, and the managing underwriter will distribute copies of the preliminary prospectus and form his underwriting syndicate. The investment firms in the syndicate will obtain additional copies of the prospectus and distribute them to their account executives, who will then start calling clients.

While no sales can be made until they have a final effective prospectus on the day of the offering, the underwriters do take "indications of interest" from clients. While the indications are not legally binding, the managing underwriter develops a good estimate of the market's receptivity to the proposed offering at the indicated offering price.

There is a lot of gamesmanship between the syndicate departments. For example, if it appears that the new issue is going to be a "hot" deal—that is, one which will be oversubscribed and quickly sell at a premium—a syndicate department that may be underwriting 5,000 shares, but only has indications of interest in 3,000, will ask for 6,000 shares because it does not want to be caught short. Through all this gamesmanship, a good managing underwriter will usually be able to determine within narrow limits the proper price.

Underwriters do not price a security offering with a crystal ball, but rather with some very practical tools. Good underwriters should have a similarity of interest with the client, which is to price the new issue at the highest price commensurate with a successful offering and a favorable long-term after-market.

Floor Discussion

Question: Am I correct in assuming that the price is not finally determined until essentially the last minute?

Joseph: You are correct. Usually it is not finally set until the day before the offering.

Question: It would seem that someone who is putting a lot of his very tender eggs into the managing underwriter's basket is naturally concerned about this uncertainty. Just as an ultimate control, can he at the last moment abrogate? Does he have any authority so that no matter what the price, he can pull out of it at the last moment if he decides it is not acceptable?

Joseph: He is free to pull out at the last moment. On all offerings, there is no firm underwriting agreement signed until after the final price has been set, which typically is the day before the issue. Neither the underwriter nor company is bound until they sign that document, usually early on the day that the company is actually going to issue the security. Therefore, the people do have an "out" if they want to exercise it.

On the other hand, I think a company or an underwriter would be unwise to go through the cost, time, and publicity of pursuing an issue that they do not intend to consummate.

We seldom have that last-minute crisis, but I think part of the answer is that we make a great effort to maintain close communication with the company throughout the entire offering period.

There are three alternatives available to the issuer at the wire. First, let us assume the situation is that President Kennedy has just been assassinated. It could be disastrous to try to come to market in the face of such confidence-shaking news. You always have the option of reducing price. But the odds are good that an investment banker would advocate not reducing price since it would be a mistake to come in on such a market.

The second alternative is to reduce the size of the offering. This is usually a sign of weakness. The entire financial community knows how much stock has been filed for offering, and a last-minute reduction in size may cause defections from indications of interest.

The third and most probable alternative in such a crisis would be to defer temporarily the new issue.

Question: We have been discussing coal companies here. How appropriate is this to the glamour industries?

Joseph: Not very. Pricing a glamour issue is much more difficult, but I think it is worth pointing out that the investing community has a couple of habits you can count on.

One is that they set up groups. If your company does not belong in a specific industry group, they will probably put you in one.

Secondly, they have a tendency to overdo things. When insurance companies were in favor in 1963, they were probably too much in favor. When electronics companies were in favor in 1961, they were also excessively favored. But when the pendulum swung, some companies in both groups were excessively depressed. Since the pendulum will always swing back, a responsible investment banker must price an issue realistically, despite short-term glamour.

Question: I would like to know how far in advance you would forecast a specific industry as to price/earnings ratio.

Joseph: For about one day. We will run a complete comparative pricing schedule following the close of business on the day preceding the offering. We are not predicting beyond that. We may think that an industry group is overpriced and that the particular company will be overpriced by the public, which raises the "hot issue" problem. The fact that an unsophisticated individual may be willing to pay a ridiculous price for 100 shares is not the basis on which a company should establish its initial investment banking and public ownership relationships.

We had a recent situation where a company was very much in the public eye in a community on the West Coast. We did a comparative pricing analysis of that company and priced it at 12 or 13 times earnings. This was further supported by our analysis that the company's rate of earnings growth would be relatively modest over a long period.

We brought the stock out at 13—at the upper end of our range. Within a day or two it was trading at 20 because everyone in that town wanted to own the stock. Within two months it was back down to 13, where it really belonged.

Question: When you are in your initial conversations with your client and you give him some kind of idea on the pricing, how far do you forecast the specific industry?

Exhibit I. Coal Company Comparative Pricing Schedule

Market Company Fiscal Year Ended	OTC A Coal Co. 12/31/66	OTC B Coal Co. 12/31/66	ASE C Coal Co. 6/30/67	OTC D Coal Co. 3/31/66	NYSE E Coal Co. 12/31/66	OTC F Coal Co. 12/31/66	NYSE G Coal Co. 12/31/66
Company Size (000):							
Net Sales	$29,310	$40,326	$62,009	$40,334	$32,517	$17,441	$233,923
Net Income	2,581	4,006	3,669	(2,695)	1,686	638	26,280
Net Worth	25,458	39,413	52,094	16,209	24,483	13,411	179,460
Long-term Debt	1,048	7,000	29,376	23,995	11,250	405	79,372
No. Common Shares	1,162	1,029	790	1,982	1,617	477	9,879
Earnings Per Share: 1968E	$ 2.75E	$ 3.25E	$ 4.50E	N.A.	$ 1.60E	$ 3.00E	$ 3.00E
Latest 12 Months	2.60	3.16	4.56	($ 1.36)	1.43	2.68	2.81
1967	2.60	3.16	4.64	N.A.	1.43	2.75E	2.90E
1966	2.40	3.89	4.31	(1.36)	1.04	1.53	2.64
1965	2.05	2.76	4.88	0.16	0.71	2.14	2.27
1964	1.94	2.69	4.97	1.01	1.01	2.12	2.16
1963	1.19	2.30	4.11	1.57	0.92	1.50	1.74
Compound Annual Growth Rate (1963-67)	21.5%	8.2%	3.0%	—	11.7%	16.4%	13.6%
1967-68E Percent Increase	5.8%	2.8%	(3.0%)	—	11.9%	9.1%	3.4%
Book Value Per Share	$23.64	$38.29	$65.93	$ 6.82	$15.14	$28.34	$ 17.72
Indicated Dividend Per Share	1.20	1.35	1.00	Nil	0.60	1.00	1.00
Market Price (Mar. 4, 1968)	$32	$46	$74¾	$ 7	$17¾	$29¾	$ 42

Price/Earnings Ratio: 1968E	14.0X	9.9X	11.1X	N.A.	16.5X	14.2X	11.6X
Latest 12 months	14.9X	11.1X	12.4X	—	16.3X	14.6X	12.3X
1967	14.5X	10.8X	12.4X	N.A.	16.0X	14.6X	12.3X
Price/Book Value	2.4X	1.0X	1.2X	1.0X	1.1X	1.2X	1.4X
Indicated Yield	2.4%	3.4%	3.4%	Nil	1.3%	2.9%	3.8%
Net Sales (000): 1968E	$260,000E	$20,000E	$42,000E	N.A.	$62,000E	$43,000E	$33,000E
1967	245,000E	18,500E	37,150	$42,000	62,009	41,596	31,559
1966	233,923	17,440	32,517	40,334	61,438	40,326	29,310
1965	208,301	17,600	26,562	32,104	60,150	27,371	26,363
1964	188,650	17,370	26,762	33,306	59,643	23,000	25,031
1963	159,881	16,620	25,837	38,137	56,494	21,550	22,994
Compound Annual Growth Rate (1963-67)	11.3%E	2.7%E	9.5%	2.7%	2.3%	17.9%	8.2%
1967-68E Percent Increase	6.1%	8.1%	13.1%	N.A.	—	3.4%	4.6%
Net Income (000): 1968E	$ 30,000E	$ 1,400E	$ 2,500E	N.A.	$ 3,550E	$ 3,350E	$ 3,200E
1967	28,650E	1,300E	2,321	N.A.	3,669	3,258	2,831
1966	26,280	638	1,686	($ 2,695)	3,403	4,006	2,581
1965	22,501	1,025	1,130	323	3,853	2,851	2,211
1964	21,339	1,010	1,615	1,913	3,927	2,448	2,086
1963	17,246	717	1,469	2,755	3,250	2,109	1,407
Compound Annual Growth Rate (1963-67)	13.6%	16.1%	12.1%	—	3.1%	11.5%	19.0%
1967-68E Percent Increase	4.7%	7.7%	7.7%	—	(3.2%)	2.8%	13.0%
Effective Tax Rate—1966	29.5%	*	23.2%	N.A.	24.6%	21.5%	15.5%
Current Ratio	1.4X	3.5X	2.4X	0.8X	2.2X	3.5X	2.0X
Long-term Debt (000)	$ 79,372	$ 405	$11,250	$23,995	$29,375	$ 7,000	$ 1,048
Preferred Stock (000)	4,702	Nil	Nil	2,500	Nil	Nil	Nil
Common Equity (000)	174,758	13,411	24,483	13,709	52,094	39,413	25,458
Total Capitalization (000)	258,832	13,816	35,733	40,204	81,470	46,413	26,506

Exhibit I. Coal Company Comparative Pricing Schedule (Continued)

Market Company Fiscal Year Ended	OTC A Coal Co. 12/31/66	OTC B Coal Co. 12/31/66	ASE C Coal Co. 6/30/67	OTC D Coal Co. 3/31/66	NYSE E Coal Co. 12/31/66	OTC F Coal Co. 12/31/66	NYSE G Coal Co. 12/31/66
10X Lease Payments/Year (000)	3,120	N.A.	N.R.	N.R.	N.R.	N.A.	N.R.
Adjusted Capitalization (000)	29,626	46,413	81,470	40,204	35,733	13,816	258,832
Debt & 10X Leases/Adj. Capitalization	14.1%	15.1%	36.1%	59.7%	31.5%	2.9%	30.7%
Return on Common Equity (1967/1966)	11.1%	8.3%	7.0%	N.A.	9.5%	9.7%	16.0%
Return on Total Capitalization (1967/1966)	10.7%	7.0%	4.5%	N.A.	6.5%	9.4%	11.1%
Return on Adjusted Capitalization (1967/1966)	9.6%	7.0%	4.5%	N.A.	6.5%	9.4%	11.1%
Coal Production or Shipments (000 tons):							
1967	—	—	8,728	8,800	—	—	—
1966	6,266	10,239	8,374	9,381	7,453	4,245	62,390
1965	5,848	6,881	8,109	8,919	5,984	4,468	56,000
1964	5,452	5,813	8,253	8,155	6,125	4,353	50,100
1963	4,841	5,363	7,856	6,142	5,921	4,205	42,400
1962	4,308	5,014	7,482	4,668	5,988	4,289	34,400
Compound Annual Growth (1962-66)	9.8%	19.6%	2.8%	19.0%	5.6%	—	16.1%
Coal Reserves (000 tons)	326,500	N.A.	1,343,000	600,000	820,000	N.A.	5,150,000
Sales—Latest Year: Utilities	51%	N.A.	68%	N.A.	82%	N.A.	75%
Industrial	20%	N.A.	29%	N.A.	18%	—	22%
Other	21%	—	3%	—	—	—	3%
Exports	8%	—	—	28%	—	—	—

N.A.—Not Available   E—Estimated   * Credit of $100,000.

N.R.—None Reported

86

Joseph: What we try to do is indicate the price at which we think we can bring the new issue into the market at that time—in the context of the general economic, political, market, industrial, and your own particular business conditions—and have a successful offering and good after-market. It must, of course, be subject to actual market conditions at the time of the offering compared to those at the time of our initial conversations.

Accounting Policies and Auditing Procedures

When a company is getting ready to go public, management must give close attention to accounting and auditing matters. This is a somewhat technical area, but these technical matters have to be closely watched and satisfactorily resolved if the process of going public is to be completed.

Financial Statement Requirements

There is a series of registration forms (the one most commonly used being Form S-1), which the SEC requires to be filed for the initial offering of securities to the public. Form S-1 usually comes out as a booklet containing instructions for preparing the registration statement and prospectus. It includes a series of requirements in different areas; the ones now being focused on are those in the financial statement area.

Mr. Stimpson is a Partner in the accounting firm of Price Waterhouse & Co.

Form S-1 calls for a variety of financial statements under different circumstances and conditions. In most cases, it only specifies a balance sheet and income statements for the registering company. It also points to a separate regulation which governs the form and content of the financial statements, as well as the qualifications of the auditor and certification standards for the statements that are required to be included.

The form states that a company registering for the first time must file: certified income statements for at least the last three years; a certified balance sheet dated as of the end of the income statements' period; and a most recent balance sheet within 90 days of the initial filing. Although balance sheets are generally certified, this most recent one need not be.

In addition to the three years of certified income statements, income statements must be provided for at least two additional preceding years, or in some cases even more. Thus, if a company has been in business at least five years, it must be prepared to put in five-year income statements. All of these statements must meet the SEC accounting requirements. Of course, if it has only been in business for, say, two or three years, then financial statements are required only from the start of business.

Accepted Accounting Principles

When preparing financial statements, it is necessary to observe what are referred to as "generally accepted accounting principles." While there are certain alternatives available to some companies, as a practical matter generally accepted accounting principles appropriate in the circumstances will keep most companies confined within a very narrow area.

Insofar as accepted accounting is concerned, the primary concern is fair presentation. Many times, a company's methods

89

are selected with an eye on the tax collector, because most companies that do not have public ownership are more concerned with conserving cash than with putting their best foot forward in showing all the income they have really earned. Consequently, they are quite conservative in such things as rapidly depreciating various capital additions, writing down inventories or pricing inventories low. Because these practices do not conform to generally accepted accounting principles, a company following them but going public must make some important changes. Sometimes such accounting can be retained for Internal Revenue purposes and accepted accounting used for financial reporting purposes. At most times, however, the tax accounting has to be changed, and the tax bill involved in that change can be a serious impediment to going public. On more than one occasion, it has caused companies to think it over and to decide not to go public.

Another matter to be concerned about in the five-year income statement is whether the company is following consistent practices from year to year. It cannot choose one principle one year, a different one the following year, and then switch back and forth. In effect, it must prepare the entire five years following the same principles throughout.

Still another thing to keep in mind when preparing financial statements for a prospectus is that they are going into what is basically a selling document. A company should be careful not to present financial statements that are so detailed and confusing as to be unintelligible and have anything but sales appeal. While care must be taken not to overstate, mislead, misrepresent, or do anything of that nature, there are a number of things that can be done with financial statements to make them more easily understood. Because a prospectus is a sales tool, it should have a highly polished, concise and understandable set of financial statements.

Troublesome Accounting Areas

The most frequent, troublesome, and important problem-causing area that private companies find when they decide to go public and start looking at their accounting—which has probably been tax oriented—is inventories. What is the inventory basis? Is it acceptable? Is it LIFO or FIFO? Is it standard cost or average cost? Are there any material amounts of unrecorded inventory on hand? These are the questions to ask. A number of companies price their inventories without including any overhead. That apparently is well accepted for tax purposes, but generally accepted accounting procedures and the SEC absolutely insist that inventories be priced by including an appropriate portion of overhead.

If a company is going to get a certificate from a qualified auditor and if it is going to get its new offering approved by the SEC, it must compute or price inventories with overhead in them, whatever the right proportion might be determined to be. Since this, too, has to be done on a consistent basis, it is necessary to think in terms of five-year inventories. It is possible to go back and reprice inventories if the proper information is available, such as quantities and cost records, and that sort of thing.

Accrual Accounting

A number of other items are frequently recorded on a cash basis. Accepted accounting, however, requires a company to reflect accrual accounting, which includes elements of income as well as elements of expense that normally might only be recorded on a cash basis.

For example, a company might have some sale-and-lease-back transactions. Companies from time to time, for various

91

financing purposes, may have sold properties and leased them back under circumstances where the company appeared to realize a profit. In most cases of this kind, accepted accounting will require that such profit be deferred and amortized over the life of the lease. Thus, while it is not a profit that can be recognized, it does serve in the future to reduce lease expense.

Deferred compensation contracts are something that have to be considered; deferred compensation has to be accounted for during the period in which it is earned. Many types of deferred compensation to be paid after a man retires must be provided for now, which will again serve to reduce reported income.

Financial Arrangements

Another problem that has proved to be troublesome and embarrassing to management results when the officers and directors have been financing their personal activities through the corporation. One of the schedules that has to be filed as part of the registration statement has to do with advances or loans to officers and directors. If such advances or loans are in excess of $20,000 at any one time to any one individual during the most recent three-year period, it becomes necessary to file a schedule. There is really no way to get out of it, even if it is in the first year of the three-year period and it has been paid back. It must be reported in the schedule.

Sometimes private companies have salary arrangements which are not what they would be for a publicly owned company. When a company plans to go public and decides to change the salary arrangements, and the new salary arrangements will result in increased compensation or in increased charges in the income statement, this has to be disclosed in some manner.

92

Specific Rules

I mentioned earlier that the SEC has a specific regulation which deals with the form and content of financial statements and their certification. This is Regulation S-X. It is broken into several different parts. There are special rules that apply not only to commercial and industrial companies but to insurance companies—one for life companies, another for casualty companies—and special rules for investment companies, companies in the development state, as well as a series of other special rules for banks, bank holding companies, and others.

Any company thinking about going public would be well advised to get copies of Regulation S-X and of Form S-1, to see just what the accounting instructions and requirements really are.

Other Requirements

Besides these specific rules, there are far greater and more complex areas of what are referred to as administrative practices. These are the things the SEC is currently requiring with respect to a wide range of problems in different types of companies. One of the main challenges to accountants in SEC practice is to keep abreast of what is going on. There were some 4,000 prospectuses issued in 1969. Most practitioners try to get their hands on them to keep current, and this is quite a job. There are many visits to the SEC and negotiations and discussions with them, all designed to find out really what the SEC requirements will be in special situations. You have to keep these in mind. Unfortunately, there is no checklist that can be referred to. This is one of the areas requiring experience.

Another problem in the general accounting and financial

statement area is the need to prepare current financial statements on relatively short notice. At the outset, it was mentioned that financial statements must be filed within 90 days of the date a company first files. Depending on how long the registration statement is retained by the SEC, a first-time registrant may be required to update the financial statements before it can become effective.

For instance, if filed at the 90-day deadline and effectiveness of the registration statement, after various amendments, is delayed for longer than, say, two months, a company may be required to include more recent financial information on sales, net income, and earnings per share and possibly more complete financial statements, not only for the current period but for a similar prior-year period. Obviously, if a company does not have a good, reliable, internal accounting organization, it is not going to be able to comply on a timely basis. The independent accountant is concerned with this problem, because one of the things the underwriters want to get from him is a letter making representations about the unaudited short-period statements.

A fairly reliable internal accounting organization is needed for more reasons than providing interim statements. Cost records supporting inventories have to be reliable. Generally, a company should not even contemplate going public in the first place unless it has a reasonably reliable internal accounting organization.

The SEC also requires consolidated statements where consolidation is appropriate. This means that if there are domestic subsidiaries which are losing money, they cannot be excluded from consolidation. The SEC will also look at foreign subsidiaries and require justification for leaving them out, particularly if they are operating at a loss. If they are quite profitable, the company and the underwriters will want to include them in consolidation or separately. Many times, certification is difficult to obtain. For example, a number of companies which have small overseas subsidiaries have not bothered to require audits in the host country.

Many times, a particular business entity comprises a number of entities which take on different legal forms, other than parent-subsidiary relationships. There may be partnerships, or two or three corporations all owned by the same individual or owned by a group of individuals and not necessarily in the same proportion. In going public, it may be necessary to restructure the business in order to bring all these separate units together under one corporate parent-subsidiary umbrella. Many adjustments to these separate statements may be necessary to restate them on a combined basis. There is a lot of precedent for restating partnership financial statements on a corporate basis, usually by showing pro forma salaries and corporate income taxes.

Occasionally, a business organization has been set up in an unusual manner for various personal or financial reasons, and the owners do not want to change it until they are sure they will actually go public. However, when they file their original registration statement, they must include appropriate certified financial statements. This creates an apparent dilemma for the company.

The SEC has been rather generous in this area. The staff has permitted companies to present financial statements which reflect the accomplished reorganization, which frequently is not accomplished until just before the underwriting agreement is signed on the morning of the day the registration statement becomes effective.

The accountants have to check all this out beforehand so they can cover it with their opinion. There is a method of doing it; it is not an impediment to going public.

Independent Auditor's Role

Regulation S-X spells out the various required qualifications of the independent accountant. The foremost qualification is that he be independent, and there are certain tests that must be met for an accountant to be independent. The SEC will look at all of the relationships between the accountant and the company and its owners and management in determining whether to challenge his independence.

There are a great number of pronouncements on an accountant's independence. He must be independent during the whole period of his audit. Obviously, he cannot have any financial interest in the company during the period covered by his audit. He cannot write up the books and still be independent; he is considered to be an employee in those circumstances. His employees cannot write up the books. His organization must do the audit. He cannot certify the company's accounts in reliance on another auditor's prior work. This would be severely criticized by the SEC. Moreover, the auditor cannot be an officer, director, promoter, or have any kind of involvement that might otherwise affect his attitude toward a company.

Relatives pose a very complex area of independence. Generally, the auditor cannot have a close relative in the employ of a company. Occasionally, a situation arises where one brother is president of a company and another brother is a partner of an independent accounting firm. This gets to be rather difficult, although there are cases that are quite legitimate. The SEC is always willing to discuss these problems.

An even more complex area of independence arises when the auditor is too closely identified with his client. They go on vacation together, they play bridge together every Friday night, and they do many other things together. The auditor gets so involved with his advice to the client and in so many of his client's business matters that it is hard for him to stand back and take an objective, unbiased look at the company. While a relationship such as this is not specifically prohibited by the SEC's rules, it does have an independence problem inherent in it and it needs to be watched.

The consequences of the auditors not being independent are that the required certification has not been provided. A company must make sure its auditor is, in fact, independent.

Scope of the Audit

This is another troublesome area, and a principal reason why companies have to plan ahead when they are going public. For many years, the SEC accepted a form of opinion in which an auditor would in effect say, "I wasn't around to observe the inventories when they were taken at the end of the prior periods, but I came in and observed the last inventory, and, based on tests, I have no reason to believe the other inventories weren't properly taken. With this explanation I believe the accounts are reasonable."

Seven or eight years ago the SEC had some difficulty with a couple of filings, and decided that from then on it would no longer accept that form of prior-period opinion from independent auditors.

Today, the independent auditor has to be fully satisfied. He has to give a clean opinion, and in most cases to do this he has to have been around to observe the inventory at the time it was taken at the beginning and end of a series of years.

In those situations where a company has good inventory and financial records, an auditor may be able to satisfy himself enough to give a clean opinion—particularly if he has observed two or three inventories—without the necessity of his having to have examined at least four in order to cover that three-year period. But a company never can be sure. If it is thinking of going public, it should plan about three years ahead of time in the auditing area. Without proper certification a company cannot go public. The SEC does not waive its rules in this area.

If a company is involved in litigation or in a tax contention, the independent accountant can express his opinion subject to the ultimate outcome of the litigation or tax settlement.

Importance of Timing

Finally, there is the timetable that must be worked out among the groups mainly involved in the new security offering, the company and its owners, the underwriters, the respective attorneys, the accountants, and the printer. The timetable is important because many problems require days, weeks, or even months to solve.

Thus, if any group cannot meet the timetable, the company will have to put off going public until some other future date.

Concluding Note

Following is a kind of brief checklist of the financial accounting and auditing matters a company should take into consideration if it is planning to make an initial public offering in the future.

One of the first things should be to determine that the auditor really is independent within the meaning of the SEC requirements, then to make sure that he carries out an audit that is adequate to express a clean opinion, particularly in the inventory area.

The next thing should be adequate plans for the preparation of financial statements on a timely basis. This requires a reliable internal accounting organization and good inventory and other financial records.

Then, accounting principles should be reviewed to make sure they are appropriate and generally accepted so that they will meet with SEC approval.

Finally, the structure of the business should be examined to see whether it needs to be reorganized in some manner in order to have an economic entity for which appropriate financial statements can be prepared.

Preparations for
Financial Public Relations

Whatever your business experience in the past might have been with public relations, it becomes an entirely different matter when you step into the area of investment community relations—whether at the national or regional level. In the financial world, your exposure and acceptance can spell dollars and cents to the success of the first public offering of your common stock.

Common Fallacies

However, let me point out at the outset the fact that you should really drop the corporate image fallacy in a discussion of public relations, because such images to the financial world

---

Mr. Pincus is President, The Financial Relations Board, Inc., a national consulting firm with offices in Chicago, New York, Los Angeles, Minneapolis, and Toronto. He is the author of numerous articles on shareholder and investor relations in leading business publications.

are something that just are not there. Rather, in your financial public relations—above any other types of communications you have—you are bound by legal and other restrictions to talk about things that are there.

A contemporary example of image building is something that happened to me not long ago. Basically, I am a straight-laced, retiring fellow, but my wife decided to change my image. She had me grow sideburns and wear wide ties in an attempt to make a swinger out of me. The result was that I simply ended up to all my friends as being a straight-laced, re-tiring fellow with sideburns and wide ties. And the lesson in this applies, really, to a company that is trying to be something that it is not.

'The Record Speaks for Itself'

Yet, at the other extreme, there is a tremendous amount of conservatism inherent among privately held companies. Another common fallacy found today among private—and even among publicly held companies—is the one that reads, "Let our record speak for itself."

In a textbook marketplace where some wondrous computer would enable everyone of the nation's 22 million investors to know everything there was to know about every conceivable publicly held security, then that statement might hold true; the record would probably speak for itself, and a price/earnings ratio would surely reflect the precise indication of a company's inherent worth.

But all of us know only too well that such is not the case in today's marketplace. Records simply do not speak for themselves, and the financial laryngitis that so many companies have becomes quite acute at the beginning of the process when a company is first going public.

Let us assume that as of the moment, and for a number of years in the past, you have been accustomed to having perhaps only a dozen or so competitors in the product marketplace. All this is suddenly going to change. You will find in going public that you now have some 6,500 actively traded, publicly held "competitors," as well as perhaps 55,000 others that are technically public. Financial public relations can help you to compete successfully under these circumstances.

'Why Lift a Finger'

Before getting into some of the financial public relations techniques of how you can help your record and potential to speak for themselves, I would like to discuss briefly why you should lift a finger to do so at all. In point of fact, there are many companies, including some very large and well-known ones, today whose management still have this "Why should we" attitude. Conversely, this year publicly held companies in the United States will spend in the range of $300 million on something called financial relations.

At one extreme, even some of the most hard-headed business executives, who eschew financial public relations, usually answer the question of "why" by stating that their return on investment is merely the so-called improvement of their "corporate image." At the other extreme, some businessmen confide, not without some embarrassment, that through their financial public relations program "We are hoping in the back of our minds it will help run up the price of our stock."

Both extremes are dead wrong. I believe most of us would agree that good financial public relations is not, and should not be, the stock promotion business. However, to be tangibly effective, it cannot merely be a foggy function of corporate image building; it has to be public relations with an above-the-board purpose.

'Active' Programs

The plain fact is that truly effective financial public relations must have an "active" format, as opposed to the "passive" kind. By passive, I mean those that simply comply with the ordinary statutory regulations of the SEC, the stock exchanges, and so forth, for the release of information.

Obviously, an active financial public relations program is not for every company. It certainly will be of no benefit to a company that is really going nowhere, and here I am not referring to a company that is going into bankruptcy. Rather, I am thinking of a company whose story basically is on the surface and there is nothing more to tell. An illustration of this would be a company with a track record and long-term outlook that is quite unimpressive by overall investment community standards. Realistically, that company could never hope to achieve a significantly higher price/earnings ratio, or to attract greater investor attention than it would nominally receive after a modest public issue. To those companies going nowhere, then, financial public relations can offer scant value. Nevertheless, many of them today waste their time, effort, and money in a fruitless quest for the pot of gold at the end of the rainbow.

Professional Analyst Target

To those companies going somewhere—the ones with genuine short-term and long-range plans, with proven growth records, and with good prospects for even greater growth both internally and externally—a sound program of financial relations can be of quite exceptional value. The fundamental reason why I make such a strong claim is that the financial community today is a tremendous pyramid, whose broad base contains the nation's 22 million investors or shareholders and whose top is made up of a relatively small number of professional security analysts who are exercising an increasing amount of influence on the overall buy-and-sell decisions.

Today, with 10, 15, and 18 million shares being traded daily in the marketplace, the average broker has much less time available in which to be his own security analyst. Beyond him, the average individual has even less time to devote to his own pursuit of security analysis. Thus the burden falls increasingly on the shoulders of the professional security analysts, of whom there are currently a record 10,500 in this country, compared with less than half that number just five years ago.

It goes without saying that a tremendous amount of expertise is being built up by the ranks of those professional security analysts today, and your corporate fate in going public rests more in their hands than anywhere else. In fact, in terms of expertise, those professionals have reached the point where they have even made a distinctive separation within their own ranks; they now have a Chartered Financial Analyst ranking which the most erudite, most learned of them can achieve.

Important Objectives

In viewing the professional security analyst audience and in putting together some tangible reasons why you should try to reach that influential group with your corporate communications, there are some very definite goals that you should keep in mind which extend far beyond simply building a better corporate image.

Primary Markets

First of all, there are primary markets for a company whose securities are traded over-the-counter, as yours would surely be on going public, since your managing underwriter almost invariably whosesale markets your securities and he thereby becomes, in effect, your "stock exchange."

However, in the over-the-counter market, one of your major goals should be to achieve breadth in that stock exchange. In other words, you want to have not only a broad coverage of wholesale activity in your own backyard, but also in all the important financial centers from coast to coast. Major headway toward broadening investor awareness and interest can therefore come from the primary dealers in those marketplaces.

The number of firms in the securities industry that are giving active retail sponsorship to your offering—not because they have any allegiance or ties to you through the managing underwriter but simply because they regard your company as a very attractive investment—is one of the most important aspects of your stock's seasoning and your maturity as a publicly held company.

Geographical Interest

Another major goal is to sustain broad geographical interest for your public offering in the retail after-market. You can have a successful managing underwriter, and you can also have broad coverage that takes your securities to the four corners of the country, but sustaining the after-market interest is an important consideration because of the danger that the stock might otherwise gravitate right back to where it started. If the interest of the investors, brokers, and professional security analysts in those regions distant from your headquarters and plants is not maintained, then this gravitation back is the natural evolution. Along these lines, you should also strive to generate fresh interest in other areas of the country, as well as in your own region, that have previously shown little or no interest in your original underwriting.

The point here is that to be ideally successful the market for a company's stock should show a full range of geographical scope across the country, and an increasingly broader base of stock ownership.

Additional Goals

The above major considerations lead to still other objectives, one of which is stock exchange qualification. There have been pros and cons debated for years over the advantages and disadvantages of a stock exchange listing, and many people still maintain a company enjoys some distinct benefits in remaining over-the-counter, even after it qualifies for an exchange. Of course, if you should follow the advice of someone who feels that an exchange would benefit your securities, then the groundwork has to be laid for meeting those many rigid qualifications.

Another goal should be satisfactory liquidity for your securities. Liquidity is achieved basically through an active trading volume so that when an investor buys or sells 500 or 1,000 of your shares on a given day, the price of your stock comes under no pressure. In other words, satisfactory liquidity maintains a stable market and provides one very important boost toward your stock's maturity.

Lastly, a worthy goal, and perhaps the most important one of all to the growth of your company, is a maximum *sustainable* price/earnings ratio. I emphasize the word "sustainable," because companies often, for short-term benefits, make concerted efforts to see that their price/earnings ratio increases to the maximum point possible. But in the long run more than one company has almost invariably found that to really be of value—that is, to preserve the company's reputation in the investment community, and to retain the confidence that people have in the company and in its management—you have to strive not for a maximum, but for a maximum sustainable price/earnings ratio.

Early Head Start

Now, let us turn our attention to some of the considerations that you should be thinking about in this area of financial public relations prior to your public issue. First, we feel concerted action should begin approximately one year prior to when you plan to actually have your public issue. There are two valid reasons for making an early head start.

One reason is the fact that you want to establish believ- ability, and financial public relations helps to develop such *third-party* endorsements for your company. Nowhere else is believability more important than in the financial community —although it might certainly have some importance in the consumer community among product claims, and so forth—in maintaining and building a company's reputation among investors whose savings are involved.

Consistent Pattern

The second reason for starting a year early is to establish a clear and consistent pattern, and this is very important from an SEC standpoint. Some companies have tried to promote themselves too quickly in the last month or two prior to a public issue, and have found that because suddenly on short notice they have come out of the closet to let the world know exactly who they are and what they are doing, the SEC has in several instances delayed the offering. The SEC claims, and its laws point more and more in this direction, that those companies are purposely preconditioning an investment audience.

However, if you have established a consistent pattern of allowing the press access to your company, of even issuing annual and interim reports prior to going public, and of putting to good use a number of other techniques which I shall cover in a moment, then this pattern can simply be a normal part of your corporate life before your public issue. In other words, start acting like a publicly held company a long time in advance of when you actually become one.

Vital PR Elements

One technique is being available to the press for comments about your industry. You may be the fourth or fifth, or eighth largest firm in your industry, despite the fact that you are private. Actually, the business and financial media do not really care whether you are public or private as far as your expertise in your own industry is concerned. Often their articles have an investment slant, but the main thrust of the information that the business press wants to get across is what is going on in a particular industry. And you know what is going on in yours as well as the next man—whether you are public or private.

Another element in developing rapport with the financial press is the extent to which you can arrange profile articles on your company, especially if it happens to be somewhat different from other companies in your industry. Certainly, you cannot discuss what your company's financial prospects are—as a publicly held company may do—but there are many newsworthy editorial elements that you can go into, and we PR specialists see companies using this technique quite often.

Moreover, the issuance of news releases on new contracts, financial performance, acquisitions, and other elements is also extremely valuable if done consistently.

Issuing an annual report is another public relations element that many privately held companies fail to consider, and yet this is a natural and ideal way to get your company's story across before going public. The annual report may not have to be as detailed as those that follow your public issue, but it is a vehicle for introducing many people for the first time to what your company is doing and what its progress has been.

Developing capable speakers among top management is another very important part of this going public preparatory process. When you are public, you will find that one man alone can no longer handle the job of being a corporate spokesman—at least it is extremely difficult. The president or chief executive officer has a great deal of work to do just watching the store, much less talking to security analysts and financial editors. Thus the greater depth you can put together as far as articulating management talent, the better off your company is going to be just prior to, during, and following your public issue.

Development of good visual aids is another important part of this program. Many companies have only catalog sheets or product literature of the drabbest sort conceivable. Other wide-awake companies have annual and quarterly reports, press kits containing editorial material on the company and how it operates and on how the industry operates, and well-organized slide films. Of course, putting a comprehensive package of visual aids together can be a time-consuming process, and so your head start is an excellent period to begin work on that.

As the date of public issue approaches, your financial public relations advisers, attorneys, underwriter, and others will all advise that you will have to call a halt to every bit of the activity that I have just mentioned in compliance with SEC regulations.

Company Profile

During the registration period, one other aspect is quite important, we feel, and that is to develop a complete company profile. The prospectus serves one purpose; but to bring your company to the attention of the investment community immediately following the post-registration period, one technique that we have found to be most effective is to issue a comprehensive report in the same format and with the same objectivity as a brokerage firm or investment adviser would do.

In other words, put together a profile of your company which is not an annual report or a corporate history—because investors care very little about history, really—but a report focused on what your competitive position is currently, spelling out as much information in as well-organized a fashion as you can, and on the overall market outlook for your industry.

If you happen to be in the steel business, there would be very little necessity for that, because brokerage offices have reams of material on what the market outlook is for the steel industry. However, if you are in a more specialized or new and lesser known field, this can be of immense help. You might for example have good earnings this year, and you might have an excellent competitive position. But if the after-market in the investment community does not know it, then that is just going to be one more stumbling block to sustaining the kind of financial public relations program that can help continue and build the reputation you have begun during the underwriting period.

Legal Matters
Prior to Going Public

From the standpoint of considering legal matters prior to going public, both your corporate counsel and the counsel for the managing underwriter you finally select will be interested in a number of things.

First, of course, they will be interested in knowing that the company has been validly organized. They will examine your corporate charter, your by-laws, and—even worse—your minute books. In many instances, counsel finds in doing this corporate examination that since, say, 1923 no one has bothered to keep any minutes.

This is no cause for alarm or panic, because it happens quite naturally in a closely held company—where one or two families have been involved—that no one bothers to call annual meetings. The principal stockholder runs his company, and if

Mr. Faletti is a Partner in the Chicago law firm of Winston, Strawn, Smith & Patterson.

he did have directors, they would merely give their blessing to what he proposed to do.

But when it comes to the point of considering a first public offering, then these things do have to be given some close attention.

It is quite easy while the private company is still controlled by one or two individuals to hold a meeting in which important corporate action can be ratified. For example, you can have the stockholders elect the directors who have purported to be your directors, and then the directors can turn around and elect the officers who have purported to be your officers.

By this process of ratification of past acts, they become just as valid as if they had been initially approved.

In some instances, of course, it may be necessary to obtain affidavits from executives who have been around the company for a long time as to what may or may not have been done in the past. I am thinking particularly of your stock record book. As lawyers, we are interested in seeing that the stock that you think you have issued and have outstanding actually has been issued and actually is outstanding—and that it has been paid for. All this is important because we have to give an opinion that your outstanding stock is validly issued, fully paid, and nonassessable.

Sometimes, it is difficult to establish that issued stock has actually been paid for due either to the sequence of transactions when old certificates have come in for transfer to other names, or to the fact that the old certificates are missing from the stock records. In such a case, again, an officer of the company can probably provide an affidavit as to what did in fact happen.

Retention of Control

Generally speaking, the officers in control of the small, closely held company will wish to retain control after going public. One device that can be effectively used is the noncumulative voting procedure pursuant to which holders of 51% of the company's shares can elect the entire board of directors.

If your company happens to be an Illinois corporation or an Ohio corporation, for example, where you are required to have cumulative voting in the election of directors, the only way to solve the problem is to reincorporate your company in a state such as Delaware which does not require cumulative voting. This sort of thing can be done quite easily when you have only a handful of stockholders. In fact, the action can even be taken by written consent of the stockholders.

However, if you are unsure whether you want to go to the expense of doing a reincorporation in Delaware, you can postpone this step until just about the time the underwriters are ready to offer your stock publicly. Then, you can do it just about concurrently. In that way, if the deal does fall through, you will usually save the out-of-pocket expense of reincorporation.

One problem with noncumulative voting, which you should be aware of, is that the State of California—particularly, the Commissioner of Corporations in California—does not permit it. In order to qualify your stock for sale under the California Blue-Sky Law, a disclosure has to be made in prominent, bold-faced type in your prospectus that your stock does not have cumulative voting rights.

Corporate Directors

Another device often used to retain corporate control is the classified board of directors—that is, a third of the board

113

is elected each year and each director serves a three-year term. While I think it is fair to say that most underwriters really do not care for this kind of control, it is nevertheless a decision to make as you go along in the discussions with your investment banker.

From the standpoint of providing corporate democracy, and perhaps of avoiding the headache of noisy dissidents at your stockholders' meetings, a wiser course might well be to shun the classified board of directors.

With respect to the number of directors serving on your board, decisions will have to be made on such questions as: Are all of them to be inside directors? Are there to be some outside directors? If outside directors, should they come from your banking connections? Or, for example, should one of the partners of your investment banking firm also be one of your directors?

Here, again, the investment banker you select to work with you will have some definite recommendations to make regarding the composition of your board of directors.

There are so many problems with respect to a director's liability that it is becoming increasingly difficult to get outsiders to serve on company boards. Outsiders, who have respected names either in your community or in a particular industry, may have a great deal of hesitancy about exposure to stockholders' suits which can impose serious liabilities on directors.

Preemptive Rights

Another question to consider is whether or not your stockholders should have preemptive rights. These permit existing stockholders to purchase a proportionate share of any future issue of stock or convertible securities the company may wish to sell.

Some underwriters feel, however, that if stock first has to be offered to your existing stockholders, it becomes a little more expensive in connection with the public distribution because of the waiting period while the shareholders determine whether they want to exercise their preemptive rights. Under the rules of the New York Stock Exchange, for example, the stockholders have to be given 14 days in which to exercise their rights. And, if any of the stockholders live west of the Mississippi River, they have to be given 16 days.

During this waiting period, the underwriting syndicate—which is committed to buy all the shares not purchased by the existing stockholders—is exposed to market risks. Thus the spread of the commission, which the syndicate underwriters are going to insist on for handling a rights offering, will be greater than if they were not exposed to such market risks.

Again, this is an item that should be arranged before you go public rather than after you are publicly held. As a private company with comparatively few stockholders, it is much easier to amend your charter by either unanimous written consent of the stockholders, or by an actual stockholders' meeting than it is as a public company to circulate proxy statements and to hold a meeting of 2,000 or 3,000 stockholders.

Restrictive Rights

Other matters of interest to the lawyers will be restrictions found in loan agreements, debenture or bond indentures, first mortgages, bank term loan agreements, and the like.

If you have done any term loan financing, you are aware that the insurance company or bank lenders attempt to operate your business through the loan agreement. A typical restriction which might be found is a limitation against the payment of dividends. Usually, an earnings test is imposed so that you possibly may be permitted to pay dividends out of 50% of your profits, earned from a period commencing with the date the loan is made to the date at which the test is being applied. If such an earnings test is not met, then you are not permitted to pay a dividend.

Thus the extent to which dividends can be paid out of your current earnings becomes a question that may relate to the pricing of your new issue, because the ability to pay dividends may be an important consideration with respect to your particular company.

Other Restrictions

Once in a while, there is a restriction concerning the type of business in which you may engage. The lender knows that you are knowledgeable about the business you are now in, and he may decide to restrict you by making you promise that you will not engage in any other business about which you may know very little.

If part of your future plans does entail getting into some other business, this restriction is one with which you may have to contend.

Another type of restrictive agreement is a voting trust where the stock certificates are actually lodged with a trustee who has the power to vote the stock. This is sometimes used as a device for maintaining control of the company. Usually, the president of the private company is the voting trustee and he, having all the voting powers, can elect the board of directors each year, and in turn cause the board to elect the company officers.

116

However, the voting trust may create difficult problems, particularly if you are contemplating a listing on the New York Stock Exchange whose rules prohibit this kind of restrictive agreement.

Still another kind of limitation is the stockholder restrictive agreement. In many closely held companies, the family that developed the business operation, or the family which controls it, in order to keep capable employees will make some of the common stock available to employees—but subject to an agreement requiring that the stock be sold back either to the company or to the family stockholders.

Frequently, if two or three families have participated in the organization of a company, the restrictive agreement may require that the stock be offered on a first-refusal basis to members of the other families in the event any one particular family wishes to dispose of its holdings.

Moreover, as one of the conditions in this stockholder restrictive agreement, the price at which the stock is to be resold to the company or to the other stockholders is often predetermined either on a fixed basis such as book value or on some kind of a formula basis.

The particular problem of using a formula for pricing the stock is that it becomes very inappropriate once you undertake an initial equity offering and the public establishes a market for your stock. The reason why it is inappropriate is that the public will undoubtedly put an appraised value on your stock which departs substantially from the value to be derived by the application of the fixed formula basis in the restrictive agreement.

In many cases, you will find it will be in your best interest to cancel such restrictive agreements. In other cases, it can be continued in a way that is compatible with your first public offering.

Public Disclosure

Before deciding to do a security offering, one important question that must be answered is whether or not your company can live with the public disclosures that you will have to make in the registration statement and in the prospectus. The Securities Act of 1933 requires disclosure of all material facts concerning the company, and provides liabilities for omissions or misstatements of any material facts.

Some companies, of course, feel very strongly about disclosing their operating methods and financial information. This disinclination may either be from a personal management reluctance to disclose such things as executive compensation and bonus and profit-sharing arrangements, or from a corporate reluctance to disclose sources of supply, profit margins, patent arrangements, and so forth, that might be of value to competitors.

Now, if you feel that the disclosure of such information to your competition is going to affect your company adversely, you are going to give the matter a lot of careful thought before becoming a publicly held company.

Company-Management Transactions

In another area, all transactions between the company and its officers, directors, and any stockholders owning 10% of its security, as well as all transactions between these groups of people and other companies or partnerships in which they are affiliated or associated, must be disclosed in the registration statement.

All the Securities Act is actually interested in is your making full and complete disclosure, and it is not its purpose to keep you from going public. Frequently, however, disclosure may prove to be embarrassing. Therefore, you should carefully consider whether or not you can live with what we call the "truth and accuracy" part of the registration under the Securities Act.

These matters should be covered at an early stage with counsel, because it is often in this very area that you really get into the question of whether or not you are actually going to have a public offering.

For example, it is not enough just for you to say, "The corporation has been lending us money; we will stop the practice." That is all well and good for the future, but the loan transactions which have occurred in the previous three years must be disclosed.

In Illinois, for instance, it is a violation of the Criminal Laws for a corporation to loan money to its officers. Many executives do not know this and, in their closely held companies, they think nothing of borrowing from the company to pay their income taxes, and then paying it back a month or two later or having it deducted out of their salaries. I personally do not know whether any corporate executive has actually been prosecuted for violation of this particular law, but it certainly is something you should think about before deciding that you are going to make the disclosure.

If you are undergoing a tax audit at the time you file a registration statement, one of the first things an Internal Revenue agent will look at in the prospectus is disclosure of transactions between management and the company to see if he can find items of interest in connection with your personal income tax return.

Thus it is in this area that a great deal of soul searching must go on, and I think it is here that the lawyer performs his most essential function, because he is going to be under quite severe pressure to approve the nondisclosure of certain things.

Sometimes, we find that in the past the company has issued stock in violation of the Securities Act. Not necessarily has this been done intentionally; in fact, the company may not even know that the manner in which it issued the securities was in violation of the Act.

If such a violation has occurred within the past three years, disclosure of the fact has to be made in Part 2 of the registration statement, and this could create some problems for the company in its dealings with the Securities and Exchange Commission. The SEC staff will undoubtedly ask you to explain exactly why the securities were issued in violation of the Act.

Usually, means can be found for satisfying the Commission with respect to such securities issuances.

Corporate Recapitalization

Another preliminary consideration to be made prior to going public is whether or not your company should be recapitalized. For example, let us assume that your managing underwriter— on the basis of his analyses and examinations—recommends that your stock be brought to market at a price somewhere between $15 and $20 a share, and that this price is to be based on a multiple of 10 times your company's most recent year's earnings. In this case, only a very unusual company would have the right number of shares to be offered publicly, so that the new stock issue could be priced in accordance with the formula the underwriter wanted to follow.

Let us assume that you are earning $50 a share. Using a multiple of 10, your stock would have to be priced at $500 a share. Unless your firm happens to be named IBM, not many members of the public are going to buy your stock at that price. Therefore, your investment banker will probably recommend a 25-for-1 split of your stock, and something like this is what I mean when I use the word "recapitalization."

Prior to the time when you go public, it is easy to amend your charter and thereby enable your company to have the desired number of shares which will earn $2 a share. Then, when the earnings multiple of 10 is applied, you derive a price of $20 a share.

I have seen some recapitalizations which involved splits of the stock as high as 1,000 to 1, 2,000 to 1, and 3,000 to 1. The reason for such high ratios is that in small privately held companies it is not at all unusual to find that there are only 100 or 200 outstanding shares.

Dividend Payout

In connection with your discussions with your investment banker, he is going to be interested in the dividend policy your company intends to follow. Unless, of course, your company happens to be in a phenomenal growth area where the public is going to be interested in buying your stock, in spite of the fact that it pays no dividends, serious consideration is going to have to be given to a dividend payout.

This can create problems in cases where the sole owner, or the two or three people in control of the closely held company, because of individual income tax situations, may not have cared about dividends each year. The argument frequently heard is, "Why should I take the dividend and then come out and pay 50% or 60% income tax on it? I need the money in the company. I will just leave it there and let it build up the earned surplus of the company, and avoid the personal taxes."

Again, unless you happen to be in that unique category of a company which can sell its stock publicly without any dividends at all, you are going to have to seriously consider a

121

payout of perhaps 30%, 40%, or 50% of the corporate earnings.

Now there are various methods used to keep the present proprietors from receiving dividends while still satisfying the public. One device is to recapitalize and provide two classes of shares. One is called Class A stock, the other Class B stock, and both have voting rights.

The distinction between the two is that the Class A stock is retained by present management and is not entitled to dividends, whereas the Class B stock is sold to the public and is entitled to dividends. However, this can present what we call a Section 306 tax problem.

Dividend Waiver

As a result, another device is preferably used, and that is the dividend waiver.

Pursuant to the dividend waiver, the controlling interests of the company that do not care much about receiving a payout agree to waive receipt of dividends either on all, or on a certain percentage, of their stock for a definite period of time. The waiver can relate to receiving no payout whatsoever for three years, or to receiving dividends only on 20% each year until the company's earnings have been built up.

The difficulty with the dividend waiver is that the Internal Revenue Service must rule on the question whether giving up the dividend constituted imputed income to the stockholder making the waiver.

However, with respect to a company going public for the first time, most tax lawyers will give an opinion that the dividend waiver will work. Their reasoning is that if this device is necessary to enable the company to establish a public market for its stock, the stockholder who values his dividends is contributing to that corporate purpose.

Pattern of Compensation

A further consideration which must be given preliminary examination is the present and future pattern of executive compensation and fringe benefits in your closely held business that may or may not be compatible with a publicly held company.

In operating your own business, you probably have never thought of having an employment contract. However, now that you are planning to go public, you may desire to have one so that you have some protection in your job.

Then, again, you still may not care about an employment contract because of your unique contributions to the company. Nevertheless, the managing underwriter may insist that you have a contract for a 5-, 6-, or 10-year period for the very reason that you are so uniquely important to your company. After all, the underwriter wants to make sure that you are going to be in there continuing to run the company once you are able to afford, say, vacations on the Riviera or your own yacht.

If your company has no pension plan, profit-sharing plan, or stock-option plan, the appropriate time to consider whether or not one should be established and put into effect is during the course of negotiating with your managing underwriter.

It is a lot easier to do these things before—not after—you make your first public offering.

Floor Discussion

Question: I have two questions. First, by definition, what is a public offering? And second, what determines whether a public offering has to be registered with the SEC?

Faletti: Taking your questions in reverse order, if it is indeed a public offering by a privately held company, then it

123

must be registered with the Securities and Exchange Commission—with one exception. That exception is when the new issue is confined to what we call an intrastate offering. However, there are serious limitations with respect to trying to come in under this exemption.

There are, of course, other exemptions relating to exempt securities such as those of banks and railroads.

The definition of a public offering is an extremely complex, difficult question involving quite a bit of know-how, expertise, and a detailed knowledge of the facts of the particular situation.

There is an exemption under Section 402 of the Securities Act known as the Private Offering Exemption, and if—on consideration of all the facts—your offering is a so-called private offering rather than a public offering, then you have an exemption and you don't have to register with the SEC.

But making this determination is very difficult.

Many years ago, the SEC followed a rule of thumb that if there are no more than 25 offerees, it would take no action on its own to say that you have made a public offering. However, this SEC rule of thumb was in terms of the number of people to whom an offer was made, not the actual number who ultimately bought the securities.

The potential danger is that any person who bought the securities, even if the offering was to less than 25, could in case it went sour always go into court and say, "It was indeed a public offering and I want to rescind. I want my money back with interest."

In this area, the Private Offering Exemption usually is used in connection with a placement with insurance companies and banks where the offerees are sophisticated investors. They are able on their own to procure from you the information that an ordinary investor would have to get out of your registration statement and prospectus. Generally speaking, when you have

25 offerees, you are approaching the area of a public offering.

Question: Do pending acquisitions have to be disclosed?

Faletti: This is frequently a very difficult question to resolve. Usually, the lawyers do try to pin down their clients as to how far they have gone in any acquisition talks.

Some kind of a disclosure will probably have to be made when you are having discussions about acquiring another company. If the negotiation has gotten beyond the point of discussion, however, to where there is an understanding, then you would have to disclose that you propose to acquire it—even though you may not have a signed contract.

Question: Say you don't have a contract or a letter of intent. You are just talking to 20 companies—you know, any good businessman is talking to lots of companies—do you still have to make a disclosure?

Faletti: Yes, but in this case the disclosure would be just worded to the effect that "the company has been having acquisition discussions with a number of companies, which could lead to one or more acquisitions, but to date there are no commitments, understandings, or agreements, written or oral."

Question: In going back to a point you mentioned earlier, suppose you are a multidivision company and you report your annual sales, not by separate divisions but as a group. Then, further suppose that at your stockholders' meeting someone asks you the question, "What are your sales and profits on this product?" Can you refuse to answer that on the grounds that you feel this is privileged information for management?

Faletti: Certainly, at a stockholders' meeting, management can take the position that "this information is of a nature we would not like to divulge to our competitors, and therefore we don't care to divulge it at this meeting."

Of course, the stockholder does have a right to examine the books of the company. This, however, could require a considerable investment of his time and money in hiring a lawyer to enforce his rights.

You are initially going to run into this question in connection with your registration statement, since the SEC has been pushing toward financial reporting on a divisional basis. In regard to the registration statement, if you are a multiproduct company, sales of any single product which constitutes 15% or more of your gross sales would have to be disclosed separately. Moreover, you would either have to include a statement that the profit margins of all your products were substantially the same, or a statement as to how they were different.

And you will recall, earlier I did mention that consideration has to be given to this kind of disclosure with respect to your competitive situation. It may be that you couldn't live with such disclosures, but in connection with the registration process, they would have to be made.

Question: Is there any minimum requirement on sales and profits for going public on the over-the-counter market?

Faletti: There is no minimum. Newspaper quotations of stocks in the so-called over-the-counter market result from the application of rules of the National Association of Securities Dealers. The NASD has certain tests with respect to the number of public stockholders you have and the areas in which those stockholders are located, and the association works closely with the newspaper publishers in defining standards that they will follow before a company's name is included in the list.

After all, the newspapers don't like to have these things keep expanding all the time, because their space is limited. This has nothing to do with sales or profits of the company.

Any discussion of sales and net earnings is normally confined to the investment banking house in making its decision whether or not it is interested in a particular company or situation.

Question: Is there a minimum amount of trading required before some publicity appears in the newspaper? Does there have to be a minimum amount of trading per day?

Faletti: The trading volume is not one of the significant criteria with respect to the newspaper reporting of over-the-counter prices.

Question: How much information must you give to a minority stockholder—assuming that he has tapped his attorney on the shoulder and said, "I want information"—because your competitor can be a stockholder?

Faletti: Well, he would be entitled, in pursuing his legal remedies, to disclosure of at least that information which is revealed on your books and records.

Question: In order to go public, which one of these four would you suggest that my company approach first. The underwriter? The attorney? The accountant? Or the public relations man?

Faletti: Usually, I have found that in most small closely held companies there is either a very close relationship between the ownership and the attorney, or between the ownership and the accountant. Doing a new public issue is something that probably should be discussed with one or both of these individuals. Then, I think your next step would be to find a prospective underwriter or investment banker.

Question: If you have Class A and Class B stock, can one be entitled to a stock dividend and the other to a cash dividend?

Faletti: That is certainly possible. However, I see no particular advantage in it. If you are going to make stock dividends on a security which, in itself, is not entitled to cash dividends, there is really little purpose in it.

Question: Wouldn't it be an offset of obtaining more stock in the corporation against the person that receives cash in lieu of stock?

Faletti: Usually, the nondividend stock is not the type of stock you are going to be able to use, either from the standpoint of selling to the public or of exchanging that stock in connection with acquisitions and mergers.

Class A stock is usually created for the ownership people who aren't interested in paying a lot of income taxes on dividends.

But it certainly could be done from a corporate standpoint, to answer your question.

Question: You mentioned that in investigating the books and records of a corporation that is potentially going public you might find that it should have registered its securities, or at least some of them with the SEC previously, and you mentioned there are certain alternatives to remedy that situation. What are some of those alternatives? How do you go about this?

Faletti: Going back to my statement, if there was a flagrant violation of the Securities Act, there probably would be no remedy.

Chances are, however, if it was done unintentionally and depending on the length of time which has elapsed, that the SEC will not take any criminal action against you.

The people who bought that stock do have rights to tender it back to you at the purchase price plus interest during a period of time running three years from the date it was issued.

However, if your company has become so successful that you are going to have a public offering, from a practical standpoint there is very little risk of recision.

Arrangements with the
Investment Banker

Selecting an investment banker, I think, is one of the most critical financial decisions that a company can make. This decision is somewhat akin to picking a wife, but in some ways perhaps more difficult and some may think even more important than picking a wife!

A logical starting point is not to think of the relationship with an investment banker in the customary terms of credit and money. You are not buying a commodity. Rather, you should approach it from the viewpoint that the relationship, if it is to be successful, will have to be a rewarding one for both parties and that it will be based on *mutual confidence,*

Mr. Detwiler is a Vice President and Director of E. F. Hutton & Co. Inc. He is also Chairman of the Finance Committee, member of the Executive Committee, and on the Board of Directors of Continental Mortgage Insurance. He is a member of the Executive Committee and Board of Directors of Tesoro Petroleum Corp., and additionally serves on the Board of Directors of Handleman Co. and Hayes-Albion Corp., as well as others.

trust, and *respect,* and frequently a close personal relationship.

When you associate with an investment banker, both in the financial community and in the business world, you take on the stamp of that investment banker. If your company is new to the public and not known in the financial community, people will associate the investment banker with you. His successes and failures to a great degree affect you. And so if you associate yourself with one who has had some deals that have run into difficulty, you are going to be tarred with that same brush.

There are a great many varieties of investment bankers, and their standards vary when it comes to eliminating such things as conflicts of interest, and other "problem areas." However, any top-flight investment banking firm insists on what I call "clean deals" and thus avoids a lot of built-in problems that could possibly come back to haunt both parties later on. Accordingly, the selection process is a two-way affair, with the reputable investment banker choosing his clients at least as carefully as the company should the banking firm.

The standards of a top-flight investment banking firm are much higher than the legal requirements of the SEC, the stock exchanges, and NASD and the state regulatory authorities. The reputable investment banker is determined not only to do a good job of raising capital for the company, but also to protect the public interest. In short, he desires to build something which both parties will be proud of, and which will be in the company's and the public's interest over a period of many years. And so, corporate management should look forward to building a solid, lifetime relationship with the investment banker.

The investment banker puts a tremendous amount of work into the first financing for a company and he hopes to amortize his investment in this undertaking over a period of years and

130

in a number of other deals. The company, too, has a large investment in the undertaking, because of its identification with the investment banker and because of its cost of assembling materials for the investment banker and educating him in the company's business. Therefore, it is very important to pick an investment banker for the long pull.

Investment banking firms deal with many industries, and it probably is unreasonable for a given company, after the investment banker has done an underwriting for that company, to assume that the investment banker will not do a public offering for another company in the same industry. After all, there are only so many industries in the country, and if the banker did only one public offering in each industry, I am sure you can see that after a period of time there would be nothing further he could do.

However, in the event there might be a potential conflict of interest, I do think that the investment banker has an obligation to discuss this in advance with his client and, generally, this problem will be satisfactorily resolved.

In many instances, the company owners may feel there is a significant advantage in having an investment banking firm that specializes, say, in insurance company deals, retail trade, the petroleum industry, or what have you, because this specialized knowledge may enable the firm to do a more accurate appraisal.

Actually, the potential conflict of interest may be a hidden advantage. The confidential nature of the relationship is vital, and a company should consider its arrangements with the investment banker as similar to dealing with its own attorneys and accountants. Top-flight firms do not misuse insider information, strictly as a matter of policy quite apart from any legal ramifications.

Screening the Investment Banker

There are a number of different kinds of investment banking firms. There are small firms that cater to regional or local areas, large national firms, and firms in different areas of activity. For instance:

• There are wholesale investment banking firms which do not conduct a large brokerage business or actually engage to a great extent in the sale of securities. They are simply underwriters, who make financial commitments, arrange private placements, and handle mergers; their retail brokerage business is somewhat of a side line.

• There are retail investment firms that do a large brokerage business and only a little investment banking.

• There are integrated firms that do a large investment banking business and a large retail brokerage business.

• There is a further group of investment firms, frequently "wholesale firms," that do only large deals for America's leading corporations. This, in itself, is a highly specialized area of the investment banking business. The clients of such specialized organizations are typically in America's top 500, and it would be very unusual for any of these companies to change their investment banking relationships. Such relationships may have endured over many decades.

Key Questions

An investment banker's interest in a potential corporate relationship is important, but not all investment firms, for one reason or another, are interested in every type of company. In view of this, I think it is important for the issuer to appraise the potential interests of the investment firm.

Further, what is the firm's track record? Of its last ten deals, how many have gone up or down? Have any of the deals run into legal entanglements, such as SEC problems? Just how has this firm performed? How carefully has it done the job of analysis, the job of selling, and the job of after-market follow-through? How aggressive or conservative is the firm? This, I think, can be again looked at in the light of the firm's track record.

Is there an opportunity for a mutually rewarding relationship between the investment banking firm and the company? I am speaking financially, because we are all in business to make money, and the compensation of investment bankers usually—but not always—is based on the consummation of some sort of investment banking transaction. If there is no immediate transaction in prospect, it may be difficult for the issuing company to interest or motivate the investment banking firm.

I think you have to be realistic and analyze whether the relationship can be mutually rewarding. Is there a warm feeling? Do you like the people? Are they going to be easy to work with? You do not usually have a successful relationship with a lawyer or a doctor or an investment banker unless you like them and get along satisfactorily.

You certainly want to look at the standards of the investment banking firm. Are they high? Will those standards fit your company in terms of your size and type of deal?

In regard to costs, most large investment banking firms' fees are relatively similar. The differentiation between firms is not in the fees that they charge, but rather, it is in the quality of work they do. For example, most large firms do not take cheap stock, warrants, or options as part of their investment banking compensation. There is a belief—and I think it certainly is a correct one—that if a deal requires an inordinate compensation to sell, then it must be set up incorrectly or priced too high. A deal should be set up so that it is an attractive piece of merchandise compared to other investment opportunities and, therefore, it sells itself.

Be sure to consider carefully the qualifications of the individuals in the investment banking firm. What is their experience? What is their background in different industries? What is the breadth of the firm's facilities? Is it the kind of firm that handles only one type of investment banking transaction? Or is it the kind of firm that handles virtually the entire range of financial services?

Approaching the Investment Banker

There can be a problem of going too early to an investment banker with nothing more specific in mind except that ultimately, say, in 1975, you want your company to be publicly owned. This can be a financial problem because in the interim period, where there is no specific deal to focus on, time is costly for both the company and the investment banker.

On the other hand, if you approach the investment banker too late, with many critical decisions made, sometimes these are difficult—or utterly impossible—to change and that can present a serious problem.

As a generalization, I would say that you should approach your investment banker about a year in advance of your proposed offering and perhaps even longer in advance than that, especially if there has been no history of audits with "clean certificates."

Approaching investment bankers is relatively easy, I think. An investment banker usually has a well-known reputation. Most of the things that he does are published in *The Wall Street Journal* and in the business and finance sections of other newspapers. You can check his track record. There are any number of ways to check on investment bankers and to approach them. Some of the sources that immediately come to mind are the firm's clients, commercial banks, attorneys, and accountants. By "accountants," I am referring particularly to the national firms.

In addition, discussions on a very preliminary basis with several investment banking firms can be useful, but there is a big danger in doing so. "Shopping" a deal can do a company about as much harm as anything. No investment banker likes to think that he is getting a thrice-rejected deal that no one else liked. Further, some of the firms that might have rejected a potential piece of investment banking business might ultimately reject participation in the underwriting syndicate.

You see, we are a funny business. On the buying or corporate finance side, which is the area of our business involved with setting up, negotiating, and readying a deal for market, we all compete aggressively with one another.

On the other side, our syndicate partners are out having lunch and playing golf together because they all have to cooperate with each other in bringing a syndicate together and in marketing the security. And so beware of shopping a deal.

Choosing the investment banking firm is something that has to be done carefully and without creating too many ripples in the financial community which, by the way, is not very easy to do.

Compensating the Firm

In terms of compensation, most investment firms prefer it to result from the performance of some specific task, such as bringing a new issue to market or handling a private placement. Fees are usually a modest percentage of the amount of money involved, but a successful deal can have a tremendous impact on the corporation.

Investment banking firms, of course, have to determine where they are going to devote their time. As I indicated before, a mutually rewarding relationship is really the only one that is going to work. I think it is important that the investment banking firm and the company be perfectly frank with one another in discussing compensation to head off potential problems that might arise in this area.

Sometimes companies may be anticipating doing a public offering, but the timing of it may be two years or more away. In such a case, the company may set up a retainer arrangement with the investment banker to provide him with modest compensation over the interim period, during which various analyses and reports might be prepared. But basically, the investment banker looks to the successful conclusion of a deal for his compensation.

Usually, companies prefer to concentrate their business with investment banking firms rather than disperse it. For instance, the brokerage business from the company's pension fund or from the owner's personal accounts makes the company a more important client to the investment banking firm, and creates a desire within the investment firm to devote more time and effort to an even larger relationship.

Secondary Service

In addition to the raising of money, investment banking firms perform a variety of other services, some of which can frequently be more important than the initial public offering. I think that the great responsibility begins *after* the securities are offered publicly.

After-market sponsorship and follow-through are important responsibilities of all investment bankers, but the way in which the individual firm does this varies tremendously. Does it prepare periodic research reports? Do the research analysts keep themselves abreast of all developments in a firm's group of investment banking clients? Typically, other firms will call the banker's analyst who is following a given company and expect him to be better informed than anyone else in the financial community through in-depth study from publicly available information.

Investment banking firms usually will make an over-the-counter market in a given company's securities after an offering and for an indefinite period of time in the future.

There is the question of assistance in the handling of a listing on the American or New York Stock Exchange, or of assistance and guidance in mergers and acquisitions. Investment banking firms frequently have important contacts with other companies which might be potential customers or suppliers. These contacts can be very helpful to their clients.

From time to time, investment banking people are invited to sit on corporate boards. They can be a valuable source of general financial guidance in the early years of a company, and particularly in its first year after a public offering.

Forming the Syndicate

I want to discuss just briefly the important job of an investment banker in forming the underwriting syndicate. A typical underwriting for a small offering, let us say, of 200,000 shares at $10 a share will consist of a syndicate group, a managing underwriter, and perhaps 25 other underwriting firms.

Each of these firms makes a financial commitment to underwrite a certain number of shares, and once the agreement among the syndicate underwriters is signed, each virtually unconditionally agrees to buy those shares.

How does this come about? First of all, major retail firms,

which may be underwriting as many as five to seven new issues or more a week, will seldom have the time to examine every aspect of the issuing company. Therefore, they will have to rely on other things. Certainly, they will read the prospectus and the underwriting documents, but they will basically rely on the good reputation of the manager.

The manager will attempt to have a few of the most prominent firms in his syndicate. Once he persuades these firms to join in the underwriting, usually the smaller firms—seeing not only a well-known manager, but several extremely well-known and successful firms in the underwriting field—readily come in: "What is good enough for these firms, must be good enough for us."

The Short Position

During the period that the issue is being readied for market, the manager has been getting indications of interest from the "selling group." A firm that might have put down for 8,000 shares as an underwriter, for example, might have only a retail indication among its customers for 4,000 shares, and so the syndicate manager is constantly adjusting and shuffling these shares over to another firm that is, say, committed to 3,000 but has demand for 8,000.

Ultimately, after all this is done—and it requires a high degree of judgment—at the time of the offering, the syndicate manager has a retail demand for at least 200,000 shares. Let us assume, in this case, that he has a retail demand for 215,000 shares, and is thus selling 15,000 shares short to provide stabilization in the after-market.

This short position is one of the most misunderstood areas of our activity. It sounds bearish if somebody has a short-position stock but it is actually very bullish. The larger the

138

short position, the more bullish it may be for the offering, because the more stock there is that has to be bought. The old saying is, "He who sells that which wasn't his'n, buys it back or goes to prison." We have to repurchase those shares we sold short. The expression we use is that we "burn up the short"—hopefully at premium bids over the offering price, which means we lose money on each share repurchased.

Concluding Note

I think that any company considering a public offering in a year or so is in a good position to start to assemble a file. Watch *The Wall Street Journal*. Read the advertisements of the deals that have come to market and pick those firms that are doing the most comparable offerings to your own. Then, watch their after-market performance.

Have your secretary just automatically clip *The Wall Street Journal*. Then, six weeks or eight weeks later, or at some other point downstream, run a comparison on how the stocks have done in the market compared to offering price. Also compare the price/earnings ratios of the securities at the time of offering and in the after-market, and the gross underwriting spreads that are charged.

You can usually obtain a copy of a prospectus from any investment banking firm. Then, when you get it, on the cover of the prospectus you will see the pricing table, which shows exactly how the underwriter is being compensated. Look at the fine print right under that table, and you will also see any warrants or options or cheap stock or reimbursed expenses that the underwriter is receiving in addition. In this fashion, you can become more sophisticated in selecting a firm that has done a good job with the most comparable offerings to yours, and see what the cost would be to have such a firm do it.

Floor Discussion

Question: Can the underwriter buy some of the stock for his own personal account?

Detwiler: If the deal is a good deal, the answer is "No." If nobody wants to buy the security and it looks like it will fall out of bed, I guess it is probably all right. But the underwriters can never take a free ride on a hot issue.

Question: What do you think about listing on the National Securities Exchange?

Detwiler: Just as it can be a mistake to go public too soon, so it can be a mistake to get listed too soon. The problem with listing prematurely is that you then have only one man—a specialist on the floor of the Exchange—making a market. The "depth" in the market varies widely with the amount of capital of the specialist, with the volume of activity in the stock, and with other factors. The specialist may have no continuing contact with the investing public, and he is not sponsoring your security at all.

We have seen instances where companies have listed prematurely and the market activity in the stock just dried up. No one was sponsoring the stock and no one was talking about the company.

The National Exchange is a small exchange, and some of the companies that are going on it, of course, are only meeting extremely low requirements. Whether or not it will work out well in terms of a good market is something that remains to be seen. It is still too new to express an opinion on.

When a company considers listing, one of the important things to think about is the customers of *which* firms own its stock. If its over-the-counter market has been primarily made by nonmember firms, or if the company was underwritten by nonmember firms—and presumably the customers of nonmember firms own your stock—and the company lists, the demand might be substantially diminished. This can serve to depress the price of the stock.

By contrast, if the firms making the over-the-counter market are member firms primarily and the stock lists on an exchange, this market is usually quite bullish after the stock has been seasoned.

Question: Let us assume that I was recommended to an underwriting firm and I started a preliminary relationship. However, after a period of time, I didn't like the way things were going one way or the other, and there was a falling out. Then, let's further assume that I decided to go to another firm and went through with the underwriting. Am I obligated in any way for the fact that I decided not to go with the original firm?

Detwiler: There are no legal obligations, of course, until the transaction is consummated, because there is no binding legal document until then. I know of one instance where the company did arrange to compensate the original investment banking firm, but I would say it is not typical at all.

Question: You indicated that there is a period of negotiation between the underwriter and the company in prospect. How do you evaluate and what should you look for in this negotiation?

Detwiler: I think I would look for two things: a high degree of professionalism and high ethical standards, and an attractive deal.

Question: How about the money?

Detwiler: There is a very definite area of negotiation. What is the cost to you, the issuer, of doing the offering? The gross spread will vary widely depending on the size and nature of the financing.

We will put down on our spread sheet all the most comparable offerings that have been done and what their gross spreads were, so that the issuer has a clear idea of what the parameters are.

It is desirable to appraise the underwriter carefully in terms of his personnel and the continuing services that he is going to provide at no cost to the issue. But once a company has done an underwriting, the kind of services that you can expect are, first of all, to make a market in the stock if it is traded over-the-counter, as most initial public offerings are, and continuing research reports. The kinds of questions that I would ask of an underwriter are: "I noted you did this deal last year. Have you put out any research reports since then? May I see them? Who are your clients?"

The size of the firm is an important consideration. For instance, if it is an average firm with the bare minimum of requirements to do an offering, you may be neglected as the client of the firm in terms of acquisitions and other things.

If it is a small firm, on the other hand, and the decision is made entirely on the offering price, you may decide that you will go with this firm because it has indicated a willingness to bring your stock to market at, say, $15 a share, whereas the best preliminary indication you have from any other firm is a lower figure. If your decision is made on that basis, the odds are very great you will go with the least desirable firm.

The firm will be motivated primarily by the gross underwriting spread, the profits that it will make on selling the stock, and it will assume no risk in terms of the after-market stabilization in taking a short position.

Question: Is that what the warrants are used to do? To protect the short position?

Detwiler: No, the warrants are purely an additional compensation to the underwriter—"We would like you to have a real stake in our company because we want you to continue to do various things for us."

But the major firms have come to the line of reasoning that if they cannot do an offering at a conventional minimum gross spread, they probably shouldn't do it anyway. It has very negative implications for the other participating underwriters and for the investing public as a whole when you see the underwriter getting all kinds of special deals for himself.

As a rule of thumb on a $2 million offering, an underwriting may cost about 10% of the amount of the issue, including the gross underwriting spread which is typically in the area of about 8% with another 2% covering the legal, printing, and accounting costs. This is assuming that the underwriter would be coming on year-end audit figures.

Question: What about the retainer fee? Wouldn't that fall in the same category?

Detwiler: Retainer fees are uncommon. However, where relationships are established and no immediate transaction is in prospect, and the underwriter is called on to give a lot of advice and guidance well ahead of the offering, there are, occasionally, retainer arrangements.

There are also retainers in connection with a merger program where the company owner says that he wants to buy.

Question: This may be a matter of semantics, but you call yourselves "investment bankers." I know what commercial banking is. Can we use the term "investment banking" synonymously with "underwriting?" Is this a carry-over from the old days?

Detwiler: Commercial banks typically are depositories of funds and lend relatively short-term money. Investment banks purchase, or underwrite, the distribution of securities. The two terms, "investment banker" and "underwriter" are synonymous. But the term "investment banker" is usually applied to a broader area than merely underwriting. It includes doing private placement—that is, providing long-term capital privately—and negotiating mergers. The three principal activities are underwriting public offerings of securities, mergers, and private placements. In other words, an investment banker deals in all sources of capital—usually long-term capital—while commercial banks deal in only one.

Question: Commercial banks can also do underwritings, for instance, of municipal bonds?

Detwiler: Yes, but not corporate securities.

Question: Is the extent of the short position a negotiable item, or is this at the discretion of the underwriter?

Detwiler: It is not negotiable, because the way to determine the short is when you are at the moment of the offering. It is very hectic. All the participating underwriters and their syndicate managers, through their branch office systems, are getting reports from their customers' men that are filtering back to the manager. He is taking stock away from one underwriter because he feels the account is soft there and putting it with somebody else, and doing everything he can to equate supply and demand.

The size of the short will largely be determined by the syndicate manager's figures and his feel for "the account." Unfortunately, he can't be positive about this kind of thing. He doesn't even know, for instance, whether the people who have put in indications are, in fact, going to buy the stock, although by experience he does have a strong conviction in that area.

I would say from an issuer's point of view, a more important area of discussion—and we might call it negotiating with the underwriter—would be, "What are you going to do about the stabilization of the offering?"

The underwriter is only allowed under the agreement among underwriters to take a short up to 10% of the issue. That is the maximum. He can do other things, however. If the stock starts to break through the issue price and he has already used up his short position in stabilizing it, he can now swing over and start buying it long for the account of all the firms that participate under the agreement. But this is rarely an area of real negotiation. It is an area where the client wants to have the conviction that the investment banker will do a responsible job of stabilization.

Question: When a new issue goes short like that, is that when people say it is over-subscribed?

Detwiler: Yes.

Question: Where do the underwriters get those additional shares?

Detwiler: They buy them back in the after-market.

Question: If the stock goes from $10 to $15, and it does not come down, who actually dishes out the extra money?

Detwiler: The underwriters.

Question: They are the ones responsible?

Detwiler: Yes, but there is a variation on this. The issuer and underwriter together agree that an unusually large short should be taken. Under some circumstances, the underwriter may have a call on the issuer for additional shares to cover the short.

Question: Say a company issues a certain number of warrants associated with a finder's fee. Is there a suggested percentage of how many warrants it will issue and the period when these warrants will expire?

Detwiler: No. As I mentioned earlier, you will usually find that the least costly underwriters, in terms of totally effective costs, are the largest and often the best firms, and they will not take warrants. The reasoning is that if they should need additional compensation, they shouldn't do the underwriting in the first place.

The Registration and
the Offering

The Securities Act of 1933 applies to any public offering of securities made by the issuer or any person in control of the issuer; so for any method of going public, whether a sale by the issuer alone, a sale by the principals alone, or a combination of the two, the Securities Act would apply equally.

There are two aspects to the Securities Act as they apply to public offerings. One is the requirement for registration, which in a sense is mechanical. You simply must register. If you sell stock which should be registered, you violate the law if you sell it without registration. Registration is effected by the filing of a registration statement, which includes the prospectus. I am sure you have seen prospectuses and you are familiar generally with what they are.

Mr. Kramer is a Partner in the New York law firm of Shea Gallop Climenko & Gould.

The other area of potential liability under the Securities Act is based on misstatements or inaccuracies in the prospectus.

So we have the two aspects: the registration itself, and the "truth and accuracy."

Just in passing, the penalty for failure to register stock is that any person who buys the unregistered stock has an absolute, positive right—without any limitation—to rescind his purchase for a period of one year after the purchase. In other words, he has an absolute put-back to the person from whom he bought it. He can return the stock and get his money back. If he sold the stock during the period for less than he paid, he can file suit for damages for the amount of his loss.

From this point on in my discussion, I shall be talking about the registration statement and the prospectus—how to prepare them, the responsibility for preparing them, how they must be used, how they can be used, and the liabilities for misstatements or omissions in these documents.

Preparing for a Transaction

Once your stock is registered, you can sell the particular shares registered in accordance with the terms of the offering described in your particular prospectus. I think you would never get this impression by reading the Securities Act itself. The registration is really for a transaction, so if you want to make an offering of, say, 200,000 shares at $10, what you register is 200,000 shares for offering at a certain time through your underwriters at $10 a share.

You cannot register any stock you do not plan to sell. If you have more stock of your own that you are thinking of selling at some time in the future—if you will permit me a little oversimplification—I would say for practical purposes you cannot do it.

147

If you want to do a second offering later on covering your own stock, you have to have another registration statement at that time, which would be prepared in the same manner.

Once stock is registered and sold pursuant to an initial offering through the underwriters, and it is subsequently reacquired by the company, by purchase or otherwise, or if it is acquired by any controlling person, it loses its registered status, so to speak.

This is why I stress the point that the registration is, in fact although not in theory, for a transaction.

With very limited exceptions, once stock is in the hands of the public, there is no distinction between registered or unregistered stock. The real question should be:

Is registration required for the sale of a particular share by the particular seller at the particular time?

And the answer to that will depend on the circumstances of the sale and the identity of the seller.

Liabilities for Misstatements

Before we get into the mechanics, I would like to mention something I think you may find a little startling—namely, one of the liabilities for misstatements and omissions. At the end of the registration process, you produce your final prospectus, which is the document used in connection with the sale of the registered stock.

Under the Securities Act—this is a very extreme concept of liability—any purchaser of that registered stock, whether he buys it on the original offering or subsequently in the market, has a right to sue the following people: the issuer, any person in control of the issuer, every director or officer of the issuer, and every underwriter.

What he can sue them for, if he has a loss, is the amount of his loss from the offering price down to his selling price. He can sue them if the prospectus contained a misstatement of a material fact or omitted to state a material fact required to make the statements in the prospectus not misleading. In other words, everything in it must be true and there must be no omission required to make the statements true, or, to put it a little differently, there must be no half-truths. If this truth standard was not met on the effective date of the registration statement, the liability to the purchaser is absolute for the period of the statute of limitations.

This right to sue extends to anyone who buys the stock for three years after the offering, that being the statute of limitations under the relevant section of the Securities Act.

For the initial period, which I shall delineate in a minute, it is not even necessary to prove that the stockholder had ever seen the prospectus, let alone relied on it.

To illustrate, if the prospectus is in existence, any person who bought that stock has a right to sue the people I named and, except for some technical defenses which I shall not go into, he will usually recover.

Thus you can readily see it is a very extreme liability and it serves to point out the importance of preparing your documents with care.

Assuming it takes 14 or 15 months to prepare an earnings statement, the effect is that anyone who buys your new issue for 14 or 15 months after the initial offering and loses money on it—provided there is a misstatement or omission in the prospectus—can sue all those people I named for the amount of his loss. There is no necessity for him to prove that he knew the prospectus existed, that he had seen it, that he relied on it, or that he knew it was wrong or should have known it was wrong.

149

Regulation A Exception

There is a slight exception to this for small offerings, which I shall mention only in passing, and that is Regulation A. You probably have heard of this special provision which applies to offerings up to $300,000 in any one year.

Under Regulation A, the SEC requires, before you offer securities, the preparation of what is technically known as an offering circular as distinguished from the prospectus, even though the offering circular comes out looking very much like a prospectus. For all practical purposes, the nonfinancial information required is identical by the time you get through with it. However, the financial statements are somewhat less elaborate, both in the number of years covered and in the number and scope of the statements.

Technically, certification by independent accountants is not required in a Regulation A offering circular; but with this relatively unimportant exception, these documents are practically indistinguishable from the prospectus.

In my judgment, there are many disadvantages to a Regulation A offering. It does not come out a lot cheaper because there are basically the same costs, such as the printing process and legal work, and there is still a good bit of accounting to be done, even though perhaps not quite so much.

As I shall explain in more detail a little further on, a registration statement and prospectus are filed and processed by the SEC main office in Washington where the people are not only highly experienced and highly skilled, but are likely to do it faster, more professionally, and more predictably.

Most people who file Regulation A offerings find the opposite is true in every respect. In the first place, they are required to file with the nearest regional office of the SEC, of which there are nine in various parts of the country. The processing is handled by the local staff members who are conscientious and some of whom are quite able. The problem is that generally these people do not have much experience in the field.

Protecting Yourself

Let us turn our attention to some of the things you can do to protect yourself against liabilities under the Securities Act. Underwriters will always require the issuer, or sometimes the selling stockholders if there are any, to indemnify against any liabilities they may incur as a result of any misstatements or omissions in the registration statement and prospectus. This standard practice is certainly sound and no reasonable person would quarrel with it.

The underlying concept is that the facts concerning the issuer are peculiarly within the knowledge of the issuer, and any liability based on the fact that the registration statement or prospectus is inaccurate should properly be borne by the issuer who is ultimately responsible for the misstatement.

Preparing the Documents

In any discussion of the preparation of the registration documents, it is important to understand the difference between the registration statement and the prospectus. These are actually two separate documents. The prospectus, which is only one part of the registration statement, consists of a cover page that identifies the company, the kind and amount of securities to be registered, and the computation of the filing fee. The filing fee is a relatively nominal amount.

As a matter of physical preparation, the prospectus is bound right into the registration statement. It is customarily a little

151

less than eight and a half by eleven inches, although almost any size is legal, and it says, "Prospectus" right on it. If you have ever bought a new issue, a copy was delivered to you with your stock certificate.

Appropriate SEC Forms

The balance of the registration statement consists of what is known as Part 2. This part of the SEC form contains certain questions to be answered item by item. These data are more or less of a legal nature, which are not of general interest to potential investors, compared to the information required in the prospectus.

If anyone wants to see this information, he can find it in the registration statement, but the SEC does not require that it also be in the generally circulated prospectus, because it is not of enough interest or significance.

The registration statement also contains certain additional financial information, generally classified under the heading of schedules, which supports the balance sheets and income-statement items as required. Again, however, these data are not considered to be of sufficient general interest to investors to require their inclusion in the prospectus.

There are various SEC forms for registration which are more or less in question form. Some are quite routine, such as "State when the issuer was incorporated and in what state." Others are of the broadest possible scope, as, for example, "Describe the business done for the last five years and intended to be done."

Anybody who has never compiled a prospectus certainly should begin by looking at the appropriate forms. For any commercial or industrial company, there are really only two forms that are ever likely to be used by a private company. One,

152

which is the most common for any established business, is known as Form S-1. There is a separate one called Form S-2 for new businesses. The legal and practical preparation are substantially the same in either case.

Compilation Responsibility

Whose responsibility is it to prepare the prospectus? This is nowhere clearly defined. The answer is, it depends. Some underwriters like to do most of the actual preparation, at least of the business parts, themselves; also they send their own people to dig out the information. Sometimes the issuer, when the company has people who are experienced in the field, may want to take the responsibility.

The lawyers on either side may play a very active part in it. Perhaps the company, if it has a lawyer experienced in the field, will want him to do it. Then, again, perhaps the under-writers will want their own attorneys to do it. That would probably be the least likely case in terms of preparing the first draft.

In any event, the issuer must provide all the information required, and the answers will depend on the circumstances. Some businesses are considerably easier to describe than others.

For example, the proprietor of a chain of supermarkets does not have to report much more than the fact that he has a lot of competition.

On the other hand, the manufacturer of, say, five or six ex-traordinarily exotic, space-optical-type products that defy de-scription is going to have a most difficult job getting that in-formation down in such a way that others will understand. If the description is accurate, does justice to the business, and does not disclose more than is legally required, then the job is well done.

153

Filing With the SEC

When the registration documents are completed, they are filed with the Division of Corporation Finance of the SEC in Washington. Structurally, this organization of more than 1,400 employees is capped by a governing body of five commissioners. Below are various divisions, each with a director and a number of assistant directors. Within each division are several branches, and if yours is an ordinary registration with no complicating factors, the highest authority in the structure with whom you are apt to deal is a branch chief.

Branch Examination

Each registration statement that is sent into the SEC is assigned to a particular branch which includes a chief, examiners, an attorney, an analyst, and an accountant. They figuratively and almost literally take it apart and go over it looking for what they can find. It is difficult to say just what they look for. Of course, they read it to see that it complies with the requirements of the law and the applicable form, and to see whether it has internal inconsistencies. They may require the applicant to disclose, to elaborate, to tone down, or to prove some of the things that are stated in his registration documents.

They have available to them all published sources of information, and they do check these to a certain extent. I am often asked whether the SEC makes an independent investigation of the facts about a particular business. As a general rule, no; but the examiners certainly have every right to, and we must keep in mind that they have all the resources of the federal government at their disposal for that purpose.

If your company depends to any material extent on doing

154

business with other branches of the government, particularly the military or space, I think you can count on it as a matter of course that the SEC is going to check the other side of what you say with the appropriate officials.

The SEC also has experts. It has an oil and gas expert who looks at every oil and gas registration. It has a mining expert who looks at all mining registrations.

Everything depends on the facts. With an old established company, such as GM or AT&T, there is very little independent SEC investigation; the examiners know that business and the registration is going to sail right through. Conversely, when a brand new company, particularly one of a complicated nature, files a registration statement and prospectus, the process is going to take longer.

Of course, much depends on the personality of the SEC people to whom the documents are assigned, as well as on the quality of the presentation. Are the documents clear and lucid? If they are, they will perhaps get a little less going over than those for which the opposite is true.

What happens after the branch examiners have worked the registration over? A convention has grown up as a matter of practice that works very well in fact. However, there is absolutely no warrant for it in the statute. If you study the statute carefully—layman or lawyer—you will conclude, quite rightly, that a registration statement automatically becomes effective 20 days after it is filed.

Nothing could be further from the fact, especially under the existing backlog conditions at the SEC. What happens is that by voluntary act of almost every registrant, the 20-day automatic effective provision is suspended. This is accomplished by including a sentence prescribed by the SEC on the cover of the registration statement when it is filed.

Deficiency Letter

The SEC, during the period of filing, looks over your registration, reviews it as I have explained, and sends you what is known as a deficiency letter or letter of comments. This represents the views of the examining branch about what you have to do to make your prospectus accurate and complete.

If the letter, as is frequently the case, is something that can be complied with without violating any of your principles, you do so. You expand this and delete that according to suggested changes, and you are all set. You file an amendment the same way that you filed your first registration statement and incorporate the new prospectus.

The SEC will look at amendments very promptly. If there is no big problem, in a day or two you are likely to get a telephone call, or at least they will respond to your call, and they will tell you everything is all right. Then you pick your offering schedule, and you are ready to go public.

Suppose you do not agree with what the SEC says in the deficiency letter. Perhaps the examiners have missed a point, or they ask for something you cannot or would rather not do. What can you do then?

For one thing, you can face facts, which is sometimes the best idea, and comply with their suggestions at the outset.

If you do not favor this alternative, there is a very informal process, amazingly so considering what is involved. You can telephone the appropriate person at the SEC in Washington. You can usually find out readily who he is, although sometimes he is hard to reach by phone. It can be exasperating. If you get him, you try to convince him of the rightness of your position, and sometimes you succeed.

SEC staff members, by and large, try to be helpful. I have never dealt with any of them whom I thought was uncooperative. If they think something peculiar is going on, you will know it in a hurry. If they see something they think is fraudulent, you can argue in vain forever; but if you are acting in good faith, I think you will get nothing but full cooperation.

If a phone call fails to do it, there is no reason not to go to Washington for an informal conference. They will give you all the time you want, and either you convince them or not. I would say in 99 cases out of 100 you can come out with an agreement you can live with. There is not much I can say about the 100th case, but generally things go, if not smoothly, at least satisfactorily.

Using the Prospectus

During the period after the time you file your registration statement and before your effective date, what can you do legally without violating the law?

Assuming that your prospectus is not materially deficient, it is perfectly legal to give the red herring prospectus to anyone and in any quantity you want to. The concept is to disseminate the information before the offering is made.

For various technical reasons, it is hard to keep track of the people to whom you give the red herring prospectus. However, if you should make a material change in your prospectus, it may be advisable to give the revised one to everybody to whom you gave the first one, so there can be no possible contention that they were relying on false information. Apart from that possibility, which is relatively unusual, there is absolutely no limitation on the number of people to whom you can give the red herring prospectus.

There is a limitation on what else you can give them during the offering period. Again, technically, you are not allowed to give them anything else in writing—no annual reports, no advertising material, no summaries, no research reports—about the company. The red herring prospectus is the only thing that can legally be used in connection with the proposed offering during the period between filing and the effective date.

This does not apply, of course, to a letter of transmittal. You can send something out to the effect that "I am pleased to enclose a copy of this prospectus in case you are interested." That is all right, but anything other than the prospectus that might be construed as a selling document is absolutely illegal —no matter how accurate or how inoffensive it may be.

You are allowed to make oral statements during the period. You can say anything you want as long as the oral statements themselves are true and complete. This sounds like an evasion of law, but it is not so at all. This is technically the way the statute is written. You might very logically say that it would be more sensible to permit written and forbid oral statements, but that is not the way it is.

Investor Distribution

Anybody who purchases the stock must be given a copy of the final prospectus no later than the time he gets any other offering material. Usually, that will be with the confirmation from the broker or the underwriter. The confirmation is the regular little bill you get when you buy securities. The prospectus must accompany that.

In understanding the structure of the Securities Act, an important point to keep in mind is that the buyer of the stock may never have seen your preliminary prospectus; but as long as the final prospectus accompanies the confirmation, all the requirements of the law have been complied with. The concept of the distribution of the red herring is that the information was available for anybody who wanted it. The underwriters are required to make reasonable efforts to make it available to investors generally, but if someone never saw the red herring, it is nevertheless legal to sell him the stock.

When the confirmation comes from the broker, the buyer is at that moment committed. That legally is when the firm contract for purchase takes place, and still the buyer may not have seen your final prospectus. It sounds a little peculiar, but that is the way it is.

What is the theory of this? He did not have to buy your security in the first place. If he is willing to buy without seeing the red herring or without seeing the final prospectus, what he really has is a three-year insurance policy against the stock going down.

Coming full-circle to where I started with the discussion of liability, if there is something wrong in that prospectus, whether or not he knew it, or even if you tried to make him read it and he said, "I won't read it," his rights are still the same. If there was something wrong and the stock goes down, he can recover from you for three years on the basis of the misstatement or omission. The basic concept is that the burden is on the issuer to make sure that the information is right. No one has gone so far as to legislate for the protection of the issuer that the investor must read it before he buys.

Once the prospectus is effective, it is now legal to put out other material with it. Thus, if you are still offering, you can distribute anything you want in written or oral form so long as the final prospectus goes with it and everything else you say is accurate.

The prospectus is much more than a legal document for people to put in their desk drawers. There is a lot that can be done with it. Anybody who takes the approach, "Who's going to read it anyway? Just put in everything as negative and as bad as you can," is really his own and your own worst enemy.

I think you count on all your competitors reading it with maximum care. I also think your customers are going to show great interest. And so are a large number of nosey people in general.

Apart from the description of the business, there is a great amount of personal information—compensation arrangements for the executives, stock ownership, titles, and so on. Outsiders are going to find out many things about you and your company for the first time.

I would like to emphasize that everything I have said about the registration statement is equally applicable to every company that files. The size of the offering makes no difference. This is equally true whether it is the stockholders selling their own holdings, or whether it is the company selling its own securities. The rules are the same; the uses are the same; and the practicalities are the same in every case.

Attitude of the SEC

I should mention a bit more about the SEC's attitude, which is very negative for what you can say about your business. In effect, the Commission says, "Point out the risks and qualify any statement that might be considered to be optimistic."

Thus, even if you are able to prove your statements, they sometimes will not let you say anything that even smacks of prediction of improvement in volume, earnings, position, or market. However, if you think something is going to take a turn for the worse, it is always important that you say so in your prospectus.

For example, if you think your industry position is fourth and you can prove it, you can say your company is the fourth largest whatever-it-is. However, if you are positive you

160

are going to be third next year, you cannot say that. But if you think you are going down to sixth, the SEC's attitude is—and perhaps rightly—you have to put that in.

There is one other thing I do want to mention about liability and protection. Insurance against Securities Act liabilities is available in the market. All I shall say is that it is quite expensive, that the companies who write it are very selective in their risks, and that I doubt that anyone going public for the first time would be able to get it.

Perhaps the second or third time around, when there is an established market for your stock and the insurers know your business, they might be willing to consider your company as a safe risk. But generally, I would say that it is pretty much limited to large, established companies. Nevertheless, in a particular case it might be worth looking into.

If you are interested, take it up with your regular insurance broker. He may not have heard of it because it is quite rare, but he should certainly know where to go. After all, it is just another specialized kind of insurance to him.

Timing and Cost Factors

There are two aspects to the timespan involved in the registration and the offering of a new security issue. One is from the time you make up your mind to go ahead until you file with the SEC. The other is from the time you file with the SEC until your registration statement is effective.

It is easier to discuss the first—the time required from the moment you decide to proceed until you actually file. It is really up to you. The key consideration always is when the financial statements will be ready. First, you have to decide as of what day you want your financial statements, and various considerations may enter into that decision.

161

Having decided what day you want your financial statements, the next question is: *How long will it take the accountants to have them ready as of that day for inclusion in the registration statement?*

To risk an unsafe generalization—assuming the availability of your financial statements and assuming no unusual problems of any sort—for the first time going public you ought to be able to produce a filable registration statement from a blank piece of paper in about four weeks, if everybody gives it his attention.

As a practical matter, almost all registration statements are printed although the law does not require it. If you use an experienced printer in New York, Chicago, or wherever, you will save a lot of time. Any schedule I discuss will assume the use of the best financial printers. They are all expensive, and all run about the same price.

Registrations have been prepared in less than four weeks. A real rock-bottom minimum is somewhere around ten days to two weeks, and that is a schedule where you will not get home to dinner very often.

However, it also can literally take months, depending on what happens, if things start to change and drag.

Sequential Order

Once your registration statement and prospectus get to the SEC, the situation becomes a little harder to predict. These documents get assigned to a branch, as I discussed earlier, and they go to the bottom of the pile in that branch.

With minor exceptions all of the filings are dealt with by the SEC in the order in which they get there. If you can convince the Commission that you have a very compelling reason why you want to go fast, such as you have to sell your stock to meet a pressing obligation and there is no other way to meet it, or something else relatively unusual, it might help.

In the normal course, however, once it gets there, it sits until your branch examines it. Moreover, I think that the smaller and less pressing the issue looks, the longer it is apt to take. Any crisis the SEC has is likely to be at your expense. Anything that comes in which involves a legitimate rush will move ahead of you. But all of them do get done.

SEC personnel review registration statements and compile comments. How long it takes varies with how busy they are at the particular moment.

The early spring, say in March, is a slow period generally for two reasons. One is that the same SEC people who review registration statements also review proxy statements for stockholders' meetings. By and large, these meetings come in March and April and the proxy statements are mostly down there in January and February, thus increasing their burden.

The other thing that makes the early part of the year a little busier than others is the heavy volume of filings. Again as a general rule, many companies try to use their December 31 financial statements in their registration statements.

In any event, the registration process takes as long as it takes. You are free to call or have your lawyers call and check with the SEC people. If they answer your calls at all, they will tell you they are doing their best, and that they "hope to have it out by the end of the week." After four or five times, you are likely to get it.

Once you have gotten your deficiency letter, how long it takes after that really depends on whether it is a big or little deficiency, and how fast you want to go. If it is not a particularly serious one, there is no reason why you should not count on being out within two weeks after that. Once you have your comments and the Commission sees that you mean business, it does go very fast. There is no more going to the bottom of the pile. You are on the top of the pile, and it sweeps right along.

Fees and Other Expenses

How much does all this cost? Other than the underwriting compensation, the costs are fairly much the same, regardless of the size of the issue.

The SEC Filing Fee. This is a minimal amount, being 1/50th of 1% of the aggregate offering price of the securities.

Printing Cost. This is a very large expense, because financial printers get fantastic prices compared to other kinds of printing. However, considering the wages that they have to pay and the services that they perform, I personally think their prices are not out of line.

The mechanical requirements as to the form of financial statement and the presentation of the information in the registration statement are quite rigid. You should not have to worry about those; the printer should.

There are probably 20 or so printers in the country who are perfectly qualified to do this work. You want one nearby. I hate to estimate printers' fees, especially with prices going up as fast as they have in recent years. Nevertheless, to give you a rough idea of the cost factor, I would say that for a relatively small offering of $1 million to $2 million—underwritten with a regular syndicate, with not too many amendments to your registration statement, and not too great a quantity of final prospectuses—you ought to be able to do it for $15,000 to $20,000.

Some people handle printers better than others. If you make them your stenographers and every time you change a comma you order a new proof, it is going to cost more. Moreover, if everything gets down there at 4 A.M. and you want it delivered at 7 A.M., you are going to pay double for overtime. Conversely, if you can time it so it gets in on regular time, the cost is going to be less.

Legal Fees. This relates to the issuer's own legal fees. Sometimes, especially on smaller issues, the issuer will be required to pay the underwriter's counsel's legal fees and other expenses. They are going to be what they are going to be. That is a matter of negotiation.

What should your own lawyer get? It is difficult for me to answer that. Generally, it would never be less than $10,000, under existing standards, at least in New York City and environs.

How high might it go? That is also a hard question to answer, the problem being that so many other things sometimes are involved. If there is a complicated recapitalization or if you want to make up to your lawyer—when the money is coming in—for the money you should have paid over many years, it can get quite high. There is really no top but, on the other hand, it is a negotiable item.

You are going to have to pay your accountant, too.

Blue Sky. This involves complying with state securities laws. State regulatory authorities have concurrent jurisdiction with the SEC. The cost depends on how many states your underwriters want to sell in, what states they are, and how much you are offering.

The filing fee in some states for certain types of issues can run as high as $1,500. In the past, such fees have been as low as $2, which is what it was in New York until recently raised to $20. There is no way of predicting. With a $2 million offering, your normal filing fees would run no more than $2,500.

Customarily, the issuer pays the fees of the underwriter's counsel for doing the legal work in connection with Blue-Sky matters.

Miscellaneous Expenses. These include things like preparing stock certificates and paying the bank transfer agent to put them out. They do not amount to a great deal.

Floor Discussion

Question: I understood you to say that stock registered and not sold loses its registration. What effect does this have on convertible debentures? How is registration accomplished for the convertibles and also for the stock so converted later?

Kramer: I assume that your question is about the stock issuable on conversion. On a convertible debenture, taking it as a single security, the rule applies as it does to anything else. You must sell the convertible debenture itself soon after you become effective. The conversions into common stock would be deferred over a number of years.

When you register the convertible debenture, you also register the underlying common stock into which it is convertible, and no further registration is required. There is a sort of semi-exemption to that extent for the issuance of stock on conversion of convertible securities.

Question: I would like to get something clear on the liability on this new issue. Suppose you were to acquire a company that had gone public within, let's say, one or two years, and you acquired 100% of the stock. Would the acquiring company have any of that three-year liability as through misstatements or omissions in the prospectus?

Kramer: I believe it would.

Question: Let's say that a corporation, which already is registered and has stock on the market, acquires other companies that are not registered. Do they go through the same procedure in registering and issuing the prospectus in this whole thing as far as the acquiring companies? What do they have to do in regard to these newest corporate acquisitions?

Kramer: To put that in different terms, your question is: If you have a public company that acquires a private company in exchange for stock of the public company, what are the registration requirements?

There are a number of ways in which registration can be avoided. It depends entirely on the circumstances of the case.

It's possible that you would need a registration statement, but for many reasons that interrelate, I can't answer generally. Registration would be required if there were a relatively large number of stockholders in the acquired company, and you were going to acquire the stock of that company rather than merge with it or buy the assets.

If you merge or acquire their assets, there would be no registration required for the acquisition.

Question: Can you register stock that is available for issue under a stock option or stock purchase plan that may not be issued or exercised over the next year or two?

Kramer: Yes, you can. Not only can you do it, but there is a much simplified form of registration statement which doesn't amount to much more than a description of the particular plan and a five-year summary of earnings of the issuer.

Question: In your discussion of getting the prospectus on the road, who is in charge of the production timetable: the accountant, the attorney, the client, or the SEC? Who rushes the entire thing from raw copy to a finished prospectus? Who is the traffic manager, as it were?

Kramer: It will vary. It really depends on who your people are and who wants to do it. I think it would be very unlikely that it would be the underwriter, because there is only so much he can do.

It would probably be somebody on the company's side, either your counsel or some official in the company, or a combination of both, because ultimately it is the company's registration. It just depends on who is best qualified and who is willing to do it.

Question: Would it most likely be the attorney?

Kramer: It would depend on the particular attorney.

The Accountant's Role in the Registration Process

Before we can actually put the financial data into a legal form, as required by the Securities and Exchange Commission, I think consideration has to be given to the importance of constructing a time schedule so that all the principals—the company officials, the underwriters, the attorneys, the accountant, and eventually the printer—involved in the registration process know when they are expected to produce, fulfill, and discharge their respective responsibilities.

Critical Deadline

In constructing this work schedule, the most important date is the time within which the financial statements get stale. For companies which do not report annually to the SEC, the date

Mr. Wende is a Partner in the Chicago office of Haskins & Sells. His special area of interest is in supervising the work of corporations which are making public offerings.

of the balance sheet must not be more than 90 days old at the date of filing the registration statement. For example, if you are filing with respect to fiscal year-end statements, 90 days after December 31 is approximately March 30. This statement must be certified; or, if not certified, a certified balance sheet has to be filed in addition as of a date within one year. Details are spelled out in the instructions to Form S-1 and Regulation S-X.

Because most accounting firms are heavily involved in year-end audits for the greater majority of companies that have calendar-year closings, it sometimes takes 60 to 90 days subsequent to such year-end before the audited financial statements can be issued. As a result of this time requirement, the independent accountants start from the critical due date and actually work backward to the various conferences, meetings, and requirements that must be met in order to determine that the company can meet the legal 90-day financial statement deadline date in filing the registration statement, which includes the prospectus.

In this regard, many companies going public for the first time quite often do not use their regular year-end as the audit date since either they cannot meet the critical deadline dates or the financial data may be considered stale by the underwriter. Meeting the critical deadline date may be delayed as the result of some complications in getting certain legal or financial problems solved such as a corporate reorganization, an acquisition negotiation, cancellation of employment contracts, cancellation of leases between principal shareholders and the company, arrangement of observing and taking physical inventories, and so forth.

Therefore, instead of the audit being as of your regular fiscal year-end such as June 30 or December 31, you will probably arrange that the audit be extended to meet the time requirements of keeping the data from being called stale by the SEC. This does not mean the regular year-end will not be audited, but rather that the extended period will also be audited. This extension date of a June 30 year-end might be July 31 or August 31, which would give you an extra 30 or 60 days. Many companies find that they just cannot obtain the information within the 90-day deadline, particularly when they are being audited for the first time.

Physical Layout

Within the registration statement are generally financial data which cover various periods of time, and in many cases include a short or "stub" period. This latter period sometimes causes a lot of trouble, and I shall get into that shortly. But, first, let me briefly mention the actual format and the location of the financial data.

The five-year summary of earnings is so important that it is not contained physically with the remainder of the financial data; rather, it is located at the forepart of the registration statement. The preparation of this summary probably causes more problems to the company and its accountant than any other section of the registration statement. Involving as it does the underwriters, the attorneys, the company officers, and the auditors, the summary of earnings sometimes takes many days to prepare.

Since the regulations require a five-year summary of earnings as well as statements of income for the most current three years, most registrants combine the requirements in a five-year summary of earnings.

The most current three years of the statement must be covered by the public accountant's opinion. In some cases, the underwriters may request that all five years be certified, and in rare cases a ten-year certified statement has been requested, usually where a business is cyclical, all for the purpose of assisting in the sale of the securities.

Some of the difficulties encountered in compiling the five-year earnings summary are consistency in application of accounting principles; unusual adjustments or losses resulting from Internal Revenue Service examinations, or sale of a material portion of the business; acquisitions; application of accounting pronouncements that may have a retroactive effect on financial data; and so forth.

Each problem area must be carefully considered for each of the five years, for any effects prior to this period that may affect surplus or possible subsequent effects, and for related financial data presentation such as equity statements, notes, or schedules. The thoroughness of consideration given to these problems and the presentation of the financial data take considerable if not a major share of the preparation time.

Emphasis on the technical competence of the individuals, or the company or professional advisers who are compiling this information, cannot be overstressed. Deficiencies in this area cause almost more comment from the SEC staff reviewer than any other area of the financial information in the registration statement.

Preceding the summary of earnings is an introductory paragraph which explains that this statement has been examined for certain specified periods by the independent certified public accountant and that his opinion appears elsewhere in the registration statement. In the event that a stub period is included in the summary, it also explains that in the opinion of management all adjustments necessary for a fair presentation have been included in the unaudited financials, and that such adjustments include only normal recurring accruals. If the adjustments are other than normal recurring adjustments, the registrants must furnish a letter to the SEC staff describing the nature and amount of such adjustments. The introductory paragraph also refers the reader to the other related financial statements and notes included in the registration statement.

This preparation may sound relatively simple, but it covers a multitude of items, and serious consideration must be given to each phase—format, content, and overall results and possible interpretation thereof by outsiders. If a company fails to give all the information that is asked for, or what we know from discussions with the SEC staff is required, then after the registration statement is filed the company will get a letter of comment commonly called a "deficiency" letter from the SEC which will require a correcting amendment.

Naturally, all of us would prefer to hold such SEC comments to a minimum, because these could easily delay the final effective date of the registration statement as well as cost the company additional money for preparation of the data.

The format is reasonably described in Regulation S-X and instructions to Form S-1, the latter form being the one most often used for any established business. (There is a separate Form S-2 for any new business.) The significant problems are not in the layout of the form, but in the application of such technical areas as consistency of accounting principles for the entire period covered.

Hopefully, at this point in the registration and offering process, all the accounting and related auditing problems have already been solved. Even so, many times as the physical layout is made and each earnings statement is put side by side, suddenly it becomes apparent that there are certain items that will either have to be explained or will require corrective adjustment.

If the company has any foreign operations or domestic subsidiary operations throughout this period, there may be more complications since, if material, they must be included in the financial data presentation. This is why various accounting problems, or any auditing problems related thereto, should be solved early. Careful thought and analysis of each reporting period will make the final process of compiling the earnings summary much easier and will avoid the pitfalls of unpleasant surprises at a late date.

Explanatory Notes

The statement of earnings includes notes which describe certain material factors that affect various income or expense items in the presentation or computations such as per-share earnings. The notes to this statement follow the style of the statement format and if possible are shown at the bottom of the same page.

An example of such notes would be an explanation to the effect that there had been a stock split or a recapitalization which had affected the per-share earnings. The statement itself, being a very complex instrument, requires any number of notes to explain such items as "What is the company's pension plan policy?"

In such cases, at the bottom of the financial statement, there will probably be a note that, in effect, says, "See page 19 of the company financial statement for a description of these various items." This reference may be to the forepart of the registration statement, or to the financial notes presented with the other financial statements.

The back part of the registration statement contains the balance sheet, the statement of earned surplus, and possibly capital surplus or additional paid-in surplus—whatever the title happens to be—notes to financial statements, and the accountants' opinion. The notes and surplus statements cover

174

not only the current period for the balance sheet, but also the most current three years and the stub period, if applicable.

Here again, the company must be careful. One of the more common deficiencies in the preparation of the registration statement is failure to cover in the financial notes a particular year. The notes may cover everything in the current year and in the year immediately prior, but the company may have inadvertently omitted some reference to one of the prior periods or to the stub period.

Stub Period Data

I think another important item is the stub or interim period unaudited financial statements that may be required for a current date and for the comparable period of the preceding year. These statements cover the balance sheet, income and surplus statements, and notes. For example, if your audited information is to be as of June 30, 1970 and you are filing on October 15, 1970, you may have an interim period of, say, one or two months. In this case, it would be July 31 and August 31, 1970, and the same stub period for July 31 and August 31, 1969.

Generally, the greatest problems sometimes arise in getting the comparable information for that prior stub period. The reasons are varied. Some companies do not maintain perpetual inventory records and do not take interim physical inventories, and therefore do not have the necessary inventory information available; others have not calculated depreciation on a monthly basis; and so forth. Again, these are the kinds of problems, hopefully, that have been solved prior to this time.

Ideally, as the audit has been carried on, someone in the company has been trying to put together on at least a preliminary basis most of this prior period information, and to lay it out, even if some of it may be discarded later. At least, in this way, you have a start and begin to find out what problems must be solved. And this is why we, as accountants, insist that our clients assign someone who can be working with the auditors, the lawyers, and the underwriters to compile this necessary stub period financial data while other data for the registration statement are being prepared.

Some of the problems related to the audited period are that you have to apply the same closing and accounting techniques to this stub period as you do in preparing the financial statements for the full fiscal years. You cannot just decide that you are going to put some figures and not others in the stub period.

Inventories, depreciation, and federal income taxes (the latter computation sometimes is a complicated transaction in the interim periods) must all be presented on the same basis as applied to all your other financial data. The introductory paragraph preceding the earnings statement states that management has included all normal, recurring adjustments in the audited stub period necessary for a fair presentation.

In the past, the unaudited periods have been a very fertile field for litigious-minded people who felt that they did not get full disclosure in the registration statement, and followed subsequently with a stockholder's suit. One of their common methods now is to sue everyone who has had any connection whatsoever with the registration statement.

Although it is sometimes difficult to get good, clear answers for unusual interim or period swings and fluctuations that are shown in the earnings statement, these must be explained somewhere in the registration statement. Generally, such explanations may be inserted in the forepart immediately following the notes to the earnings statement.

In addition, there may be a reference to the notes to your summary of earnings or to notes to the financial statements which are at the back part of the prospectus and registration statement. If these explanations are not included in the registration statement, you will certainly get a comment from the SEC requiring that you do so.

Other Considerations

As the registration statement compilation proceeds, the accountant may have to refer to another accountant for an opinion. This normally happens when he is using financial statements that have previously been covered in the earlier years by some other accountant.

Here again, arrangements must be made prior to the final due date in order to obtain that other accountant's opinion and consent for the use of that data.

Another requirement is that certain supplemental financial data must be supplied in the registration statement but not the prospectus. This information is for review and consideration of the SEC staff, but is not considered necessary for issuance to the prospective purchaser of the securities being registered. Again, the rules covering the schedules to be filed are outlined in Regulation S-X. This information is located at the end of the registration statement.

Some of the more common supporting schedules are reserves covering doubtful accounts and depreciation; intangible assets, property, plant and equipment, capital shares, and supplementary profit and loss information. The schedules which relate to the audited financial statements must be certified by the independent accountant.

Except for the schedule of capital shares, the other schedules such as reserves and supplementary profit-and-loss information must include financial data for the most current three years and stub periods, if applicable.

Reviewing the Statement

One important part of the accountant's role in the registration process is to review the entire registration statement. This is in addition to the financial statements, because he wants to be sure there is no conflict as to what is being said about the company's business in the registration statement with what the financial statements show. This requires careful discussions with everyone—the company officials, the lawyers, and the underwriters.

Of course, the accountant also reviews the accounting information to make sure that full disclosure and, if necessary, any financial impact is shown in your published statement of earnings, balance sheet, or other financial statements and schedules.

At this point of review, it is well to again consider any pending clearance from government agencies or legal counsel on such matters as internal revenue service rulings, lawsuits, renegotiation, and so on. Certain financial presentation or other factual presentation may have been made on the assumption of approval; either no approval or no answer may require further disclosure in notes to financial statements or other data within the registration statement.

Underwriting Agreement. The accountant next turns his attention to the underwriting agreement. This is important to the accountant, because among other conditions it usually asks him to carry out certain specified procedures, read certain unaudited financial statements, and give the underwriters a letter—called a "comfort letter"—at the time of the closing.

The comfort letter itself sometimes requires a significant amount of field work—I am referring now to a fairly good-sized corporation. One of the reasons for this is that the comfort letter devotes a great deal of time to the interim or stub period.

The letter also requires that the accountant read financial data in the forepart such as tables disclosing sales by product, sales by territory, assets by location, long-term debt, stock options, and so forth.

Included in the comfort letter is a further statement that the accountant has read the minutes of the board of directors, shareholders, and executive committee subsequent to the date of the balance sheet right up to the effective date of the registration statement or closing date. Further, it requires a reading of any unaudited interim financial statements available (subsequent to the balance sheet date).

Based on performing these various procedures, the auditor is generally in a position to give negative assurance that there were no material adverse changes in financial position or results of operations.

Processing the Proofs

Once the registration statement is put together, it is sent to the printer, and proofs are given to all the parties involved in the preparation process. Understandably, each interested party—the accountant, the underwriters, the attorneys, and the company officials—makes his own corrections.

For example, in our company, we try to funnel all corrections through one individual, who is generally one of the attorneys. In that way, the processing of printer's proofs is done efficiently, a small but important point to keep in mind when there are sometimes as many as 20 sets of proofs.

The more care you take—that is, the more preplanning you put into the actual preparation of the registration document—the fewer numbers of times you need to have revised proofs. Conversely, the more times you have revised proofs, the higher your printing bill.

Once the registration document is printed, there is the actual signing of the registration itself. This is also in the accountant's area, because he must sign his opinion and his consent for use in the registration statement. Generally, we sign enough copies for filing with the SEC and for distribution to the underwriters, the attorneys, and the client.

Correcting the Deficiencies

Following the filing, a period of from four to twelve weeks may pass (particularly for a company which is filing a Form S-1 for the first time) before the letter of comment is received from the SEC. The deficiency letter states what must be done to correct or clarify the registration statement to make it more complete, accurate, or acceptable to the SEC.

Assuming we have all done a careful editing job and have had a high degree of technical skill in compiling the information for Form S-1, the deficiencies should be at a minimum. However, when a company goes public for the first time, the SEC sometimes has a few more comments than would otherwise be the case had the company been to the market before.

As a matter of fact, we have had many experiences where the SEC staff examiner contacts the attorneys, the underwriters, or the accountants directly by telephone, and discusses certain areas, mainly for his own clarification. In many cases, it is possible to resolve a number of the examiner's questions over the telephone. But if a telephone call fails to convince the staff examiner of the company's position on the presentation, it is still possible to arrange an informal meeting with the SEC officials in Washington.

In most instances, however, meetings are arranged with the SEC prior to the filing, and even prior to the preparation

180

process of Form S-1, whenever it is believed that there may be serious problems in obtaining official clearance on presentation of certain financial data.

In the case of correcting amendments, the registration statement is filed in the same processing procedures as the original filing. The SEC will usually look at it promptly and, assuming everything is now in order, the staff examiner will notify you that everything is satisfactory.

As of November 21, 1968, the Corporate Finance Division of the SEC adopted a cursory review procedure for all registration statements, rather than the standard review and attendant letter of comment. This procedure was adopted due to the unprecedented work load of the staff arising from the number of registration statements filed with the SEC.

The responsibility of the statutory burden of full disclosure is on the issuer, its affiliates, the underwriters, and the other experts. The SEC division officer will make a cursory review of every registration statement and will make one of the following three decisions: 1) that the filing is unacceptable and no oral or written comments will be issued; 2) that the staff has made only a cursory review, issue no comments, and require written confirmation from auditors, chief financial officer, and managing underwriter that they understand that only a cursory review has been made and that they understand their statutory responsibilities; 3) that the filing will be subject to the regular review process.

Due Diligence Meeting. Once the corrected registration statement has been filed, there will be a due diligence meeting with the underwriters in which everyone party to the registration preparation is a participant. The purpose of this meeting is to allow the underwriters and their counsel to ask questions relative to the information that is included in the registration statement.

In summary, by going public you will be embarking on a potentially tedious, litigious, and expensive process. Furthermore, in most cases this process of reporting to the SEC generally does not end with this initial filing but requires annual, semiannual, and quarterly reporting. From this point forward, your financial life will be subject to public scrutiny to an extent never experienced previously.

The Uses of
the Prospectus

At this point in the registration and offering process, you have gone through a series of auditing and legal steps, and you have filed your registration statement and prospectus with the SEC. Normally, it will be three to six weeks or longer before the SEC declares that your prospectus is effective, but in the interim period the offering of your securities is made by your managing underwriter. He will distribute copies of your preliminary prospectus to national and regional firms he hopes to interest in his underwriting syndicate. They will then redistribute copies to their account executives, who will in turn start calling clients.

Of course, they cannot legally make sales until they have a final effective prospectus on the day that you are actually going to issue your securities. The concept is to disseminate the

Mr. Marcus is Vice President and member of the Board of Directors of E. F. Hutton & Company, Inc., a leading investment banking and brokerage firm.

information as broadly as possible in advance of the issue date in order to get indications of interest from potential buyers.

As a Sales Document

During the waiting period when you are using your preliminary or "red herring" prospectus, you cannot legally distribute anything at all in writing other than the prospectus. You will be called down, in fact, if you use any other promotional data, or if your public relations people do anything to create unusual activity during the registration period. For all practical purposes, your preliminary prospectus is your only sales document.

This prospectus will look like the final effective document, but there will be a legend printed on the front cover in red ink, hence the name "red herring." In effect, the legend states that this prospectus is not yet effective, subject to change, and so on.

Distribution to Dealers

Numerically, for a $2 million offering, let us say, you should probably print about 5,000 or 6,000 copies of your red herring. The first use of it would then be to mail one copy each to about 200 dealer firms around the country which your managing underwriter has chosen. This would be just to inform those firms that your offering had been filed.

Now those 200, I should add, are out of some 3,700 member firms of the National Association of Security Dealers. But by mailing your prospectus to them, your managing underwriter would have selected perhaps nine or ten times the actual number of dealer firms that he hopes to have in his syndicate. Psychologically, the underwriter would rather have them ask to participate as underwriters than have to ask them to join in forming a syndicate to handle the offering of your securities.

In the weeks that follow, he will probably meet and talk with several of the major national firms, which are usually headquartered in New York, that he would like to have participate with him as underwriters. Typically, they will have read the red herring prospectus very carefully. They will also have given it to members of their research departments who are specialists in your company's particular industry to read; members of the syndicate departments will have read it, and quite possibly members of their corporate finance departments who make the actual buying decision will have read it.

The managing underwriter would like to talk personally to all these people, but often he does not. In fact, sometimes they take it as a sign of weakness if he insists on a meeting. Therefore, even with the national firms that are going to make significant underwriting commitments, the only communication may often be the red herring prospectus itself.

Then, very quickly by telephone, the managing underwriter will bring in the regional firms he would like to have participate in this offering in order to make sure that he is giving you an effective and broad geographical distribution of your securities throughout the United States. In an average public offering, his hope is to have ten national firms and possibly fifteen leading regional firms in his syndicate to assure effective coverage.

All of these underwriters will be given as many copies of the red herring prospectus as their requirements dictate. In turn, they will distribute them to their branch officers and to their account executives. The account executives will mail your preliminary prospectus to clients on an interest-only basis, and normally each interested client will then contact his particular account executive or broker for any further discussion.

185

Because of the pyramid structure of the investment market, this entire chain of events happens very quickly. Usually, all of these contacts from top to bottom and back again with indications of interest in your securities take place within a couple of weeks.

As an Information Source

As I noted earlier, your only effective means of communication is the red herring prospectus. You cannot vacate the responsibility of using it as a sales document. Therefore, we at Hutton, and I am sure this is true of many investment banking firms, spend many hours negotiating with our own attorneys, and the client company's attorneys on how to make the preliminary prospectus most effective.

Accordingly, we prefer to write the first draft of the red herring. We feel that one of the important abilities we can bring to a company is our expertise in communicating and projecting the company in the frame of reference of the investing community. It can be very difficult for company officers to explain what their company does in terms that a layman might understand.

I well remember many hours of debate that we had with the officers of a valuable foundry. Now this in itself may not sound too complicated, but they really could not speak about their company without describing the various grades of iron they produced. Typically, that kind of talk is not of any particular interest to the investing public.

For the Security Analysts

You should keep clearly in mind that the prospectus, besides being a sales document used in conjunction with the offering, is also the single most important source of information available to the professional security analysts and to the potential institutional and individual investors in the financial community for a period—usually for a year—following the offering of your securities.

Moreover, if the underwriters are providing good service to you, this may be the last communication to your shareholders or to the public until your annual report, which would normally be nine to twelve months away from the effective date of the actual issuance of your securities.

Your prospectus has a charismatic aura about it. Even though it says in big letters on the front that it has not been approved by the SEC, every potential investor knows that the SEC has functioned on it, and that the Commission must obviously have some independent judgment concerning the issue. If the prospectus is effective, then after the 90-day waiting period is over you will find the professional security analysts writing reports about your company based on the information contained in it.

For the Reporting Services

Probably one of the most important reporting services on any publicly held company is the so-called Standard & Poor's Report which, I am sure, most readers are familiar with. Every brokerage firm in the country has this report. It consists of tear sheets covering all listed companies, and a great number of over-the-counter companies.

Here is a typical example of how a reporting service uses the prospectus. Several years ago, we underwrote an offering for the Bali Company, and the Standard & Poor's tear sheet was taken verbatim out of the company's prospectus. It was only a brief passage, but in terms of what the company was doing and in the way the company executives wanted it expressed, we considered the information to be most important:

"The Bali Company manufactures quality brassieres. It sells exclusively through the nation's major department stores, ladies' specialty stores, and selected corset shops. . . .

"High quality is emphasized in an effort to assure proper fit, support, comfort, and durability. Bali concentrates on basic types and colors rather than short-lived promotional items."

This information was incorporated in the prospectus and cleared by the SEC. In our role as the investment banker, we were able to verify that what was said in the prospectus was in fact quite true. Moreover, it would not have appeared in the Standard & Poor's Report if it had not been effectively presented in the prospectus.

Now these were all positive facts in terms of the image and problems that a company in the garment industry might have. As a result, at least partially, this was responsible, we think, for Bali selling at an extraordinarily high multiple for a company in this industry.

Bali had an excellent report; its earnings had been outstanding from the time of inception, and in early 1969 its securities were selling at a multiple of 19 or 20 times earnings.

As an Intangible Benefit

In the preparation of the registration statement and prospectus document, we will typically write the first draft, as mentioned previously. There is a fundamental reason for our doing so. We agree 100% with the lawyers and the SEC that everything in the prospectus has got to be absolutely true. As the underwriter, we share in the liability for misstatements or inaccuracies in the prospectus, although we are indemnified, which is another case of being accused on the front page and being acquitted in the obituary section. The prospectus is what we call the "truth and accuracy" part of the registration document, and we want to be quite certain in our own minds that it is; hence, we prefer to prepare the first draft of it.

Illustrative Example

Along these lines, we recently underwrote a company that we believed to be the "major" producer of safety and armament fusing devices for nuclear weapons. We said that in the prospectus, and the company believed it absolutely.

Following the filing of the red herring, we prepared a so-called "probable deficiency memorandum" for the company to alert the executives as to what the SEC might ask them to clarify or prove 60 days or so out.

We went through the prospectus (we were really doing this all the while we were preparing it) and we pulled out all the items we thought the SEC might question. Then in our memorandum, we recommended to the company ways of preparing to respond to the SEC's letter of comments.

For example, if you want to say you are the "major" producer, you know that the SEC is going to come back to you and say, "Prove it." Thus, if you can obtain telegrams from your leading competitors or from your leading customers, or if there are industry associations that can tell you whether you are the major producer, these can be effective in your conferences with the SEC.

Now we had a problem regarding this particular major producer, because there is very little information released on how many nuclear weapons are manufactured and stockpiled each year in this country. This is top-secret information.

Therefore, we checked with the people in the government purchasing agencies that the company was dealing with. They assured us that our client was the major producer. Thus, on the basis of this, we requested that the SEC talk to them. However, the SEC declined to do so, saying, "It is not our job to check with other government agencies. If you can't prove your claim from outside sources, you'll have to delete it."

Naturally, since no outside sources buy nuclear armaments, we were stymied. The upshot was that we had to delete the word "major" from the final prospectus. Ironically, we learned later that the SEC had talked with the agencies in question and the purchasing agents had indeed told the Commission our client was the major producer. Apparently, because of the secretive safety and arming devices, or what have you, and despite the fact we could prove beyond a shadow of a doubt that our client company was the major producer, the SEC still said, "No."

You are not going to win them all, but the red herring did have the word "major" in it, and we think it had a beneficial effect in the national and regional investment communities.

In summary, the primary functions of your prospectus— aside from meeting the obvious legal requirements—are providing truthful and accurate information about your company, getting your story told in the simplest possible terms, and creating a beneficial effect on potential institutional and individual investors throughout the country.

Floor Discussion

Question: What incentive does the underwriter have other than maintaining his reputation and maximizing commissions to try to get the highest price possible for the specific offering?

Marcus: The incentive that the underwriter has in getting his client the highest possible price is the very fact he doesn't anticipate that his relationship with that client is going to end on the day of that filing.

190

Let's take a hypothetical case of a company that is selling $2,000,000 worth of securities, and there is an effective gross commission or discount of $150,000.

The managing underwriter will get a percentage. Let's say in this particular case he is going to get 15% of that fee, or $20,000 for his work. This is the underwriter's profit, per se, for acting as manager.

In addition to that, his firm may—as some underwriting firms normally do—distribute no more than 25% of the issue itself. Thus, if the manager is selling 40,000 shares of the securities to his own clients, he may get an additional gross of about $40,000, to use a round number.

Therefore, out of the effective $150,000 which you are paying as a commission or discount, the manager's total gross may be $60,000. Now out of that, he has to pay his account executives and cover a great many other costs, as well as make a necessary distribution within his own firm of these monies. So you can see that the net the manager actually takes down is not a fantastic windfall.

It is far more important that we maintain any client on a long-range basis. Just from a dollars and cents standpoint, we think that by keeping the client happy and by maintaining a good relationship, he will possibly at some future point in time have an additional offering in the same securities; he may tell his friends that we did a good job for him, and this could therefore bring us additional investment banking business.

We are not going to look good if a client's stock comes in today at $12 and tomorrow it is $24. Remember, in dealing with a client, we and our fellow underwriters are agreeing to buy and to commit ourselves to the purchase of his complete issue at a specific price. The fact that some individual investor is willing to pay $24 for 100 shares of an offering which we paid $12 for the day before has no meaning to us, because we are talking millions of shares and he is talking hundreds.

We are going to try at all times to get the client the best possible price that is reasonably competitive with the market at the time of purchase.

What market price the public puts on the company's securities thereafter is created by the investment decisions of thousands of individuals, whereas the managing underwriter and his syndicate have to consider the one major purchase of the complete offering.

Question: At what period prior to the offering can the investment broker start accepting commitments for that stock? Is there any particular date when he can start accepting these commitments?

Marcus: Actually, the first notice the public has of the fact that there is an issue contemplated would normally be found in the minutes of the Securities and Exchange Commission, which are put together every Friday night for issuance on the following Monday morning.

There also is the Elliott Sharp Letter, which is circulated within our industry on a daily basis. Elliott Sharp has a reporter covering the SEC all the time, and news of a contemplated issuance normally would appear in the letter within a week after the date of filing.

Some underwriters, because of the fact that they may have knowledge of a particular company, or who in some cases may feel that the investment banker managing the issue has a particularly good track record, will get on the phone almost immediately and say, "Count me in."

As the managing underwriter, we can accept indications of interest once the filing date is commenced, but we cannot confirm, nor can they in turn confirm any of the securities to their clients.

Question: Is the normal procedure, then, to have indications of interest for a good portion of that stock prior to the offer date?

Marcus: We surely hope so.

Question: Usually, what percent is "spoken for" prior?

Marcus: If we are talking about an equity offering, we would like to have on the offering date 100% of that equity covered by indications of interest.

If we accomplish that, it is certainly also going to be to the client's benefit because, if we are committing 100%, we don't think the stabilization problems are going to be any greater. Probably there will be some premiums from the offering price. This is best for all involved. The company certainly wants to start out with its shareholders having a profit instead of a loss in their equity in the first week.

Question: How much do the advance indications of interest you get influence the price of the stock? I would think that would make a tremendous difference if you oversold, say, by 50% or so. Wouldn't that come up with a difference in the price that you actually offer at?

Marcus: You have to remember that in the original registration statement filing of the S-1 there is a price affixed to the statement. This is normally considered to be the maximum filing price, so that it would be unusual for that price to be increased because of the demand.

We feel that this maximum filing price is a fair price. People are deciding whether to buy the securities on the basis of the numbers they find in the financial information of the registration statement and prospectus, and on the maximum filing price.

Now if that price goes up suddenly by 20% or 30% on the offering price, a lot of those anticipated orders are not going to materialize.

193

Alternative Sources
of Capital

In a discussion of sources of long-term capital, alternative to a primary public issue of equities, it is important to cover not only long-term sources, but also some renewable short-term sources of capital as well. If you are successful in obtaining short-term funds, frequently they can be rolled over to serve the same purposes as long-term funds.

I am going to exclude from my discussion the public issuance of new equity capital, because I expect that you may anticipate feeling the same way a company president did at his first stockholders meeting after having gone public.

It turned out that he had asked for comments and questions from his new stockholders. One gentleman was very quick to take the floor. He was not one of the well-known corporate gadflies, but he very quickly launched an attack

Dr. Marple is Chairman of the Department of Finance and Insurance and Associate Professor of Finance, Northeastern University. He specializes in corporate financial matters and is an active consultant to industry.

when he said, "Mr. President, is it true that your retirement plan is funded to provide 80% of your annual current income?" The president blushed and acknowledged this was so.

The man pressed his attack further when he said, "Is it true that your son, the one who is interested in sports cars and who is a vice president of the firm, spent only twelve days on the premises last year, and that those days generally were toward the end of the month?"

The president acknowledged that this was likewise true. Then he felt he had better take the offensive, and he asked his inquirer, "Sir, I would like to know what your interest in our company is."

IIis adversary responded by saying, "Well, Mr. President, I am short 20,000 shares."

The point of this is that you may decide the known benefits from a public issue will be swamped by the unknown risks not all of which are financial. You may simply decide that you are not willing to change your style of doing business. In recognition of some of the reasons that a public issue may not be appropriate, I have organized my comments into three parts.

First, I shall start out with some general observations about the task which you have set for yourself in trying to find additional sources of funds.

Second, I shall focus on specific sources of funds.

Third, I shall concentrate on how you can organize to tap some of these sources of capital.

General Observations

Let us begin with the assumption that the book value or net worth of your company is in the vicinity of $200,000. A preliminary check of company executives attending "going public" seminars indicates that this is a very reasonable premise.

On the one hand, in comparison with what most of us are accustomed to thinking about in terms of personal wealth, this is a handsome sum. On the other hand, in the corporate universe, where companies that have net worths exceeding $200,-000 number about 100,000, this is not too big a sum.

When you consider that the 500 largest U.S. corporations account for about half of the gross national product, that there are only 1,300 companies listed on the New York Stock Exchange and just about twice that number listed on all the other organized U.S. exchanges, and that there are only about 24,000 U.S. corporations which are traded over-the-counter, we begin to realize that a company with $200,000 of net worth is not a major factor in the capital markets of this country.

Thus my assumption that your company may have a net worth of about $200,000 indicates that your company is not in the major stream of financing activities of corporate enterprise in this country.

As a result, the search for additional capital is extremely difficult for a variety of reasons. The principal one of these is that a company of this size is perceived by the lenders as affording extremely high business risk, in part because it more often than not offers a single product, frequently in a regional market, and in part because it is likely to be very thin in the upper ranges of its management.

It is also a firm which needs, in terms of the financier's alternatives, a relatively small amount of money. This means that his return for the time invested in investigating an unknown company and a new financing opportunity is relatively small, even though the compensation as a percentage of the funds provided may be quite high.

Therefore, because his firm is starting with some competitive disadvantages, it behooves the manager looking for nonequity capital to plan his needs well and to be, like Caesar's wife, above reproach in approaching the capital markets in which he is not an esteemed participant.

Accordingly, the first step in searching for funds is to plan carefully the uses of those funds and to develop as accurate and as justified a figure of capital needs as possible.

There are two principal ways of doing this: one is through the development of pro forma income and balance sheet statements; the other is through the development of pro forma cash-flow statements. Most standard texts in business finance describe approaches for making these estimates. If competence in-house is lacking, your accounting firms will be able to help you do this.

Make your capital needs forecast as accurate as you possibly can, and your forecast will stand you in good stead in the difficult negotiations that lie ahead.

While you know that the purpose for which you are obtaining funds is sound and has good future commercial prospects, the provider of funds is inherently skeptical. You must, therefore, share your vision of the future with him. Pro forma financial statements will help to make your future operations appear achievable and justify your request for funds. I shall return to this point later.

Having placed your need for capital in perspective and urged you to plan your needs carefully, we should think about specific fund sources. There are three areas or aspects of new fund sources to which I shall refer. These factors are risk, income, and control, from the point of view of the majority stockholder in the company. I assume that it is his interests which will be served by the new funds and he will be interested in the effect of the new funds on the risks he will run, the income he will enjoy, and his ability to direct the affairs of the company.

I would like to use the concept of the cost of capital for these various sources of funds as a further differentiating device. By this term I mean the financial return expected by the provider of the funds which prompted him to make them available to your company.

Sources of Funds

Let us turn now to the second major part of this chapter, which is a discussion of the specific sources of funds.

I find a good way to organize this discussion is to be guided by a balance sheet. You realize that a decrease in an asset is a source of funds as much as is an increase in a liability. Perhaps if you think about your alternatives in this way, new ideas about possible funds sources may occur to you.

Balance Sheet Assets

Let us go down the asset side of the balance sheet first and see what financing opportunities are available.

Cash Account. Is there any possibility of wringing some funds out of this account? Or, alternatively, is there any way of planning your cash needs more carefully than you have in the past so that present balances will support more business activity?

Is your operation such that you can speed up the processing of accounts receivable? Is it possible that if you change your payment dates for wages or your purchasing dates for materials you will even out your cash flow over the month and, therefore, be able to get by with a smaller cash balance?

All of these alternatives have been used with some success in reducing needs for cash, as well as in freeing cash for other corporate purposes. Your commercial banker will be able to advise you about ways to speed up your cash collections and to suggest ways of making your cash work harder for you.

Accounts Receivable. Is it possible to manage your accounts receivable more aggressively? Do you really need to have the amount of capital committed to accounts receivable that appears in your balance sheet? Have you been too lenient with some accounts? Is it possible that you could press some of them for payment without losing either their business or their goodwill?

Some people may very quickly say, "Well, maybe we could speed up the collection of our accounts receivable and reduce the commitment of funds to accounts receivable by offering a cash discount."

However, this is a very expensive way of realizing funds. If the standard two-ten net 30 discount provides a company with 20 days' additional capital, the annual interest rate associated with the discount is approximately 36%.

Customarily, when thinking about accounts receivable, your thoughts turn to the possibility of factoring them. This may be cheaper than offering a cash discount on the accounts receivable, but factoring carries with it a substantial expense. When you consider the cost of the borrowed funds and the cost of managing the accounts receivable, the cost of funds may run between 14% and 20%.

Inventory Account. You may also want to ask yourself whether inventory needs to be as high as it is. Is it possible that your inventory control system has not been designed as carefully or structured as well as it ought to be? Is it possible to change your method of production so that commitments to goods in process inventory may be reduced? Likewise, is it possible that you are selling in a market which is such that you do not have to sell from a large finished goods inventory?

All of these factors may lead you to conclude that funds

can be wrung out of your inventory account through closer and more careful management of this so-often substantial investment. If you decide that reduction of inventory is not possible, it may be that it would provide the basis for a secured loan under a warehouse arrangement at less cost than would be possible with factored accounts receivable.

Fixed Assets. Going further down the balance sheet, a company sometimes finds that there is a substantial source of funds in its fixed assets account.

Is there machinery that has salvage value which might be sold? Some companies routinely sell idle machinery and plant for which there is no planned use even though it may later become necessary to buy a particular item back. Searching such items out may provide a good source of cash. Is it possible that machinery or plant presently owned could be leased, and the funds realized by such a sale-and-lease-back arrangement could be put to work in some critical area of the business?

It may turn out, too, that on the asset side of the balance sheet you will find that you have capitalized an item which has some market value—although usually it turns out that the owner-manager has expensed whatever he possibly could for income tax purposes. There might be a patent or other intangible item which you are not presently using that has a market value.

A final item that can frequently provide an additional source of funds is payment of your insurance on an annual rather than three-year basis. The small additional premium may make this a relatively inexpensive source of funds.

Balance Sheet Liabilities

Let us turn now to the balance sheet liabilities, for this is the side that is generally thought of as illustrating the richer array of financing opportunities, particularly in the long term, because a source such as a loan immediately appears here.

Accounts Payable: Here, I believe, is an excellent source of funds because a customer's accounts receivable is a valuable investment from the point of view of a supplier. If you look on your supplier's accounts receivable from you as being analogous to a capital investment, you may be surprised at the rate of return that supplier is anticipating by continuing to have you as a customer. I shall illustrate this.

Assume for a moment that you are a customer for $120,000 worth of the supplier's merchandise a year, that he is selling to you at a time when he has surplus plant capacity, that his variable costs associated with your business are $60,000, and that his accounted after-tax profit on sales is 5% or, in this case, $6,000. Without your account, his profits before tax would drop by the difference between his sales to you and variable costs on your purchases, or $60,000. If he had been selling you on 30-day terms, his average investment in your account was $10,000. If he were to increase his credit terms to 90 days, he could still realize more than a 200% return on his investment in your account of $30,000. In fact, if the perceived risk associated with you as a borrower would justify an interest rate of, say, 15%, you could point out to him that your annual business alone would afford a return equal to that on a $400,000 capital investment. Thus, if your suppliers have unused capacity, you probably have the leverage to negotiate favorable payment terms and thereby to gain substantial amounts of working capital.

If you are unable to negotiate extended payment terms, it might be possible for you to negotiate a loan at a relatively favorable interest rate from a supplier who views you as an important source of marginal profitability when he does not have a ready customer to take your place.

It may be sobering to view the requests of your customers for long payment terms in light of the discussion above.

Bank Loans. No doubt you are familiar with the short-term bank loans designed to meet cyclical, usually seasonal, needs for funds generated on the asset side of your balance sheet. These are usually self-liquidating loans. That is, when the need disappears, the funds are automatically provided as is the case with short-term loans for seasonal inventory or accounts receivable. They are usually not difficult to obtain, so I shall explicitly omit them from this discussion of alternative sources of capital.

Long-term loans, however, are an entirely different matter. A long-term loan is one which you would probably expect not to roll over, but rather to replace through retained earnings or refund on maturity.

Banks will probably be reluctant to give you a long-term loan. They are, unfortunately, going to look for good security for a long-term loan, such as a multipurpose building or securities, because they are probably not going to regard your business as a good risk in view of some of the factors I have discussed.

A salable plant on which a bank might be able to take a mortgage lien or a source of assured income may enhance the willingness of the loan officer to talk to you, but he will probably be skeptical about your qualifying for a long-term loan.

Occasionally, bankers and borrowers will enter into a short-term loan agreement which is expected to be renewed on maturity rather than repaid. Such an arrangement provides added risk for the borrower, giving the lender greater power than he would enjoy with a longer-term loan. They are poor substitutes for long-term funds even though they may serve like long-term loans.

Nonbanking Loans. The foregoing discussion implies that

if you are interested in long-term funds you are probably going to have to go to nonbanking sources which, because of the risks involved, will usually want more than interest compensation.

In that case, you will probably be called on not only to pay high rates of interest, but also to offer the possibility of attractive capital gains, generally in the form of warrants or a conversion feature to the loan.

You might say, "If they are going to demand warrants and the right to buy our stock, why don't we try to sell these venture capital firms, or small business investment corporations, some of our equity capital initially?"

The problem with this line of reasoning is that most of these venture capital firms do not want just an equity position in your firm, because a minority interest in your business is not going to give them the protection they desire. They desire the claim of a loan and the market appreciation of the equity kicker to meet their risk and return preferences. In view of this, most of the deals offered to you by venture capital firms will likely be unattractive.

Your size will probably preclude your borrowing from insurance companies and other institutions, although some of these firms will make loans of $50,000 to $100,000. Even though it is sometimes deprecated, the Small Business Administration has frequently been a good source of last resort either for a guarantee of an otherwise unobtainable bank loan or even for a direct loan.

I would like to digress for a moment to make some observations about determining the capacity of your firm to use debt. It may well be that if you use analytical devices different from those customarily used by lenders in appraising debt capacity, you will be able to talk yourself into a larger loan than the lender would find justified by looking at your balance sheet.

The approach bankers sometimes use is based on the percentage of your debt to total long-term capital, or on the percentage of your current liabilities plus long-term debt to total assets. The resulting ratios are compared with established norms for your industry.

However, these ratios do not focus on the factors which really determine your ability to utilize debt, for they imply that the loan will be repaid from the book value of your assets in liquidation. Instead, you hope to amortize your debt through the cash flows that your business produces in its successful operation.

With this in mind, you should be prepared to demonstrate that you are able to handle the requested loan by indicating how the cash flows from your business will enable you to pay the interest on, and reduce the principal of, a debt of the term and size you find desirable.

If you really want to jack the amount up, and if you have not been persuaded by your financial advisor that there is a ratio of debt to equity which lenders consider inviolate for companies of your particular business category, you might say something to this effect:

"There will be a cash flow available from our business if we are operating successfully. However, in the event we find our business is not operating as planned because of a turndown in sales, there will be cash flowing in through the automatic liquidation of our working assets, particularly inventory and accounts receivable. Either of these sources will be adequate to meet our debt service obligations."

Capital realized from the liquidation of assets, added to the cash flowing from business operations, provides a debt-repaying capacity in periods of financial adversity. This is considerably different from looking to assets on liquidation to repay the loan.

As we have already seen, there is the possibility of obtaining a loan from your key supplier. It may also happen that you are a valued supplier for some customer, and that he might also be willing to lend you funds in order to ensure himself the continued supply of a product critical to his activity.

Equity Capital. The last of the items on the liability side of a balance sheet is the equity account. Let us talk about the preferred, common stock, and retained earnings components of this account.

It is improbable that a private company could or would issue preferred stock to the public. It is likewise unlikely that it could be issued on a private basis. As you know, the dividends of preferred stock are not tax deductible to the issuer and the holders of preferred stock are in a less preferred position than that of the creditor. Therefore, debt is usually selected over preferred stock because of advantages to both the issuer and the holder.

On the other hand, there is one advantage to preferred stock from the point of view of a corporate investor. In such a case, 85% of the preferred stock dividends are free of federal income tax. Thus you may be able to structure a deal that will meet the particular needs of a corporate provider of capital, even though at somewhat higher expense to you than debt, because you are able to give him this preferred stock dividend income at an effective tax rate of only 7.5% of the dividend.

Turning now to the possibility of the use of equity capital outside of having a public issue, you may possibly find it both desirable and feasible to take into your company some additional partners on a private placement basis. Frequently, underwriting firms which feel that a company of your size is on the threshold of going public but not quite ready for the public

205

market will take an equity position in its stock. The partners sometimes do this for their personal accounts, or for the firm's, or they will arrange for a private placement with a friendly venture capital firm.

It is also possible that you can approach a number of wealthy individuals in your community or your employee group as a way of providing capital. Turning to employees does compound their personal risk, and if you have a paternalistic regard for the welfare of your employees, you may question the wisdom of their committing not only their salaries to your fortune, but also their savings as well.

I would be remiss in any discussion of the equity account not to mention retained earnings, but for my assumption that no one here pays dividends. Most owner-managers prefer to build up their personal wealth through retained earnings, rather than through the payment of dividends, thereby avoiding the ordinary income taxes to which dividends are subject. In some cases, diverse needs of common equity holders necessitate the payment of some dividend. It may be possible in such a situation to restructure the capitalization of the company to give just them an income-paying security such as a convertible preferred stock, thereby reducing the cash flowing out of the company.

Other Possibilities

There are various other ways of getting funds which do not fall into the balance sheet framework and I shall briefly review them for you.

One, of course, is the minimization of taxes. If you can increase the amount of operating income you shield from tax, you will be adding to your cash flow. You are probably already depreciating and expensing everything you possibly can, and there is clearly an advantage to your so doing inasmuch as you are a private company not overly concerned with reported after-tax profits.

If you are successful in persuading another firm to merge with your company, you may be able to minimize taxes by restructuring your operations to increase the number of tax entities in the resulting operation in order to increase the amount of income which will be taxed at the basic, rather than the surtax, rate.

Another way of getting capital into a business would be through a merger with a company that has either liquid assets or unused debt capacity. However, it is important to you to be sure that your partner is bringing the funds that you did not possess all along.

The disadvantage of going the merger route obviously is the potential loss of control of your own operation. Nevertheless, it is possible that you will be able to find a partner with whom you feel you could live. You may foresee the possibility of greater personal wealth—as a result of using the assets that he would bring—which would justify your giving up the personal satisfaction of being the principal in a smaller company.

The possibility of acquiring another company's assets is somewhat less likely, unless for some reason you already have a public currency and you are unwilling to go to the public market to raise additional funds. However, some of the large companies listed on the New York Stock Exchange have been highly successful in building their assets through thoughtful acquisitions.

Judicious use of leases may give you the assets you need at a cost not far removed from what you would pay if you borrowed the needed funds and then bought the equipment. Leasing has the advantage of not showing up on the balance sheet, which may make it possible to obtain added financing that would not be available had you borrowed and then bought. Also, companies which are not good candidates for loans usually can lease, making this a prime source of funds for the small company.

There is also the possibility of obtaining additional funds through the joint ownership with another company of a subsidiary. This arrangement could provide funds to develop an opportunity that you would be unable to fund by yourself. Such a joint-ownership arrangement might well be more desirable than trying to obtain capital for your firm or merging with another.

Two other possibilities related to this are the licensing of a process, which you would exploit but for the lack of funds, or the granting of franchise rights.

Tapping the Sources

The final topic that I shall discuss with you is how you can organize to tap some sources of capital, as well as some of the things you might consider doing when you find it desirable to obtain additional funds.

I have mentioned the importance of having a well-developed plan and a well-developed analysis to support your need for funds. Now I would like to reiterate the importance of having an exhibit to show your potential supplier of funds that you (a) have thought through your need for funds, (b) have come up with realistic expectations of the amount of capital you need, and (c) have a program for the profitable employment of these monies in your business.

It is important for you to be fully prepared to articulate both the risk which you perceive the financier may face and the likelihood that he will have a satisfactory experience by providing funds to your business.

Be prepared to discuss with him your forecasts of sales and your anticipated levels of profits.

Be prepared to talk about where you expect those sales to come from and how you estimate your operating expenses.

In other words, have a forecast and a plan, and share your vision of the future with your potential source of funds. That dream of the future is all you have to sell, and it is going to determine whether or not you will be able to obtain the capital you need. If your plans have been well conceived, you will increase your chances both of obtaining the desired capital and of having your venture turn out successfully.

Floor Discussion

Question: The thought occurred to me that perhaps your assumption of net worth of the companies represented here is very low. Let's assume that their net worth would be between $1 million and $2 million. Would this change significantly some of your comments?

Marple: Yes, it would. I think you would then be in a position to go to some institutional lenders and obtain substantial amounts of debt capital on terms just slightly above the rate that firms of similar risk would have to pay on the public market. I would say that typically a well-regarded investment banker would desire a net worth in the area of $3 million. Certainly, anyone who has a net worth approaching $2 million should seek a more conventional method of financing. With that type of picture, the company should be able to explore term bank loans at a rate associated with the prime rate or private placements with insurance companies, and so on.

Question: You said something about acquiring or merging subsidiary corporations, or creating a subsidiary corporation, that this would provide a lower tax base. How?

Marple: The first $25,000 of income is taxed at 22%, and then everything above that is taxed at 48%. Therefore, if it is possible to have two corporate entities, you shield another $25,000 from that large surtax rate of 26%.

You have much more opportunity to break your firm up, or to set up separate corporate entities, if you do this at the time of formation or acquisition. You can't do this solely for tax reasons with an established corporate entity. For instance, if you were buying a chain of stores all under a single ownership, there is a possibility of establishing a number of corporations to buy these stores separately and to avoid that 26% surtax.

Question: I understand that, but I thought you said you could do it under the same corporate umbrella.

Marple: No, sir.

Question: In small companies, have you had any experience in a company just, say, offering preferred stock or debentures? Has this been a successful avenue, or have there been problems?

Marple: It is very difficult for a small company to offer debentures, unless there is some kind of sweetener in the form of a conversion feature, and I suspect that in a small company a lender is going to want to get as much protection as he possibly can. He would, therefore, prefer to have some lien on an asset, rather than to take an unsecured debenture.

I think that debt with warrants is a less attractive sweetener than convertible debt. The company can force the conversion by calling the debentures, whereas the initiative to exercise the warrant lies with the holder. Also, if converted to stock, the convertible debt need not be repaid but the debt associated with the warrants has to be retired.

Preferred stock has sometimes been used with corporate investors because of the dividend exclusion for federal tax purposes which I described. There have been some intriguing mixtures of personal and corporate resources centering around the use of preferred stock. From time to time wealthy corporate owners have guaranteed the payment of dividends when they felt that the corporation alone would be considered too risky. Others have also provided a put so that the stock could be redeemed out of their personal assets if there were a question about the corporation's performance justifying a satisfactory price or providing the resources for redemption.

I believe that preferred stock is not nearly as attractive to the corporation as debt because of the tax deductibility of the interest. I believe that a corporation that could sell preferred stock would also be able to sell debt.

Private Placement:
The 'New' Money Game

All last year, Roy Chapin, President of American Motors Corporation was driving down a road that seemed to have no end. Having run in the red for two straight years, American Motors needed both time and money if it were to turn itself around. But where do you get either one of these when you are in trouble? Not only that, a big bank loan was falling due even as Chapin was trying to build up a dealer network and expand his plant enough to put more cars in their showrooms.

But then, Chapin found a place to get his money. True, the money was not cheap. In fact, it was fairly dear. In return for a 20-year note for $35 million, the company had to give not only a 6% coupon, it had to make the note convertible into AMC common stock at $12 a share. AMC further sweetened

Miss Hershman is a Senior Editor on the staff of *Dun's*.

Reprinted by special permission from *Dun's Review*, February 1969. Copyright 1969, Dun & Bradstreet Publications Corporation.

the pot with 875,000 warrants to buy AMC stock, again at $12 a share.

A leading investment banker, an expert in private-placement financing, explains how struggling AMC managed to make a deal with the cold-eyed men of Wall Street. He says frankly: "They could never have sold the AMC debt publicly because it had to be done on the basis of projections, which the SEC will not allow in a prospectus. But the investment men at the pension funds, insurance companies, and mutual funds could make their own determinations on the basis of AMC's figures. They were the only choice."

Forgotten Financial Instrument

The experience of AMC and a lot of companies like it is the reason that a comparatively forgotten financial instrument —the private placement—is now attracting the attention of corporate treasurers and investors alike.

As old as the banks of Rome, popularized in America in the 1930s by a Lehman Brothers partner and then resurrected in our time by no less a financial figure than James J. Ling, the private placement is currently in a boom all its own. In 1965, the estimated total dollar volume of private placements came to $10 billion, up from $4.2 billion as recently as 1959.

Three Distinct Purposes

But there is more to the popularity of private placement than tight money. For all its hoary old age, the private placement has been fashioned into a remarkably versatile financial instrument. In fact, corporate treasurers currently are using it for at least three distinct purposes:

• When a company needs cash to turn itself around. Like AMC, the company in such a situation cannot spell out its hopes in a prospectus to raise money; the Securities and Exchange Commission, rightfully, simply will not allow investors to be swayed by projections. But sophisticated investors can make a value judgment on the company's prospects and then put up the money "for investment purposes only."

• For the company that wants to raise money for special purposes, such as a takeover, a private placement can raise millions in as little time as 96 hours.

• Finally, the private placement can give the privately held company the kind of financial muscle it needs before it goes public—and can do it at a comparatively cheap rate.

One measure of the range of the private placement can be seen in the kinds of companies that are turning to it. Besides AMC, Lytton Financial Corporation—the mismanaged California savings and loan institution—recapitalized late in 1968 through private borrowing. And University Computing, Gulf + Western, Collins Radio, and City Investing all have used the same money-raising gambit in recent months, either to bolster their working capital or to finance acquisitions.

For all its somewhat forbidding name, the private placement is nothing more than a loan to a company. Sometimes it is a note, sometimes a debenture, and more often these days— it is in the form of common stock. But whatever the type, the Securities and Exchange Act of 1933 exempts such borrowing from public registration simply because it is, both legally and literally, a private matter. (Much of today's highly controversial "letter" stock, the type that caused the Mates Fund to suspend trading in its own shares, is a private placement.)

As simple a device as it is, the private loan can be easily tailored to fit almost any kind of condition in the money market. Right now, of course, investors want capital gains, not income. So private placements now are being sweetened by making the loan convertible into common stock, as in the AMC

214

deal, or by throwing in the added lure of warrants to round out the package.

"It's safe to say," notes Robert Madden of Kidder, Peabody, "that well over half of the current deals include some kind of equity sweetener, as against a pre-1966 count of less than 25%."

As still another inducement, an attractive price can be put on the warrants. After City Investing snapped up Rheem Manufacturing last year, for example, President George Scharffenberger found himself with a $50-million bank loan to pay off. But how? The Federal Reserve System had already started tightening money, and City would lose all its vaunted leverage if it tried issuing common stock.

So Scharffenberger set up a formula that pegged the warrants to a price that was a few dollars under the market price of City Investing stock. In effect, then, the lenders got not only the interest on their money but a guaranteed capital gain. As one Wall Streeter comments: "The deal sold out in a matter of weeks because institutional buyers don't need much time to analyze a package like that."

Back in the Financial Swing

The versatility of the private placement, the number of adjustments that can be made in it, is one feature that rings all through its history. As Herman Kahn, a partner in Lehman Brothers points out: "Private placement is basically what the businessmen of Rome used as their financing."

Kahn should know. He was a prime mover in bringing the private placement into the twentieth century. Shortly after Franklin D. Roosevelt and the New Deal set up the SEC Act of 1933, business went into a deep freeze. Corporations still needed money to continue their operations, and, though it was in the depths of the Depression, other companies were still being formed.

But businessmen understandably were too frightened to try to register stock. They feared that if the SEC found even a single material fact that had not been disclosed in a prospectus, the company executives would be thrown in jail. So deep was this fear that one registration of the time, for American Water Works, had a prospectus as thick as the Manhattan telephone directory.

The only way around it, of course, was to avoid a public issue. So the then 25-year old Herman Kahn, remembering the Romans, hit on just the way to finance Boston's Jordan Marsh Department Store. He simply went to Equitable Life and Metropolitan Life and got the two insurance companies to lend the money. All the parties were delighted with the arrangement—and private placement was back in the financial swing.

It remained for Jimmy Ling to adapt this instrument to the inflationary 1960s. Nearly every executive remembers Ling's famed takeover of Wilson & Co. in 1967. With money tight, Wall Street figured that Ling could not possibly raise the funds to take over Wilson. Ling himself, in a surprise move, went to Europe, where he managed to raise the money.

Not so well known, except to moneymen, though, is the fact that not all of those funds came from Europe. In the U.S., Ling raised another $30 million through a private placement. To get the money, however, he sold three-year notes with not just a 6¾% coupon; he also added five-year warrants to the package.

Additional Advantages

And a new day was born in finance: the man who wanted to take over a company could simply finance such a transaction

216

through a private loan. Adding to the advantages, the risk in the Ling deal was so short-term that even some mutual funds bought into the deal, along with the usual collection of sophisticated, well-heeled investors. The Convertible Securities Fund of Los Angeles picked up $500,000 worth, for example, and even the conservative Puritan Fund of Boston was emboldened to put in $2 million.

As an added lure, the private placement can bring in merger money fast, fast, fast. By way of proof, consider the experience of Joseph McKinney, the 38-year-old head of two-year-old Saturn Industries. Previously a manager of the corporate finance department at Goodbody & Co. and Ling & Co., the firm run by Jimmy Ling's kid brother, McKinney was trying to swing a merger with Tyler Pipe. McKinney had been negotiating with M. J. Harvey, Tyler's major stockholder, for some time. Finally, Harvey agreed to an offer of $40 per share (the price over the counter was $31 to $32), with the proviso that Saturn would arrange the financing.

But McKinney was worried. Although the price was 3 times Tyler's book value and 15 times its prior year's earnings, if the deal leaked out other bidders could easily come in and push the price even higher. So McKinney and his executive vice president, C. A. Rundell, set themselves a two-week time limit for raising the $42.5 million they needed.

Monday afternoon, August 12, McKinney and Rundell boarded a jet for New York and Tuesday morning began the round of visiting bankers. By Thursday afternoon they had commitments from three banks for a total of $30 million. But the bankers put strings on the deal: Saturn would have to raise the remaining $12.5 million from private placements of subordinated debt. It would also have to make a public offering to retire $15 million of the debt within a year. "From then on," says the executive vice president, "it was the private

217

placement that was instrumental in putting the deal over."

Meanwhile, Smith, Barney sold the $12.5 million in three-year notes with the three-year warrants to Morgan Guaranty, Chase Manhattan, Chemical Bank, and Marine Midland as trustees for pension fund accounts and to the Wisconsin Alumni Research Foundation. "These buyers look upon a three-year debt from a time standpoint as not being so subordinate," explains Rundell. "It's just a matter of betting that nothing will go wrong for three years."

A mere two weeks later, the tender offer ad appeared in *The Wall Street Journal* and the deal was essentially closed. As a footnote to these events, Rundell points out that Saturn's stock doubled as a result of the acquisition and the company easily went to the public with a convertible debenture within three months. Thus Saturn was able to put the financing to bed and yet give up only one third of its stockholders' equity while doubling in size. "We also plan to apply for a New York Stock Exchange listing," Rundell says modestly.

There is even more to the story. The young company was able to raise so much money simply because, on the strength of the private placement, the lenders knew they could get their money back in just three years. As Ed Dugan of Smith, Barney, who managed the deal, points out: "Before the advent of three-year paper, a relatively unknown company like Saturn never would have been able to pull off the deal."

Experience Essential

Why do not even more companies use private funds, then? "There's a large amount of money around for this kind of financing," says Lester Kaufman of Applied Devices Corporation, "but it's no game for the unwary." Among the hazards, observes Kaufman, are insiders who do not think the same as management and go-go fund managers who want immediate gains. As Kaufman further points out, dealing directly with institutions requires experience.

But many of the younger breed of financial managers who know the ropes are very willing to go out to raise capital without the help of Wall Street. Banks, insurance companies, and the newly popular venture capital companies are eager lenders. According to the investment bankers, the Prudential has an office of thirty in Chicago who comb the midwestern region looking for companies that need capital. The bankers, too, have tried to stop the loan-business seepage by setting up captive SBIC's to invest in companies not eligible for regular bank credit.

But the corporate moneyman still must know his way around. Consider Lester Kaufman himself. Applied Devices Corporation is a systems design defense contractor that had been taken over by a new management team of youngbloods from Teledyne. ADC stock moved up smartly, but the company last year still needed about $750,000 to bolster working capital.

Equity, of course, was out of the question. Even with ADC stock rising, it would have been taken as a sign of trouble; the security would have been clobbered. But Kaufman knew just the way out. He borrowed the funds from a medical foundation that was personally known to ADC management. Not only that, he got it with a 6½% coupon and with warrants set at 10% above the market—nothing like the lavish discount that many go-go funds insist on.

New Twist to Old Uses

One of the newest twists of all in private placement involves one of its older uses. This is, of course, the use of a loan to bolster a small company's internal financial condition. Now, though, the money-seekers use the loan to beef up their net worth and earnings power preparatory to going public.

What is more, it adds muscle fairly cheaply. When a fledgling company tries to raise perhaps $1 million through an issue of stock, a comparatively small sum as capital markets go these days, costs may run well over $150,000. No less than 10% of the face amount will go to the underwriter. And usually the investment bankers will demand warrants on the deal.

Added to that are such other typical expenses as a $25,000 finder's fee and $15,000 in legal expenses to get the prospectus past the watchful eye of the SEC. Then there is another $7,500 or so for the accountants, since registration requires a certified audit. Printing expenses will run $10,000, and there's usually another $15,000 for a public relations firm to handle the annual report and another $15,000 in "blue-sky" or otherwise unaccountable extras. All these must come out of the $1 million, of course. So in a typical case, a company can wind up selling, say, 40% of itself to raise perhaps only a little more than $800,000.

One way or another, then, the private placement has succeeded in making itself a key part of our financial system. Indeed, most astute investment men suspect that it is only beginning to make its force felt. "The sound barrier was 6% interest," says Peter Solomon of Lehman Brothers. "When the corporate treasurers broke through that level, the sky became the limit and it was even all right for your sister to smoke pot."

Public Versus Other Financing

The key to a decision as to whether a company is ready to go public is the company's readiness in terms of sales volume, earnings, growth record, and expected after-market investor interest. Irreparable damage can be done to the corporation if premature public financing is undertaken. The step of "going public" is one which compares in severity with the action of Lot's wife. There is no turning back, no retracing of steps—one must march forward for better or for worse. Therefore, it is a decision which should be weighed carefully over a long period of time and in association with sound financial advice.

Introductory Considerations

There are many brokers who have no experience in the field of investment banking, and the investment firm's record

---

Mr. Selby is Managing Partner in the investment banking firm of Graham Loving & Co. in New York City. The firm has managed a number of public underwritings and private placements.

221

in obtaining capital should be carefully examined. The resulting after-market support given to the company "brought public" may be influenced by the after-market success of past under-writings issued by the investment banker.

There are no fixed rules as to the price at which the new stock issue should be brought out, timing of going public, number of shares to be issued, and so forth. The number of opinions obtained from investment bankers varies in direct proportion to the number of parties with whom discussions are undertaken.

For example, well-regarded investment banking houses, as a general rule, do not recommend "Regulation A's," do not recommend an issue price of less than $5 per share (since many leading brokerage houses do not pay commissions to salesmen for stock selling at lesser amounts), and have internal rules regarding the firm's years in business, earnings, and volume. In addition, major investment banking firms prefer a minimum six months' relationship with a client prior to the public financing.

In most cases, the corporation is best served by obtaining the services of an investment banker who is able to make a national or international distribution of the stock, rather than a local one. Some companies prefer a New York investment banker, since he may have regional branches or the means to obtain co-underwriters or members of the selling group located in other parts of the United States or abroad.

The number of shares to be outstanding is an important factor in making a decision of public versus alternative methods of financing. An orderly market cannot be maintained with too few shares in the hands of the public. A postponement of a public issue might be in order until an offering can be structured with an optimum number of shares.

The reception of an issue is enhanced by the fact that

a well-regarded investment firm's name appears on the prospectus, and the client company should not forget that the relationship does not stop on the date the issue becomes "effective." Thus the investment banker should be utilized for obtaining advice on questions about the issuing of interim and annual reports, the selection of an investment-oriented public relations firm, future financings, acquisitions and mergers, analytical reports prepared by brokerage houses, selection of securities firms which will "make a market" in the stock, methods of selling large blocks of stock held by insiders, and many other questions which may arise as the firm matures.

The corporation seeking financing should consider these factors:

- State of the money market.
- The atmosphere prevailing in the stock market.
- Short- and long-term plans of the company.
- Plans of the ownership of the equity of the corporation.
- The earnings projections and other factors affecting the company's future outlook.
- Relationship of the firm with outside financing sources.

Alternative Sources

Frequently, a closely held company which needs financing is not ready to go public. Therefore, as a way to raise capital, making a new security offering may actually be the poorest choice of more than a dozen options which might be utilized until the company is absolutely ready to become publicly held. Here, I shall list the alternatives to public financing. Then, in the balance of this chapter, I shall take a closer look at them. Each of these alternatives is deserving of extended description, but for purposes of summation I shall present the highlights. Consider:

1. Private Placement.
2. Banking Institutions.
3. Finance Companies.
4. Debt via Individuals.
5. Family Corporations and Investment Development Companies.
6. International Agencies (export-import banks, World Bank, etc.); Federal, State, or City Government Agencies.
7. Acquisitions and Mergers.
8. SBIC's.
9. Life Insurance Companies.
10. Sale and Leaseback.
11. Franchising Rights.
12. Sale of Foreign Rights.
13. Internal Financing.

1. Private Placement

This is an increasingly more popular method of financing a publicly or privately held firm without registration of the securities with regulatory authorities. If the corporation places the shares with investors directly, an investment banker may not be involved.

An offering is generally considered private if it is made to 25 or less offerees, provided they are "sophisticated investors" who have access to information required by the Securities Exchange Act of 1933. If the offering is made available to more than approximately 25 potential investors, the private offering exemption is jeopardized. Therefore, it is important to carefully select the prospective investors on the basis of their likelihood to invest, as well as on their financial experience and acumen.

The stock usually is nonregistered investment letter stock, the purchaser being "locked in" for a particular length of time.

This disadvantage is balanced by the fact that he is purchasing the securities at an attractive discount. The discount might relate to the common stock traded on the nation's securities markets, or to a particularly attractive interest payment paid by the company to the investor, or by attractive conversion features of a note.

Recently, our firm was asked to make a private placement because the client required funds within 45 days, whereas a full SEC registration would have taken a much longer period. We successfully sold the issue to private investors, enabling the client firm to make an acquisition which greatly enhanced its attractiveness to public investors when that firm went public eight months later.

Private placement, in other words, is a method of accelerated financing, and a great percentage of the payments made to auditors, legal firms, commissions paid to brokerage houses, and printing costs is usually saved.

The private placement offers the added advantage of permitting the company to function for a period of time with needed capital during which it can practice going public. The firm can maintain its relationship with the intended investment banker, issue an annual report to its shareholders, and take other steps in the "getting ready" process.

Several funds have sprung up whose charters enable them to purchase investment letter stock and these funds are particularly interesting as potential shareholders. Also, investors in general are becoming more aware of the advantages and disadvantages of letter stock, and the market for such shares or notes is increasing.

The main disadvantage to the corporation is the fact that the private placement, notes, debentures, or shares are sold at a lower price to the investor than the price at which a public offering would be made, thereby resulting in greater dilution of the company's stock. For this reason, it is an expensive method of financing from the standpoint of the number of shares made available by ownership, but the advantages often outweigh these disadvantages.

2. Banking Institutions

There are various financing avenues which may be chosen by the corporation, but no matter what means are decided on, the corporation should form a solid relationship with one or more banking institutions. Banks can be useful in introducing corporations to other sources of capital and they are usually necessary for banking credit available for inventories, short-term financing, and so on. Banks can steer companies to suppliers who might offer favorable terms, particularly if components or products are used for the final manufactured product, and a regular and steady supply is required, such as chemicals for the detergent manufacturer, stainless steel for the sink manufacturer, and textiles for the dress manufacturer. Bankers have been known to range far afield in providing services; for instance, a bank was recently instrumental in arranging for a stock sale to general contractors in return for a construction contract.

A bank is most useful if the loan can be secured, such as if the firm in question possesses oil or mineral reserves or has definite long-term contracts for the sale of its products. Generally, commercial banks concentrate on short-term loans, but more recently many have entered the field of medium-term debt. Some have new business development divisions and several have founded small business investment corporations (SBIC's) for purposes of equity financing.

Depending on the money market, banks are assuming greater risks than heretofore—the problem is to find the right bank. The cost of financing by banks is probably as low as one may obtain because of the factor of limitation of risk. A disadvantage is, and this may strictly be a personal opinion, that the business advice obtainable from banks is limited, and rarely are the services of a good banker available as a member of a board of directors should your company not already be a major corporation.

Several U.S. banks have established "Edge Act" subsidiaries abroad whose purpose is direct foreign investment.

Try to be well-introduced to an officer of the bank, and make him totally familiar with your business to obtain an open credit line for corporate funds to be used over a specific period of time. As for venture capital, if you are strictly in the idea stage, it is virtually impossible to obtain bank financing unless you and your co-founders can pledge collateral. As a general observation, venture capital is not raised through the efforts of banks.

3. Finance Companies

These organizations provide continuing financing to business (often to new ventures of questionable quality) and generally supply good counsel. Cost of funds are high, and even today 10% to 12% figures are not unknown. It is important to point out that during periods of so-called "tight money," the quality of financing increases while an easier money market leads to the acceptance of more speculative ventures by finance companies.

4. Debt via Individuals

Start-up operations are often financed by well-to-do friends of the founders, and banks may at times lend up to 80% of requirements, providing the remaining 20% is raised by private

227

investors. With the aid of competent attorneys, a limited partnership can be established to finance the venture. These individual investors can also include customers and suppliers of the venture company.

The advantages and disadvantages are apparent. On the one hand, customer relationships could be ruined if the firm's profitability was not in line with anticipated projections. On the other hand, overdependence on individual suppliers, who were also investors, would aid in driving off competitive suppliers.

5. *Family Corporations*

Wealthy families with investment funds sometimes establish corporations. Quite often, such corporations are founded by individuals or groups who have sold privately held firms to the public or to another corporation, and who find themselves in the position of having to invest in business organizations other than their own.

An investment development company, like the family corporation, carefully examines applications for loans or hires an outside review board to make its investment decisions, and my judgment is that more than 90% of all such applications are rejected. Because they are dependent on the business judgment of their advisers, these firms often prefer to take an equity position in the companies they finance and attempt to place one of their own members on the board.

The individuals who back investment companies are generally in the high tax brackets. Therefore, their losses might well work out to be only a small portion of any actual losses, and they are of course interested in capital gains to take advantage of the lower tax rates. The services of a member of one of these firms as a member of your board of directors might aid you considerably, both in terms of prestige and in obtaining usually excellent business advice.

Such investors may invest in more speculative situations because their major income is often derived from other sources. Family corporations generally have excellent analytical staffs that are in a position to devote full time to possible investments.

6. *International Agencies*

If you are selling capital goods overseas, it is at times possible to claim that you are aiding the balance of payments. Thus you may win support from such authorities as export-import banks, the World Bank, and so on. There are federal, state, and local government agencies providing grants or loans for specialized businesses which may aid health programs, the space program, social welfare, and the like. The National Institute of Health often grants aid to physicians or investors who are interested in manufacturing products to be used in the medical professions.

7. *Acquisitions and Mergers*

Does it fit your plans to sell your firm to another corporation? The disadvantage is that you are vulnerable to the whims of the acquiring corporation, particularly if it is a much larger firm than your own. Even if you give up less than 50% of the voting stock, usually you are not permitted to sell any stock to others without offering the shares to your partner in the venture—again restricting your ability to move forward. From the standpoint of the minority stockholders, if this group is constituted of individuals who are not very sophisticated or wealthy, bickering may come about as to the use of the firm's money, again restricting the progress of the firm.

8. SBIC's

These chartered corporations are regulated and licensed by the Small Business Administration. The minimum amount of $300,000 is "put up" by the founders of the SBIC, and this is matched by SBA purchases of subordinated debentures ranging from $300,000 to $700,000. Also, the SBA can lend the SBIC's up to 50% of their paid-in capital. So it works out that $700,000 in private capital can obtain $700,000 in subordinated debentures proceeds, and $2,700,000 in the form of an operating loan.

The SBIC's are restricted and can only invest up to 20% of their capital in any one company. There were approximately 750 SBIC's in operation in 1968 with capital of about $800 million. Some of them specialize, while others are very much diversified.

I might add that there are about 25 banks which have established their own SBIC's. As a personal opinion, this kind of financing can be expensive, for the SBIC's usually demand a rather large amount of stock or warrants.

9. Life Insurance Companies

These are legally restricted to certain investments, depending on the states in which they operate. They generally do not take a high degree of risk, confining their investments to high-quality issues and specializing in medium- to long-term credit. However, some insurance companies do purchase convertible debenture issues of small businesses. Again, there are some insurance companies which will take warrants to buy common stock. As a general observation, insurance companies usually do not make money available to many small businesses, but of course there are exceptions.

10. Sale and Leaseback

This method for obtaining financing is usually associated with the real estate field. Normally, such a sale is in the form of office buildings, plants, warehouses, and retail establishments to an individual or group and the leasing back of this real estate. In many cases, ownership officers of small companies rent space to their firms, but the general preference is that as soon as funds are available to the company this real estate should be purchased from the officer as a guarantee against possible conflict of interest. Other sale and leaseback transactions take place with computers, aircraft, and so forth.

11. Franchising Rights

Most businessmen are familiar with the hundreds of chain restaurants, ice cream parlors, chicken dispensers, and other franchised local enterprises. Many managements finance their corporations by selling franchises, and often this method works out very well for both parties. The major advantage is that corporate funds are not tied up in small local enterprises, while the major disadvantage is that corporations might well increase their profitability by not giving up a portion of the profits to local franchisees.

12. Sale of Foreign Rights

Many companies with patents or well thought out ideas license foreign companies or operators, and in this manner obtain funds to be used for domestic operations.

13. Internal Financing

This alternative method actually provides the bulk of the total source of funds in the United States. Existing companies with earnings records generally utilize these funds for expansion. The reasons for this are important.

First, using your earnings to finance does not create problems in having to go to outside sources; thus it relieves the tremendous loss of time on the part of officers who are engaged in seeking funds. Second, plowing back earnings avoids certain taxation. Third, more and more investors in growth companies are becoming less concerned about dividend payments.

Therefore, the price of stock in a company paying dividends usually is unaffected if earnings growth is maintained.

In Summary

Usually, there is more money available than there are good, sound ideas to be financed. Said another way, there are greater funds available than there are good managers to finance. The "money maker" is what the financing source is looking for; weak management may result in the failure of the firm. Thus the presentation to the financing source is important and deserves a great amount of sound preparation.

In obtaining financing, the company has one or more of a dozen options which might be utilized until the company is absolutely ready to go public.

Finally, the selection of the right source of capital is one of management's most important decisions in the lifetime of a business. Contracts and obligations entered into cannot easily be undone, and management is usually obtaining the services of a lending partner who is often not so silent.

The culmination of a firm's financing efforts is the act of "going public"—an act which will shape and dictate the firm's future. For a privately held firm, financing *other* than a public offering should be examined, and may serve as a prelude to the first public offering of the company's stock.

232

Widgets' Decision to Go Public

A well-established manufacturing company is seriously considering "going public," both to diversify the portfolio of one of its major stockholders and to raise additional capital for planned expansion. The reader will consider the range of factors which have already been treated in detail in the previous chapters of this book, culminating in the pricing of the new issue. This case study traces the company's historical background, looks at its current executive team, and then examines its decision to go public.

Historical Background

Widgets was incorporated in 1938 in Allentown, Pennsylvania, by Wesley Hayes and his brother, Thomas, who had left their jobs as engineers with a leading metal fabricating manufacturer which produced frames and fuel tanks for the aircraft industry. Wesley had independently developed a fuel gauge which had been tested by his former company and found superior in design to the ones it had been installing in its tanks. Impressed with the quality and accuracy of the gauge, Wesley's former employer signed a sizable supply contract, and Widgets, Inc. started production.

The 1940s

Within two years after the incorporation of Widgets, Wesley was supplying fuel gauges not only to his former company, but also to other aircraft manufacturers. Wesley had also established a modest R&D program to improve the design of two other standard aircraft instruments: the altimeter and airspeed indicator. Both prototypes of the redesigned instruments had tested well and they had also been well received by aircraft manufacturers. Widgets, however, lacked the necessary capital to start large-scale production and since the market for aircraft was limited, the company found it difficult to negotiate bank financing.

Wesley's older son, Andrew, who joined the company as research director after completing MIT graduate school in 1940, was anxious to continue his research in the field of optical precision measurement. Although Widgets had only limited facilities for this type of research, Wesley and Tom agreed to enter this specialized field to the extent that their limited finances would allow. They anticipated the entry of the United States into World War II, and they knew that range finders and bombsights which required high-powered lenses would be a logical extension of their standard measurement devices for wartime aviation and navigation.

With America's entry into the war, many large aircraft manufacturers, who had received prime contracts from the government and Defense Department, encouraged Widgets to undertake the expansion necessary to produce its instruments and to expand its facilities for optical research. Through their contacts and guaranteed contract commitments, these manufacturers enabled Wesley and Tom to secure the necessary financing for their company.

During the war, production facilities and employee ranks increased threefold, and Widgets' product line also increased. In addition to its gauges, the line included sensor instruments to measure the physical properties of fuel, oil, air, and water. In the control function, Widgets started to experiment with mechanical rather than manual activators which would automatically correct deviations from a predetermined standard. Likewise, Widgets had made some progress in developing recording and storage systems for data. Under government subcontract, Widgets also began manufacturing high-powered lenses for naval and aeronautical range finders and bombsights. Sales for Widgets, Inc. increased from $1.2 million in 1940 to $11.8 million in 1944.

It was obvious to Widgets' management that postwar demand for its products could not support the company's war-expanded facilities. As it was, even during the war, the development of radar-directed range finders had sharply curtailed Widgets' sales of high-powered lenses. At the estimated lower level of postwar sales, it would be difficult to maintain the research team which Widgets had assembled during the war years. Determined to hold together their production and research facilities, the brothers placed most of their wartime profits into R&D—not only to improve the present line of instrumentation for commercial aircraft, but also to diversify into other related areas.

By the end of the war, Widgets had successfully adapted its measurement, control, and recording instruments for application in the food processing and chemical industries. It also had established a commercial market for its high-powered

235

lenses for astronomical telescopes. The boom in postwar commercial aviation and the continuing need for instrumentation, which Widgets' management had anticipated, also contributed to the company's postwar earnings. Having established its name and quality product line with aircraft manufacturers, Widgets was able to change over to peacetime production without great difficulty. However, despite the success of the commercial application of its products, sales dipped substantially from a record high in 1944 of $11.8 million to $6.6 million in 1947.

Both of Wesley's sons, John and Andrew, returned from their tours of duty with the Air Force in 1946. John, who had graduated from MIT and Harvard Business School just before he entered the Air Force, assisted his father in directing the company and supervising the reorientation of Widgets' Research Department toward peacetime projects. Andrew divided his time between participating in the research for Air Force contracts and revitalizing R&D projects in his special field of precision optics.

The 1950s

When the United States began to rearm in 1948, Widgets competed aggressively for defense contracts. As a result of several large contracts awarded to Widgets by the Air Force and Navy, sales climbed to $10.4 million by 1952.

Although the company still continued to manufacture its instruments for the food-processing and chemical industries in the 1950s, the bulk of its efforts was directed toward refining and producing electrically powered recording, control, and measurement systems for military aircraft and space projects. Widgets had entered the new and rapidly developing aerospace market with the development and production of its "second generation" electrical measurement and control systems

236

for the utilization and gauging of space vehicle propulsion fuel.

Moreover, its research and production in the field of precision optics and electro-optical systems was also stimulated by a constantly increasing demand for optics for a variety of defense and space systems, such as high-powered aerial reconnaissance and panoramic cameras, and components for missile and satellite-tracking systems. In 1959, government and related Armed Force Service contracts accounted for 83% of Widgets total sales.

The 1960s

In 1962, after lengthy congressional hearings, several Defense Department contracts for which Widgets had acted as subcontractor were renegotiated. As a result of the renegotiation proceedings, the government obtained a large refund and Widgets reported sharply lower earnings.

At a family conference, the problem was discussed and John, who had urged expansion of the commercial product line, was appointed managing director of a newly formed Industrial Product Division.

During the next five years, John directed Widgets' commercial product development so successfully that by early 1968 approximately 52% of Widgets sales were commercial as compared to 46% in 1966 and less than 30% in 1960.

Through application of its products to industrial use, Widgets had well-established markets for several new commercial products: industrial metering and industrial fluid controls for the oil and natural gas industries; temperature measurement and control devices for refrigerated railroad cars and trucks; and industrial electro-mechanical indicating equipment —including electrical counters and frequency measurement equipment. In addition, Widgets expanded its optic and electro-optical product line to include refined sighting devices, precision measuring systems, and optical data processing systems which combined the technologies of precise optics and Widgets' newest technology, laser systems.

John and Andrew agreed on the vast possibilities for the commercial application of the laser, and Widgets began to develop measurement and alignment equipment for use in machine tool, aircraft, and large metal-fabricating industries. By 1967, Widgets had a few contracts from producers of numerically controlled machine tool equipment. Research was also being conducted on a chemically powered portable laser, but further experimentation with laser systems had slowed considerably due to inadequate laboratory facilities and equipment.

Although a number of competitors produced similar product lines, in 1968 some 18% of Widgets' gross sales were comprised of total measurement instrumentation systems not being manufactured by any other company. Its name had also become synonymous with the combined measurement, data, and control system which it had perfected and adapted for aviation and industrial use. The company's annual expenditure for R&D had approximated 8% of sales in recent years and in 1968 there were over 300 engineers and technicians employed in the Research Division.

The company's backlog of orders as of June 30, 1968 totaled $7.5 million as compared with $8.6 million on June 30, 1967. The percentages of total sales under government and Department of Defense prime and subcontracts had steadily decreased during the past five years and in 1968 accounted for 4% and 48%, respectively. In accordance with established government procedures, substantially all of Widgets' government contracts were subject to cancellation at the convenience of the government, and sales under such contracts were subject to renegotiation.

The company's products were distributed nationally and in a number of European countries through factory representatives, field sales offices, and international distributors. In 1967, sales were made to over 7,500 customers; and although the company's 45 largest customers accounted for 35% of the sales, no single customer accounted for more than 6% of the total. Widgets had manufacturing facilities in Pennsylvania, California, and Kansas, and planned to expand into Europe in the near future. Although Widgets had approached several companies for merger talks, none of these discussions had proven successful.

From 1962 to 1967, the number of Widgets employees increased by 25% from 1,200 to 1,500. More than 20% of the company's employees had degrees in engineering or the sciences, and an additional 40% were skilled in the professional fields. Approximately one fifth of the employees were engaged in R&D and technical service activities, two fifths in the production of instruments and components, and two fifths occupied management, administrative, and maintenance positions.

In 1967, the capital stock of Widgets consisted of 6,000 shares of common stock issued and outstanding with a par value of $10 per share. Wesley Hayes held approximately 2,300 shares or 38.3%; his brother, Tom, 1,800 shares or 30.8%; his sons Andrew and John, 725 shares each for a total of 24.2%; and three close friends of Wesley's who were employees of the company held 450 shares among them, or 7.5% of the total.

Widgets had financed its growth through short- and long-term loans. In 1952, it had issued $2 million of 5% cumulative preferred stock which was retired in 1957. In 1962, Widgets borrowed once again for the development of its new commercial product lines, and in 1968 it had notes outstanding with the Cambridge Life Insurance Company totaling $2.2 million at an interest rate of 5½% and repayable in equal installments extending to 1978.

Principals Involved

In the cast are these stockholders and management personnel of Widgets, Inc.:

- Wesley Hayes (retiring president and chairman of the board).
- Thomas Hayes (incoming chairman and brother of Wesley).
- John Hayes (incoming president and chief executive officer who is the younger son of Wesley).
- Andrew Hayes (older son of Wesley who is vice president of the R&D Division).
- Michael Phillips (treasurer).
- Benjamin Henderson (legal counsel).
- Larry Downs (corporate accountant).

Reaching the Decision

Although John Hayes had spoken casually with Widgets' lawyer, Ben Henderson, about the company going public at the beginning of 1967, three significant things happened which contributed to his decision to do so.

First, at the family's New Year's party, Wesley Hayes announced that he would retire on March 31 as the president and chairman of the board of Widgets, and he recommended the election of his son, John, to succeed him as president, and Tom, his brother, to succeed him as chairman.

Second, after the board meeting on January 5, 1967—at which the recommended appointments were unanimously confirmed—Wesley told John and Andrew of his desire to sell

1,000 shares of his Widgets' stock in order to diversify his portfolio, and asked his sons whether they would be interested in purchasing them.

Third, Andrew, who headed up Widgets' R&D activities, discussed with John the necessity for rebuilding an entire section of the Research Division if work on laser systems was to continue.

John: How much will that cost?

Andrew: About $1.5 to $2 million.

John: Are you kidding? Why don't we just throw out everything we've got and start from scratch!

Andrew: That's practically what we'll have to do. Technology costs money, and so do the people who conduct the research, the equipment they use, and the space in which they work. What I'm saying is that to progress any further with our laser program we need more of everything. And that goes for our manufacturing divisions, too. We could easily use another $750,000 for improvements in the Kansas plant.

Combined Offering Proposal

At the first board meeting over which he presided, John proposed that both the company and his father offer shares to the public through a combined offering.

John: By offering 1,000 shares of his own stock to the public, my Dad would be making a "secondary" offering and the proceeds of the sale would be for his own account. The company would be making an initial distribution, since in order to sell shares for its own account it would have to issue new shares of stock. In order to have Dad fairly compensated and to cover the costs of the needed plant expansions, I estimate that the net proceeds of the combined initial issue and secondary offering would have to total about $3 million.

Andrew: Why should we go public when all we're trying to do is sell some of Dad's shares and raise some money for some additional plant. There are plenty of alternative ways of raising money. As far as Dad's shares are concerned, we could pool our money and buy his ourselves, or he could place them privately without going to the additional trouble and expense of throwing our company to the public wolves. In regard to financing the plant, we could borrow from the bank. Our net worth could easily support more debt, and even if we were in tighter shape, we could mortgage or lease some of our fixed assets.

Think of the cost involved in going public in comparison. Not only would we have to face an underwriter's discount, but also all the legal, printing, and other incidental expenses. Our own lawyer has estimated that our total expenses could amount to from 7% to 12% of the principal amount of our offering.

Tom (frowning): Let's not be too hasty here, John. This company's been in our family for two generations, and we've really just established ourselves as part of the top 30 firms in the industry in the last decade. Going public could really jeopardize our position by requiring us not only to disclose confidential financial data to our competitors, but also to account for our actions to the stockholders.

I know statistically we would retain control over our corporation, but I don't welcome the possibility of dissident stockholders, who in some instances could inspect our books and records, challenging our management. Our actions would be constrained by the reporting, proxy, trading, and other regulations of the Securities Act and the SEC.

Michael: If you list your stock on an exchange, you can't even deal freely in what's left of your corporate stock. As officers, directors, and anyone who owns more than 10% of the outstanding shares, you would have to report your transactions to the exchange, and you could be required to pay to the company any profits made from buying and selling the stock in a six-month period.

John: Wait a minute. You're all going off in six different directions. Let's look at how going public will affect the priorities of our company. I think at least we're all agreed on the first one: we want to grow quickly and profitably. Most of our growth so far has been the result of in-house product development and while our new products have usually been natural outgrowths of an existing product line or of technical skills, this is not always going to be the case. It will be—and has been—logical for us to try to acquire a well-managed company that can profitably produce new product lines.

Tom: We haven't had much success in going the acquisition route in the past.

John: That's true. But if you look at the rough five-year plan I've sketched out, you'll see that I would like to get the company moving into the computer hardware field, and this is a tough market to cut into from scratch. But to ease our transition into it, I've had my eye on a company which manufactures electrical transformers and total assemblies for computers. And as far as expanding into areas more closely related to our established product line, I've been looking at several companies which specialize in electrical instruments and controls for ships and submarines.

Tom (*shaking his head*): Frankly, John, in view of our poor track record of merger attempts, I'm surprised that you're anxious to start the ball rolling.

John: I admit that our past merger efforts have never gotten off the ground, but I can think of at least one fairly obvious reason why. Few candidates want to merge with a closely held company and receive a nonmarketable minority interest. However, with a listed security to offer in addition to cash, we would be a more attractive bed partner tomorrow than yesterday.

Going public would also broaden our equity base and increase our net worth. This means we would be able to increase our line of credit with banks—and when you consider that most of our financing to date has consisted of short- and long-term borrowing, this becomes quite important. Once we had gone public and established a broad market, we would also have a considerable variety of financial instruments to work with—preferred stock, bond issues, convertibles.

Larry: Do you really have any idea, John, of the extent to which stockholders can make our corporate life miserable? Let me remind you of a few adjustments which, as a publicly owned corporation, we would have to make. To keep our public happy, and to attract new investors with attractive earnings, we would have to change our method of calculating depreciation. If we continued to accelerate depreciation, our tax savings would be there but our earnings statement certainly wouldn't be a real hit. On the other hand, if we were to capitalize our expenses in order to establish a better earnings position and to make our shareholders happy, our tax bill and our cash outflow would increase. And as we increased our cash outflow, the company's near-term cash position—and a large part of our corporate flexibility—would decrease.

You talked about increased borrowing power and fancy debt instruments, but you neglected to mention that the most dependable, accessible, inexpensive, and least risky source of funds—our retained earnings—would not be so accessible. When retained earnings are used to any appreciable extent for financing, the stockholders see earnings and their potential dividends decrease. Even granted that any return from an investment financed by retained earnings results in a net contribution to the company's earnings, try explaining that to a shareholder who wants his full dividend payment *now*.

244

And one other thing, although you anticipate the use of stock options to supplement, and to some extent replace, cash salary payments, if the options are offered to any great degree, the stockholder will again see a dilution in his earnings per share and market price growth.

John: While it's true that before I make a decision, I will always consider its effects on the company's cash-flow position, it's not always impossible to reconcile this managerial concern with the stockholders' interest in the company's earnings per share, dividends, and market price. Let's not forget either that even after going public, each of us would still be a substantial stockholder in his own right.

To put it very simply, I am quite willing to accept the legal and other limitations and changes in procedure to obtain what I consider the greater and necessary flexibility to achieve corporate growth. While stockholder interest would sometimes constrain us, the very fact that we would have stockholders, that we could offer stock options, and that we would have alternate methods of finance means that we would have opportunities to grow that we've never had before.

Andrew (*smiling*): I'll agree to that, but perhaps to whet our interest in this venture a little further, you should mention the benefits that we would enjoy as owners of a public stock.

John: In the first place, your stock at any one time would have a definite market value. Instead of the financial sacrifice which confronts efforts to sell stock without a market, as holders of a publicly owned stock you could sell your shares at the most opportune times in terms of personal need and market conditions. Instead of relying solely on the performance of your own company, you could easily sell a portion of your holdings and invest the proceeds in a diversified portfolio of high-quality stocks and bonds.

245

A public market for your stock would also facilitate the resolution of estate tax problems upon your death. In fact, all appraisal problems connected with gift or inheritance taxes would be alleviated by the establishment of market value for your stock.

You would also be creating a certain amount of protection from each other and from any minority shareholder who might demand a high price for his shares.

The most obvious advantage for you as a stockholder would be the appreciation in the value of your shares once we have gone public. We all know that our shares are worth more than their par or book value. I can't tell you at what price the shares would be originally offered, but at least I hope the figure would be greater than our stated or book value; and once we've created a market for our new security, we could sell our shares at this higher price.

I'd also like to remind you that even though we could probably arrange to purchase Dad's shares by conventional debt financing, or by arranging private placement, there's a problem common to both these methods which could cause considerable unpleasantness. The value of the stock would be arbitrarily fixed or, worse, would be subject to bargaining. You know Dad is not going to settle for the par value of the stock, and if we tried to have the stock placed privately, we would run the chance of settling for less than par. No one can be sure that the price he pays for the stock is a fair reflection of its value. Sorry if I've droned on.

Ben: I would worry only if you didn't discuss this. Whether to go public or not is one of the most important questions you'll have to decide on in the whole process of running this company.

John: Well, then, shall we decide?

The vote was 4 to 1 in favor of going public.

Selecting the Underwriter

Wesley Hayes listened thoughtfully to John's discussion of the board meeting and at the end remarked a bit testily that he thought the company had done very well for over 30 years without outsiders' interference. He said he had been wondering how John was going to handle the question of the value of the stock, and he suggested that John go to see Charles Wentworth, an old classmate of John's father, who was a senior partner of Wentworth, Rowles and Everest, an investment banking firm which had been on Wall Street for over half a century.

The success of the issues in which WRE had been a participant, the number and size of those participations, as well as the firm's ingenuity in the placing of the issues, all contributed to WRE's generally acknowledged strength and prestige in the financial community.

Important Criteria

On Saturday, John visited Charles Wentworth and told him about the decision of Widgets' board to go public.

Charles: Despite my long and fine friendship with your father, our firm is not the one to do your underwriting. Let me explain. In the first place, we have only rarely handled a primary offering, and in spite of the inflated condition of the market and the public's eager acceptance of new issues, for the past couple of years we haven't done any at all. Our reputation—as well as that of many other houses—is founded on our ability to place nationally large secondary debt issues—$5 million or more, in fact. The firms with whom we deal are the giants, the well-established corporations with sales and earnings in the millions.

247

Although I have great respect for your efforts to expand, your company and offering would not meet the minimum standards of size and profitability which tradition demands our clients to possess. This, of course, does not mean that many other reputable houses which specialize in primary issues would be unwilling to underwrite your offering.

John: I'm beginning to discover that the selection of an underwriting firm merits as much thought and weighing of alternatives as the original decision to go public.

Charles: Your choice is extremely important for several reasons, but chiefly because of the underwriting firm's experience in marketing issues and its knowledge of market receptiveness to a new issue. First, your underwriter may advise you not to go public at all, because of market unreceptivity, or simply and frankly because—in his opinion—your company stock is not marketable, regardless of the market condition.

Your underwriter is also largely responsible for the determination of the price of your issue, and for avoiding the mistake of overpricing which can cause a more adverse effect on the long-term market value of your stock than merely the amount by which it was overpriced.

Finally, your underwriter is responsible for the important task of marketing and shepherding the initial issue through the first weeks of trading by maintaining an active after-market for your stock.

John: Oviously, the number of firms in the investment banking field are considerable and the community as a whole has a wide range of standards. How, then, can I be sure of getting a reputable firm?

Charles: Some houses, considered in the trade as the high-grade underwriters, are very selective about the issues they will market. They have minimum standards of the size of the offering and of the size and profitability which a company

248

must meet before they will market a public security. Other investment houses are willing to work with any size or type of company, and regardless of the receptivity of the market.

The reputable underwriting firm is as interested in selecting the right company as the issuing company is in selecting the right investment house. An unmarketable issue is equally as burdensome to the offering company as it is to the underwriter.

While you will want to make sure that your underwriter is thoroughly qualified to offer your issue in terms of legal and accounting staff assistance, marketing experience, investment banking connections, and after-market responsibility; that firm will be equally interested in the quality of the public offering which you are proposing that they handle.

The age of your company, its sales and earnings record, managerial depth and competence, future growth potential, and form of capitalization are some details which the underwriters will want to know from you and to investigate for themselves. Ideally, a company with a stock of high investment quality will work through an investment house qualified to handle such an issue.

John: To arrange a happy match, do you think it would be advisable for us to employ a finder or outside consultant who has had professional experience with the underwriting community?

Charles: It all depends. Naturally, a direct approach to an underwriter is simpler. Often, the issuing company's own lawyer, commercial banker, or accountant may be qualified to act as the finder, and can provide the company with the guidance necessary for a successful underwriting.

On the other hand, unless the company is unusually well known, a finder—with his established contacts and his knowledge of the type of issue which interests a particular investment house—can be of considerable help.

If you would like me to act as a modified finder, John, I will be quite happy to introduce you to an underwriting firm which I think would handle your issue competently. Call me on Monday, and we'll arrange for a conference involving you, your accountant, your lawyer, and the underwriter's representatives.

Company Description

On Monday morning, John called in Ben Henderson and Larry Downs, and brought them up-to-date on his discussion with Wentworth. John had also made a list of some of the information which he thought would be necessary to present to the underwriters' representatives at the preliminary conference.

The data included the name and address of the company and of the principal stockholders; a brief biographical sketch of each officer, director, and middle management executive; when and where the company had been incorporated; its charter and bylaws; a description of its products and services; and a brief corporate history, indicating past growth and future plans for research and product development programs, expansion, acquisition, and diversification.

In addition, John had also included the company's audited balance sheets and profit and loss statements for the past five years, as well as the amount he wanted to raise by the public issue along with an explanation that the proceeds were to be for the company's account.

Ben: That's a good start, but you're going to need a lot more detail before the underwriter's going to be able to make a decision about this issue.

Larry: Ben's right, John, and they'll definitely want to see our latest interim balance and profit and loss statements. We'll have to include an estimate of our sales and profits for this year, too, as well as our projections of the balance sheets and operating statements for this year and next year, if we want to give them the complete picture.

Ben: Let's go back and look more closely at what you've included in your description of the business. We've got to flesh out these bare bones. For example, we'll have to explain more completely how this company works—not only what and to whom we sell, but descriptions of our major customers and a complete breakdown of the sales and profits by major product and customer categories.

Larry: Also the number and location of our plants, the kind of equipment we use, the number of employees we hire, their wage scales, our relations with them, and a description of our suppliers and competitors.

John (*smiling*): Is this trip really necessary? We might have to reschedule this meeting for next month sometime.

Ben: We're not finished yet, but you've got to realize the importance of this information. If our proposal is poorly written, incomplete, or if we sell ourselves short by not adequately using the attractive features of the business, the whole thing will be rejected. What we want to do with this information is to facilitate the underwriter's estimate that our security would be an attractive and successful public offering for him to handle.

Discussing the Offering

On Thursday of that same week, John, Andrew, Ben, Larry, and Charles Wentworth met with a group from Conrad and Lyn, Inc., an investment banking firm which was thoroughly familiar with placing new issues of corporate securities.

John presented Widgets' proposal. After reading it over carefully, Geoffrey Knox, who headed the Conrad and Lyn's delegation, asked a number of questions in an attempt to gain a general impression of Widgets' management. He was particularly interested in Widgets' plans for future R&D efforts in the field of laser development and for its ideas about acquisitions. He also questioned John carefully about the downturn in 1966 sales and earnings. John, in turn, had several questions about the services which the company could expect to receive from C&L.

John: Exactly what kind of support would you give our stock in the after-market, assuming of course you accepted the issue?

Geoffrey: I can't give you an exact answer because the type and amount of support we give depends on many variables: the size of the offering, the condition of the market, the geographical distribution of the initial offering, the general receptiveness of the investing public to a stock—to name a few.

Basically and simply, however, we try to maintain an orderly trading market for a new issue. Usually, we expect our underwriting syndicate to sell to the public 15% to 20% of the shares of a new issue purchased within the first few days. If, in the time preceding the offering, the market does not appear sufficiently strong enough to absorb this minimum amount, we will establish a short position to stabilize the market for these shares. Briefly, we establish a short position by selling several thousand more shares than the amount of the total offering with the intention of buying back the additional shares in the after-market to counter any downward pressure which might develop immediately after the shares have reached the open market.

Also, when a stock is traded over-the-counter—as your issue will be—we will support the stock when necessary until it is listed on an exchange. We attempt to keep the public's bid and asked prices for the shares in balance by buying or selling shares for our own account.

And, finally, since we have a very definite idea of the merit of the companies whose stock we underwrite, we are able to recommend—when appropriate, of course—its purchase to our customers.

John: Does Conrad and Lyn have any set policy concerning the distribution of new issues? I realize that your firm has offices throughout the country and could easily handle a national distribution, but I am questioning whether a strictly regional distribution might not be better. After all, our largest plant is in Pennsylvania, our best customers and most of our friends are in the East, and it seems only natural that Widgets would be best received in the East.

Geoffrey: When C&L acts as the managing underwriter in an initial offering, we seek to achieve through the composition of our underwriting syndicate as broad a distribution as the size of the offering will permit. If the initial offering is made in the "home town" region where friends, suppliers, and old customers are the prime investors, the issue may not reflect its true valuation relative to other investment opportunities. In such a narrow market, investors are more likely to buy or sell because of their own relationships with the management than they are because of the relative value of the stock.

We have learned from experience that home-town investors provide the strongest continuing buying support once the issue has been traded publicly. Therefore, if we, as the originating underwriters, purposefully concentrate the initial distribution in the home town, much of this necessary after-market support would be lost.

One other comforting thought about a national distribution. The larger the representation of reputable investment banking firms sponsoring your security, the larger will be the segment of the national financial community supporting your issue, following its progress, and recommending it to their clients when appropriate.

Further Investigation

After the general exchange and clarification of information had taken place, Geoffrey Knox indicated to John that he thought a public issue of Widgets' stock could be placed successfully. However, since any underwriting firm wishes to sponsor only those issues which it can readily place, a final decision would not be taken until Conrad and Lyn had conducted its own independent survey of Widgets, Inc.

During February and March, Conrad and Lyn studied Widgets' proposal in detail, reviewing the data which had been submitted and accumulating information which they felt would enable them to determine the success of the issue. Several times, Peter Davis, the partner who had been chosen to handle the issue, called on John, Ben, and Larry to ask them for further information about the company, and particularly about their earnings prospects for 1967. Peter and some of his staff members also visited the company's main plant in Pennsylvania to check out its engineering standards and potential production capacity. Peter also conferred with Andrew about the new facilities, plant, and equipment to which the proceeds of the prospective issue were to be applied.

When Peter was satisfied with the information which he had received, he requested his staff to prepare a detailed memorandum on Widgets, Inc. for circulation among the other partners of the investment banking firm. Peter also drew up a comparative pricing schedule which compared Widgets with a number of other companies engaged in the same general business whose shares were publicly held (see *Exhibit I*).

254

In March of 1967, Peter met with his fellow partners Sid Jefferies, Alex Goodman, and Joseph Hull to discuss his memo and to reach a decision as to whether to proceed with an offering for Widgets.

Sid: Well, Peter, it looks like we've got a pretty good one to start off the new month. This is certainly an unusual combination of product lines, but since Widgets is heavily committed to the field of electro-optical products which are actually part of the glamour products of the 1960s it does look all right. The growth prospects of the aerospace industry for which Widgets produces its instruments certainly is strong.

Alex: I agree. Also Widgets' relative position in the whole instrumentation industry looks pretty good. Despite its size, it seems to be meeting its competition successfully. I see your staff has confirmed Widgets' claim that 18% of their gross sales are systems not being manufactured by any other company. I'd say what this company lacks in size, it's making up for in ambition.

Joseph: This research they've started on a portable laser is quite an advanced concept. But I can see from our reports of their plant and equipment that expanded plant and facilities would help this company considerably. However, this would really be a far healthier situation if so much of their business weren't tied to government and defense-related prime and subcontracts. You recall what happened to this company in 1962, don't you? Some of its contracts were called back for renegotiation. I see from your report, Peter, that their research department is deeply involved in commercial application of their product lines, but . . .

Sid: Frankly, in looking at this comparative income statement (*Exhibit II*), I can't tell what they're doing in the area of sales and general administration. The ratio of this to gross sales jumps all over the place, and appears to be climbing

Exhibit I. Comparative Pricing Schedule

Company Market Fiscal Year Ended	Widgets — 12/31	PS NYS 12/31	CNA NYS 12/31	CF NYS 12/31	MRP NYS 12/31	BUH OTC 12/31	NRUB ASE 12/31	EP NYS 12/31	BT ASE 12/31
1967 Company Size (000)									
Net Sales	33,000	55,548	37,150	18,500	68,300	19,194	29,803	88,389	21,620
Net Income	938	3,896	2,321	1,300	2,872	2,470	953	4,400	2,612
Net Worth	10,446	19,095	24,483	13,411	34,103	10,826	11,722	39,336	11,840
Long-term Debt	2,200	3,683	11,250	405	10,210	nil	2,825	8,274	1,225
No. Common Shares	1,250	2,948	1,617	477	1,441	1,281	1,139	6,067	1,480
Market Price—10/25/68	—	25¾	17¾	29¾	39	15¾	20	33¾	26¾
Indicated Cash Dividend—1968 est.	nil	n.a.	.60	1.00	1.40	.70	.60	nil	nil
Yield	—	n.a.	3.3%	3.3%	3.6%	4.8%	3.0%	nil	nil
Price/Earnings Ratio—1968 est.	—	27.5x	11.1x	9.9x	13.6x	9.95x	18x	39x	16.3x
Earnings (E), Dividends (D) per share:	E D	E D	E D	E D	E D	E D	E D	E D	E D
1968 est.	1.20 —	.94 n.a.	1.60 .60	3.00 1.00	2.87 1.40	1.52 .70	1.11 .60	.84 nil	1.61 nil
1967	.75 .06	1.32 .13	1.43 .50	2.75 1.00	1.89 1.40	1.93 .97	.84 .60	.73 nil	1.72 nil
1966	1.10 .07	1.31 .07	.71 .50	1.53 1.00	1.99 1.40	1.50 .75	.61 .60	.66 nil	.98 nil
1965	1.20 .07	.46 .04	1.04 .50	2.14 1.00	2.06 1.40	1.58 .75	1.22 .30	.50 nil	1.45 nil
1964	.78 .02	.22 nil	1.01 .40	2.12 1.00	2.05 1.35	1.61 .70	1.43 nil	.41 nil	1.67 nil
1963	.52 .02	.18 nil	.92 .30	1.50 1.00	.81 1.32	1.21 .70	.60 nil	.38 nil	1.09 nil
Average E/S, D/S 1963-1967	.87 .05	.70 .05	1.02 .45	2.00 1.00	1.76 1.37	1.56 .77	.94 .30	.54 nil	1.38 nil
1967-1968E % increase in E/S	2.33%	(28.8%)	11.9%	9.1%	52%	(21%)	32%	15%	(6.4%)

256

Net Sales: 1968E (000)	22,441	111,596	36,626	18,391	86,500	20,000	42,000	n.a.	36,000
1967	21,594	88,389	29,803	19,194	68,432	18,500	37,150	55,548	33,000
1966	17,084	66,701	21,120	15,720	68,300	17,440	26,562	36,621	26,000
1965	17,800	56,914	23,844	16,440	77,621	17,600	32,517	22,621	27,450
1964	18,334	49,062	21,420	17,120	63,900	17,370	26,762	11,560	19,575
1963	14,838	39,599	15,110	14,330	54,625	16,620	25,837	8,746	15,225
Compound Annual Growth Rate (1963-1967)	10.7%	18.1%	15.2%	8.1%	6.6%	2.9%	9.0%	60.3%	22.6%
1967-1968 % increase (decrease)	3.8%	26.0%	22.9%	(4.2%)	10.5%	8.1%	13.1%	n.a.	9.1%
Net Income: 1968E: (000)	2,451	5,145	1,301	1,952	4,339	1,400	2,500	2,988	2,500
1967	2,612	4,400	953	2,470	2,873	1,300	2,321	3,895	937
1966	1,525	3,544	994	1,921	3,065	638	1,130	2,973	1,375
1965	2,225	2,646	1,155	2,010	3,038	1,025	1,686	1,039	1,500
1964	2,557	2,116	1,044	2,056	2,526	1,010	1,615	509	975
1963	1,678	1,929	979	1,556	1,071	717	1,469	423	650
Compound Annual Growth Rate (1963-1967)	19.8%	23.1%	(.8%)	6.2%	35.0%	26.3%	21.6%	85.5%	16.0%
1967-1968 % increase (decrease)	6.1%	16.0%	36.5%	(20.6%)	51.3%	7.6%	7.7%	(23.3%)	60.0%
Capitalization (000)									
Debt	1,225	8,274	2,800	—	10,200	405	11,250	3,683	2,200
Preferred	—	—	—	—	3,725	—	—	112	—
Common & Surplus	10,400	39,336	11,722	10,826	30,400	13,411	24,483	18,938	10,446
Total	13,065	47,610	14,522	10,826	44,325	13,816	35,733	22,778	12,646
Book Value/Share	8.00	6.48	9.86	8.44	21.15	28.34	15.14	6.50	8.35
Market as % of Book Value	325%	510%	203%	179%	184%	103%	116%	396%	—

Note: In this and in the following exhibit, the schedule has been updated to include Widgets' actual 1967 figures as well as 1968 estimated figures discussed later on in this chapter.

257

slightly. If we assume that this government business does not involve a great deal of expense, then all the rest of this has been going to their own products. And in 1966 only 46% of their sales were commercial. It would seem that their selling and administrative expenses are too high for their proprietary products.

Peter: Not at all, Sid. In fact, I asked John about this very same thing and he stated that most of those increasing expenses can be attributed to additional selling costs in 1962, representing an increase in Widgets' sales force and a new advertising program for their commercial products in the trade journals. Actually, except in 1966, there's been a corresponding increase in proprietary sales.

Sid: Let's look at this decrease in sales and earnings in 1966 a little more closely to see whether this should be a point of concern. Widgets attributes the decline to an unforeseen delay in the fourth quarter of 1966 of a congressional appropriation for a defense contract on which the company had been counting heavily, and to a slowdown of industrial orders for instrumentation systems during the credit squeeze. I know there's an old adage which states you shouldn't compare yourself to the worst, but if you look at this Comparative Pricing Schedule which Peter has prepared, you'll notice that this decrease in earnings and sales was pretty much of an industry-wide phenomenon in 1966.

Alex: What strikes me is not only the size of the earnings, but also the fact that earnings *have* fluctuated. This company is moving into the production of glamour products, and will have to compete with growth companies. Now, looking at these earnings, I wouldn't classify this company as a growth company.

Peter: Well, Alex, in a company such as this one—where 8% of earnings is applied to R&D, and in an industry in which

258

Exhibit II. Comparative Income Statement of Widgets

		1963	1964	1965	1966	1967	Six Months 1968
Gross sales less returns and allowances (000)		15,225	19,575	27,450	26,800	33,000	18,000
Cost of goods sold		10,575	13,575	19,275	18,800	25,100	12,150
Net sales		4,650	6,000	8,175	8,000	7,900	5,850
Selling and administration expenses		3,250	3,975	5,025	5,087	6,100	4,275
Income before federal income tax		1,400	2,025	3,150	2,913	1,800	1,575
Provision for federal income tax		750	1,050	1,650	1,538	963	825
Net income for period		650	975	1,500	1,375	937	750
Retained earnings beginning of period		2,100	2,725	3,675	5,087.5	6,375	7,237
Addition from net earnings		650	975	1,500	1,375	937	750
Less dividends paid		(25)	(25)	(87.5)	(87.5)	(75)	–
Addition to capital surplus		625	950	1,412.5	1,287.5	862	750
Retained earnings end of period		2,725	3,675	5,087.5	6,375	7,237	7,987
Earnings and dividends applicable to common stock calculated on 1,250,000 common shares to give effect to new issues of stock subsequently voted, July, 1968	E/S	.52	.78	1.20	1.10	.75	.60
	D/S	.02	.02	.07	.07	.06	–

Note: Years ended December 31, 1963-1967 and six months ended June 30, 1968.

R&D can be the ball game—I believe that lower earnings may be of lesser importance. The important question is: Are they a result of large currently expensed costs entailed in product development? After all, a decrease in earnings in one or for two consecutive years can conceivably be more than compensated for by a new technological breakthrough from the laboratories of Widgets.

Although sales and earnings were down in 1962, this was during the period of readjustment, when Widgets committed itself to the development of a commercial product line. And in 1966, Widgets spent quite a bit on research for the development of laser technology—its hottest item yet—and on the development of other products which has contributed to their optimism over 1967 sales and earnings.

Sid: As I see it, although in this company the potential growth in sales and earnings is tied to an element of risk in renegotiable government contracts, this risk is decreased as proprietary products account for an increasing percent of their total sales.

Does anyone have any comments to make about the management of this company? I know, Peter, that you've met the new president and other directors personally, but I'd like to avoid subjective impressions for now.

Joseph: Looking into the historical performance of this company, I must say I am particularly impressed with the managerial savvy that these scientists seem to have. You know that family is practically an institution at MIT, and John went on to business school at Harvard. That is about the happiest combination I can think of for a company—a combination of expertise in both product and management.

Peter: I'm not sure you're all aware of this, but I spoke with Ben Henderson, Widgets' lawyer, and he told me confidentially that John and Andrew have acted as the effective chief executives of this company for over 15 years. Although Wesley Hayes retained the title of president and chief executive officer of Widgets, he too has mentioned, quite proudly in fact, the contribution that his sons have made to the company.

Neither John nor Andrew will admit this, but it is important to know, as it reveals the actual extent of experience that they have had.

It was John's decision, you realize, to increase the company's commitment to standard product line in 1962, making that successful gamble of spending more for R&D and production while gross receipts from the government were off. And it was Andrew who supervised and babied along the development of their electro-optical product line.

The rest of the management team appears to have sufficient depth and staying power, I might add. All executive officers have been employed by the company for more than eight years.

Another plus is that while conducting an on-going R&D program, they have kept the company in a financially sound condition. Aside from the original capital of the company, all subsequent funds used to finance Widgets' growth have been raised through short- and long-term borrowing and through the issuance in 1952 of $2 million of 5% cumulative preferred stock which was retired in 1957. And as we've discussed with their accountant, their debt burden on these outstanding notes of $2.2 million with Cambridge Life Insurance can be handled by their cash outflow.

In fact, we've calculated that they have a debt burden coverage of about five times, which appears quite secure. And their cash position looks like it's pretty good, too. It doesn't appear, therefore, that they'll need any additional capital for their current operational needs.

Financial Proposal

Once C&L had agreed to underwrite the issue, further discussion was centered on the type, size, and timing of this issue. The decisions made by C&L were enclosed in a confidential memorandum containing a financing proposal for the consideration of Widgets' board of directors.

C&L had stated that they would be pleased to manage an underwriting syndicate for the public offering of Widgets' stock. They would organize a broad geographically distributed underwriting group, and would themselves underwrite a substantial portion of the total offering. C&L also expressed its willingness to discuss the underwriting group with John before it was formed.

Included in C&L's summary of recommendations as to the public sale was that Widgets should authorize the issue of 1,244,000 new shares of common stock at a par value of $1, and that the par value of the 6,000 shares currently issued and outstanding be reduced from $10 to $1. This would result in a total of 1,250,000 shares of $1 par value common stock issued and outstanding. C&L further suggested that as part of the recapitalization an additional 1 million shares at a par value of $1 be authorized for future issuance.

C&L invited discussion with Widgets' management as to the price at which their shares might be sold, but considered a price in the range of $10 to $20 as desirable in order to secure the broadest distribution and best investor interest in the issue. Based on its experience, C&L also recommended that in order to maintain an orderly after-market with a sufficient amount of trading stock, the original distribution should not be less than 200,000 shares. C&L's studies indicated that the market was quite receptive to the sale of equity securities and recommended that should Widgets decide to sell the stock, it proceed immediately with preparations for the new offering.

As far as underwriting fees were concerned, C&L estimated that to stimulate the interest of the syndicated underwriters and dealers who would be distributing and selling the securities, the underwriting commission should be between 6½% and 7½% of the offering price.

C&L also suggested that prior to the offering, counsel should study Widgets' charter and bylaws, since if common stock was to be issued, the rights of future stockholders would have to be clearly defined. It would be desirable to determine the necessity of new or additional provisions concerning cumulative, voting, and pre-emptive rights; the rights of directors to adopt stock bonus or option plans; the place of the annual meeting, and so forth. In 1967, Widgets had decided not to issue further dividends; Conrad and Lyn did not think it necessary for Widgets to resume dividend payments.

As soon as John finished reading the proposal he called in Ben Henderson.

John: I've just received word from C&L that they'll handle our new issue. But I wonder if you would look over this proposal. They seem to be a lot more specific about *their* registration fees and commission than they are about the price of *our* stock.

Ben (after reading the proposal): This seems quite in order to me. They've recommended an increase in issued and outstanding shares in order to give the security a range that they think is most attractive for an initial public offering. As far as the price range is concerned, although it may seem low, think of your own investment strategy. You—like most investors—prefer to buy round-lots of 100, 300, 500 shares rather than to make an equivalent dollar investment in less than 100 shares of a high-priced stock. Many investors will also buy on the theory that a stock at a price in this range has a greater chance of appreciating in value than a stock priced at a higher level.

John: It's not the price level that bothers me as much as the whole idea of a price range. Can't they be more specific? I mean I'd like to at least be able to tell Dad that I'm getting a good price for him.

Ben: No responsible underwriter would even consider giving you a specific offering price at this stage of the game. Even if our board decides to proceed immediately with the offering, a lot of preparation time is required before any sale can be made. The preparation of the registration statement requires about a month, to which must be added time for the SEC to examine it and request us to make certain modifying amendments to the original statement. My whole point is that a lot could happen to the market and investors' attitudes during this time to upset a premature pricing scheme. What really is at stake is the future market valuation of the issue.

John: You make it sound like everything that we hope to achieve through going public could go sour practically overnight.

Ben (smiling): It conceivably could, but don't look so worried. In order to assure a successful offering and a favorable after-market, underwriters almost always offer initial offerings at a slight discount from the current market prices of the most comparable securities which already have an established public market. Certainly, C&L will take responsible action in the after-market to offset any downward pressure.

John: What about the estimates for the underwriting commissions and fees?

Ben: The same type of wait-and-see logic applies. Since the selling commission varies with the anticipated difficulty and risk of placing the issue, C&L undoubtedly wishes to evaluate the buildup in investor interest and dealer attitudes before they set a firm percentage. In any case, sufficient compensation has to be paid to stimulate the interest of the dealers, as their active interest results in a higher price and wider distribution of the stock. At this early date it is impossible to tell how much of an incentive will be needed to induce the security salesmen to put forth their best efforts to place the stock with the investors.

John: I am thinking about our out-of-pocket expenses.

Ben: The management fee usually equals 15% of the gross spread, and the underwriting profit is the amount remaining after the selling commission and management fees have been deducted from the gross spread. This profit cannot be considered as all gravy, however, for each underwriter has to deduct from it legal fees, advertising expenses, and taxes which are prorated in proportion to the size of participation in the issue.

As far as redefining the rights of stockholders is concerned, I've reviewed Widgets' charter and bylaws, and I have some changes to recommend, but I'd like to talk over a few details with C&L's counsel before we present this whole package to our board for their approval.

Unexpected Setback

Widgets' going public momentum was abruptly slowed in April 1967 when John received the figures for the company's first quarter earnings. The upturn which he had predicted had not occurred; in fact, the earnings had sagged below those for the same period in 1966. A new product which John had expected to be a large sales item had to be taken off the production line for modifications, and new machinery was required to manufacture the item.

Within the week John also learned that the preliminary negotiations with one of Widgets' unions, whose contract was to expire at the end of April, had already run into difficulty and that strike action was threatened.

John and Larry Downs visited Peter Davis at his office on Monday and revealed the bad news in detail.

John: In addition to the expense in modifying our latest gauge and the machinery used to produce it, the loss of revenue due to this strike will really make this a record year. Unfortunately, I'm afraid we'll be breaking the wrong kind of records.

Larry: What's your reaction to all this, Peter? Do you see any room for optimism?

Peter: In view of the circumstances, I can only advise you to postpone any consideration of a public offer.

Larry (hopefully): What we might do now, John, while we're waiting for other axes to fall is to plan to do a little housecleaning. Since we'll be faced with heavy costs associated with the relaunching of the product and redesigning of the manufacturing machinery, and with the pending strike, why don't we write off all these extraordinary expenses this year so that we'll have an upturn in earnings, even if it isn't reflected until next year.

John: Is this something we should think about, Peter?

Peter: Well, it is something that some firms would not recommend. They hold that losing the earnings is not generally a desirable thing to do since most investors and investment bankers assume some companies are going to do this and it's generally recognized for what it is. Certainly, if an effort is made to clean up a lot of past problems for reasons other than a public offering, it would have to be footnoted and carefully set out in the prospectus. Our firm, however, feels that this type of housecleaning is a perfectly acceptable procedure. By writing off all anticipated extraordinary expenses now, next year's operations may reflect an upturn in earnings.

Resumption of Preparations

In January 1968, John showed Peter Davis the company's unaudited year-end operating statement, remarking gloomily that the figures for 1967 were as depressed as he had anticipated. Peter, suggesting that John think about the new year, recommended that Widgets hire one of the nationally recognized auditing firms to assist its regular public accountants in handling the details involved in the preparation for a new issue.

Though John was scarcely willing to start off the year by incurring this extra expense, Peter assured him that since potential investors accepted the opinion of a nationally known accounting firm more readily than that of an unfamiliar firm, the additional cost made now would be offset by the better reception in the marketplace. Peter recommended the firm of Clinton, Ross & Alexander, which had assisted several of their former clients, and John agreed to employ them.

Widgets and C&L kept in touch throughout the early spring and carefully watched the company's operations, so that when the first quarter earnings showed a marked upturn, both John and Peter were cautiously optimistic.

In July 1968, Widgets' unaudited earnings figures for the first half of 1968 (see *Exhibit III*) made the rounds of Conrad & Lyn's investment banking firm, and several of the partners including Sid Jefferies, Alex Goodman, and Joseph Hill, were on hand to question Peter's initial reaction to resume preparations for a public issue.

Sid: This is really quite a company. If these figures hold up for the rest of the year, both earnings per share and taxes will have doubled in six years, but it still can't be considered as a real growth company with those periodic dips in earnings.

Alex: I'd watch the market pretty closely on this offering.

Exhibit III. Widgets' Balance Sheet as of June 30, 1968

(Dollar figures in thousands)

Current Assets:			
Cash			$ 489
Marketable securities			243
Receivables:			
Customer		$3,551	
Other		190	
		$3,741	
Less: Allowances for bad debts		60	
			3,681
Inventories			8,887
Prepaid expenses			199
Total current assets			13,499
Property and equipment:			
Buildings		2,453	
Machinery and equipment		3,657	
Office furniture & other equipment		987	
Leasehold improvements		292	
		7,389	
Less: Accumulated depreciation and amortization		3,416	
		3,973	
Land		480	4,453
Total Assets			$17,952
Current Liabilities:			
Unsecured bank loans and current installments on long-term notes			$ 682
Accounts payable			1,444
Accrued expenses:			
Salaries, wages, and vacation pay			569
Other			724
Federal income tax			1,885
Total current liabilities			5,304
Unsecured notes, 5½%, excluding current installments			2,202
Stockholders' equity			
Common stock, par value $1 per share			
Authorized: $2,250,000			
Issued and outstanding: 1,250,000		$1,250	
Contributed capital		1,209	
Retained earnings		7,987	10,446
Total Liabilities			$17,952

If this company were to have the earnings and sales increases which the real market leaders have, an issue could still do pretty well even in a falling market. But with this uneven growth record, I don't know. Because the company can explain the dips in its earnings, it would probably do pretty well in a rising market, but run into trouble in a falling one.

Joseph: Frankly, I'm not too sure whether we should proceed. That decrease in 1967 really makes 1966 and 1965 earnings look like the exception rather than the rule. Maybe we should postpone for another year. If Widgets is the growth company you think it is, it will be even better in later years.

Peter: On the contrary, since Widgets can adequately explain the extraordinary expenses which caused the decrease in its earnings, I think there's no reason to worry. Besides, there are too many compelling reasons to go ahead with the issue. In the first place, the market is bullish, it looks like it's going to stay that way, and I'm sure we all agree that it will be necessary to offer this issue in a bull market. Secondly, and very important, is the fact that Widgets is going to use the proceeds of this offering for the expansion and modernization of its facilities. In other words, to act like a growth company in the next few years, Widgets needs this money to do it.

On June 8, Peter called John to inform him that C&L was recommending the immediate resumption of preparation for an issue, and that he also wanted to stop by John's office and drop off several copies of the time schedule which his staff had prepared (see *Exhibit IV*).

Peter further explained that the time schedule was arranged around the certification date of the required financial statements, and that the auditors had promised to complete their examination of the figures for the first half of 1968 by August 23. Therefore, if the registration statement were filed before

269

Exhibit IV. Time Schedule in Preparation for Widgets' Initial Offering

Date	Matter	Responsibility
June 10-11, 1968	Meeting to discuss proposed financing and preparation of registration statement.	Corporate management and counsel with underwriters and counsel.
June 12–July 12	Collection of information.	Corporate management and counsel.
	Interviews with company officers, and preparation of memoranda regarding history of company and its operations.	Corporate management and employees.
July 15-25	Preparation of prospectus (exclusive of financial statements) and other portions of registration statement from material forwarded by company.	Corporate counsel and underwriters' counsel.
July 25–August 5	Mimeographed draft of registration statement to be mailed to all parties.	Corporate counsel and underwriters' counsel.
August 9	Mimeographed draft of signature pages of registration statement to be approved by telephone and printed in final form.	Corporate counsel and underwriters' counsel.
August 23	Audit as of June 30, 1968 to be completed and financial statements to be furnished to printer.	Corporate accounting firm.
	Registration statement to be sent to printer for first page proofs.	Corporate counsel.
August 26–September 5	First page proofs of registration statement to be corrected and new proof pages obtained.	Corporate counsel and underwriters' counsel.
September 10	Registration statement in final form to be printed and signature pages to be signed.	Corporate directors, counsel, and accounting firm.
September 13	Registration statement to be filed with SEC in Washington, D.C.	Corporate counsel.

Date	Matter	Responsibility
September 13	Preliminary Blue-Sky survey to be distributed.	Underwriters' counsel.
	Underwriters' questionnaire to be distributed.	Underwriters' counsel.
October 1	Telegraphic delaying amendment to be filed with the SEC.	Corporate counsel.
October 21	Letter of comments to be received from SEC.	Corporate counsel.
October 21-25	Preparation of first amendment to registration statement.	Underwriters' counsel.
October 24	Underwriters due diligence meeting to be held in New York City.	Corporate management and underwriters.
October 25 (Friday)	First amendment to registration statement to be filed with letter requesting acceleration of effective date and information on distribution of pro liminary prospectus.	Corporate counsel.
October 29 (Tuesday)	Blue-Sky resolution to be adopted; agreement on initial public offering price, underwriting commission and other terms of sale; filing of Amendment No. 2 (price amendment) to be authorized; and execution of underwriting agreement to be authorized.	Corporate directors and underwriters.
October 30 (Wednesday)	A.M. Signing of underwriters agreement; price agreement to be filed.	Underwriters.
	P.M. SEC to declare registration statement effective.	
	Final Blue-Sky survey to be distributed.	Underwriters' counsel.
October 31 (Thursday)	Advertisements to be published and public offering to be commenced.	Corporate counsel.
November 8 (Friday)	Closing.	

September 30, the audited half-year balance sheet would be within 90 days of the date of filing.

Organizing the Syndicate

In July 1968, Widgets' board met and adopted the plan of refinancing which Peter Davis had suggested in his memorandum of the preceding year. Then, later that same month, Peter Davis again met with John for the purpose of introducing Kenneth Aldridge, his C&L partner in charge of syndication.

Ken: Now that the offering is progressing toward a final issue date, my function is to assist Peter in setting a final price and to form an underwriting syndicate which will do the best job possible of selling your security when the offering is made.

John: Let me remind you that the spread has all along been estimated at 6½% to 7½%. At this point in time, could you give me a more precise idea of what the final spread will be?

Ken: Although the market has traditionally provided a good reception for issues from your industry, it is still too early to tell how much of an incentive we will have to give to the underwriters who will place the issue. The best I can do, John, is to assure you that the gross spread will still be within the original 6½% to 7½% estimate.

John: Fair enough. Now let me ask you when you plan to begin organizing your syndicate.

Ken: I prefer to wait to see which firms have sufficient interest to approach C&L for participation in the issue. Once the registration statement has been filed and the newspaper reports come out, offers of participation should follow pretty quickly—if they are to be made at all. In the meantime, of course, I'll draw up a list of the syndicate underwriters and the size of the participation they have been offered. Then, with your approval, we'll begin the actual contacts.

Influential Factors

On September 20, a week after the registration statement had been filed, Kenneth Aldridge contacted John. As Ken had suspected, since Widgets was a well-known and respected name in a field which had been glamorized by the investing public, almost all of the underwriting firms included on his own list had contacted him and expressed their desire to participate in the offering.

Ken explained that several different factors had influenced his decision in organizing the syndicate. Major positions in the offering had been granted eight large nationally recognized firms, which might be considered to form the base of the syndicate pyramid. Because of the size, number, and success of previous issues which these firms originated or participated in, and because of their proven placing power, they had won respected reputations among investors that would lend prestige to the Widgets' offering.

Also included in the syndicate pyramid were 20 other smaller firms whose distribution facilities and geographic positions were vital to the successful placement of the issue. Their respective sizes of participation had been determined by such traditional factors as the amount of invested capital, number of salesmen employed, number of years in the business, and their success in previous participations.

In addition to the syndicate, Ken told John that he had also prepared another list of underwriters and brokers who wanted to receive blocks of Widgets' stock from the syndicate when the issue took place. Some of the original members of the syndicate, who wanted a larger participation in the issue than originally offered to them, had also asked to be included in this group.

On October 1, Ben Henderson filed a telegraphic delaying

amendment with the SEC, and on Ocotober 21 Widgets received the SEC's letter of comments. The requested corrections of the registration statement were relatively minor, and agreement on modification of the statement to conform to the requested changes was accomplished by Widgets' and C&L's counsel at several conferences. The modifications were filed as the first amendment to Widgets' registration statement on Friday, October 25.

Once the first amendment had been filed, clearance of the registration statement by the SEC was expected to follow quickly and the subsequent public offering to occur sometime during the following week.

For several months, Ken had been following the market closely, charting the performance of several recent new issues of unlisted securities and of industry leaders (see *Exhibit V* and *Exhibit VI*). Although the rally which had begun in April 1968 had peaked out in July, Ken saw the market make a comeback during late August and rally again in September and in the early weeks of October.

From a 1968 high of 923.72 reached on July 15, the Dow Jones industrial level had dipped to 839.27 on August 18. During September and October, however, it had recorded significant increases and on October 18 it hit 967.49. Ken had also been following the level of the National Quotation Bureau's index of 35 industrial issues traded over-the-counter. This index had risen from 394.80 recorded on August 16, 1968 to 419.29 on October 13.

Although Ken was fairly confident of the reception that the Widgets offering would receive, during the week of October 17 to 23, he telephoned members of his underwriting syndicate to learn how many "indications of interest" they had received from clients. As Ken had anticipated, the underwriters were

Exhibit V. Recently Offered Over-the-Counter Equity Issues

	Offering Dated	*Offering Price*	*October 22 Bid Price*
July			
Aydin Corporation	July 25	15	21
Bonanza International Corp.	July 11	6½	35
Camel Manufacturing Co.	July 25	9	16
Wallace Company, Inc.	July 31	9¾	15⅛
Holobeam, Inc.	July 11	12½	31½
August			
Geosciences Instrument Corp.	August 1	10	12½
Hach Chemical Co.	August 15	13	23¼
Information & Communication Applications, Inc.	August 16	4	7½
Conel Corp.	August 13	12	13⅝
Data Technology Corp.	August 27	14	33½
URS Systems Corp.	August 1	20	36¼
September			
Frequency Electronics, Inc.	September 20	9¼	14¼
Leigh Products, Inc.	September 19	16	27¾
Electro-Powerpacs Corp.	September 19	8	8¼
Electronic Data Systems Corp.	September 12	16½	30½
Vetco Offshore Industries Inc.	September 19	14½	21¼
Vega Precision Laboratories	September 19	13½	15½
October			
Cox Cable Communications	October 3	15	23¼
Sequential Information Systems, Inc.	October 8	12½	24
National Systems Corp.	October 8	48¾	51¼
MNP Electro-Systems Corp.	October 10	15	20½
Seshon Fabrics, Inc.	October 14	12	14¾

experiencing a solid demand for Widgets' stock and no problems were expected to develop.

Establishing the Price

By Friday afternoon October 25, Widgets' management was quite anxious to have a final price set for their stock. Ken and

Exhibit VI. Daily Market Quotes for Industry Leaders

		RRC	JEC
August	12	93¼	72
	13	95⅛	72⅞
	15	95¼	73⅝
	16	96¼	73⅛
	19	98	73¾
	20	97	74½
	22	95¼	74½
	23	93¾	75½
	26	93¼	75¼
	27	95	76
	29	95⅞	76⅝
	30	96½	77¼
September	3	98¾	77⅜
	5	98⅞	77⅝
	6	101⅝	78½
	9	101⅝	78¼
	10	102¾	78⅞
	12	101½	78¼
	13	103¾	79¼
	16	103⅜	79
	17	105	79⅞
	19	104½	79⅞
	20	105	80
	23	104⅝	80½
	24	105¼	80¾
	26	106⅛	81
	27	106⅞	81¾
	30	105⅞	82
October	1	105¾	83¼
	3	105⅛	83¼
	4	105⅞	83¾
	7	107⅛	85
	8	106¼	85¼
	10	106¾	85⅞
	11	106½	86¼
	14	106⅝	86½
	15	105⅞	87
	17	106⅛	87½
	18	106¼	87
	21	107	87⅞
	22	107¼	88¼
	24	107⅞	88¾
	25	108¼	88¾

276

Peter, however, argued that they wished to review the available data once more over the weekend before deciding on a firm price recommendation. They also urged John to think about the price he'd like to see the stock offered at.

John agreed and took copies of the Comparative Price Schedule, Widgets' most recent financial statements, and C&L's charts on recent market activity to study over the weekend.

On Saturday night, John, Tom, Andrew, Mike, Ben, and Larry met to discuss the pricing of Widgets' stock.

John: Now that we have all had a chance to study the figures, let's try to look at this as objectively as possible.

Larry: How about starting off with a price equal to our book value of $8.35?

Andrew (*sarcastically*): That's a good place to start. We'll have nowhere to go but up.

Tom: I really think that is way off. A price in this range would indicate a vote of no confidence in the future of the company.

Mike: I agree with you, Tom. A price of $8.35 would give us a P/E ratio of approximately 7, based on our estimated 1968 earnings, and this is quite a bit below the industry average of 16.7. As far as I'm concerned, our compounded annual growth rate in both sales and earnings—which seems pretty good to me—argues against setting a price below $10.

Larry: Trying to be very objective about this thing, I'm not sure as an investor that I would want to pay much more than $10 a share for stock in this company.

John: On an earnings basis?

Larry: Yes, on an earnings basis. Frankly, I'm very pessimistic about our 1967 earnings and somewhat suspicious of the optimistic earnings report for our first six months of 1968. In view of the fluctuations in earnings during the past years, I

277

am far from convinced that the second half of 1968 will even be as good as the first half.

I'm a little apprehensive of the fact that so much of our business is basically tied in with the government and defense, especially now when public opinion is so much against continuing the war in Vietnam.

John (*defensively*): But we are diversifying and building up our commercial product line.

Ben: You can't argue with every potential investor, John.

Larry: Now, wait a minute. Our EPS average for 1963 to 1967 is only $.87, and even assuming a P/E multiple of 10, that gives us a price of $8.70, which is still well under $10.

John: How do you see it, Andrew?

Andrew: In a much better light, basically. Instead of basing my pricing decision either on our 1968 estimated earnings or on our low earnings of 1967, I have used earnings for the last 12 months. This includes about $.60 a share during the first six months of 1968 and, assuming our earnings were evenly distributed over 1967, I add half of $.75 or, say, $.38 to come up with average earnings of about $1. Using a multiple of 10, I arrive at a price of $10.

However, I wouldn't stop here. In looking over our company, I see an indication of great promise. It's aggressive, its product line is diversified, and its research projects show great payoff potential. Looking at the sales record, which has a very high compound annual growth rate for 1963 to 1967, I would price our issue in the $12 to $14 range.

Mike: I agree with you, Andrew. I think a P/E multiple of about 11¾ applied to our 1968 earnings is logical, so that a price of about $14 makes sense. I really can't explain why, but the feel and smell of this price range seems right.

Ben: I'll go along with Andrew and Mike, too. This price

puts us roughly in line with the companies which we resemble most in the industry and, I think, takes into account the fact that we are not issuing dividends. In a slower market, I would recommend a lower multiple and price, but the market will carry this very well.

John: Good. Let's see what Ken and Peter come up with on Monday.

Last-Second Adjustment

On Monday, Widgets' management learned that Ken and Peter wanted to offer the stock at $14.75 a share.

Peter: We think Widgets most closely resembles NRUB and CNA, and so we have attempted to adjust the pricing of your issue accordingly. We have taken into consideration that both these companies are issuing dividends, and also the fact that they do have an established market. And although it is customary to calculate about a 10% underpricing in a new issue, in this bull market we have shaved that figure a bit.

John (*smiling*): That's quite agreeable with us.

Ken: We also have checked with our syndicate members and we have come to the conclusion that a gross spread of 7% is appropriate.

Peter: What this means is that instead of receiving $14.75 per share, your company will net $13.72 on each share of stock. With an offering of 230,000 shares, you'll thus net approximately $3,150,000.

John: It sounds good.

On Tuesday October 29, the Widgets' board of directors formally authorized the filing of the price amendment and the execution of the underwriting agreement. The next morning, the underwriters agreement was signed, and the price amendment filed with the SEC in Washington, D.C. In the afternoon, the SEC declared the registration statement effective.

John: We're off. Let's see how well things go.

Six days later, on November 5, 1968 the books were closed on Widgets' completely sold-out offering.

17

ALLAN KRAMER
MONROE B. SCHARFF
JOHN S. R. SHAD

Major Considerations After Going Public

The purpose of this chapter is to present three points of
view regarding what happens after a closely held company has
executed the first public offering of its security. Mr. Kramer
leads off with a discussion of *legal obligations*, Mr. Scharff then
examines the *public relations opportunities and requirements*,
and Mr. Shad concludes with the *investment banking services*
provided in the after-market.

—The Editor

Legal Obligations

There are a number of purely legal obligations that a public
company has with respect to filing and other matters which
simply do not apply to a private company.

Mr. Kramer is a Partner in the New York law firm of Shea Gallop Climenko
& Gould; Mr. Scharff is President of Monroe B. Scharff & Company, Inc., a
financial public relations firm with offices in New York and Los Angeles; and
Mr. Shad is Executive Vice President of the investment banking and brokerage
firm of E. F. Hutton & Company, Inc.

SEC Forms

First, there are reports that must be filed with the Securities and Exchange Commission. Every company that has had a registered offering must thereafter file three types of reports or SEC forms, including an annual, a semiannual, and a "when occurring" report.

The annual report is SEC Form 10-K, which must be filed within 120 days after the end of the fiscal year. This is a relatively simple form for the most part. It consists of eleven items that must be answered specifically. Some of these are mechanical—such as the number of stockholders as of a recent date; the list of the directors, and their stock holdings; the compensation of certain officers; and so forth. It would be unusual to find any problem of a substantial nature in preparing this portion of Form 10-K. However, it also requires that you include audited financial statements for the prior fiscal year, prepared in substantially the same manner and detail as those included in the registration statement.

The semiannual report is SEC Form 9-K, which must be filed within 45 days after the first six-month period of the year, but not after the end of the fiscal year. This is purely financial, and really very simple. It requires in essence an unaudited statement of sales, net income, and earnings per share. It consists of ten items, some of which are applicable in certain cases and not in others, with an opportunity to make explanations, if necessary, to clarify the figures.

The "when occurring" report is SEC Form 8-K, which must be filed by the 10th day of the month following the month in which any of the events required to be reported have occurred. The particular kinds of events that require a Form 8-K are such things as material changes in corporate capitalization, commencement of or changes in material litigation, and acquisitions or dispositions of a material amount of assets.

There is another kind of registration required of public companies in certain instances other than registration under the Securities Act of 1933. We have used the term "registration" as applicable to stock for sale. What I am now referring to uses the same word, "registration," but in an entirely unrelated manner. This is registration under the Securities Exchange Act of 1934.

Strictly speaking, the requirement for registration under the 1934 Act depends on the number of stockholders you have and on the amount of your assets. It is not directly related to the fact that you have had a public offering of your stock.

Under existing law, any company with 500 or more stockholders of record and total assets of $1 million or more is required to register. The computation is on the basis of total assets, not net worth. Liabilities are ignored.

This entirely different type of registration is by and large a question-and-answer sort of thing. It is filed only with the SEC and is not required to be delivered to stockholders.

Additional Requirements

Once a company has registered under the Securities Exchange Act, certain additional obligations are incurred that companies which do not register never have. These apply in two areas:

Proxy Statements. Prior to a stockholders' meeting, a proxy statement must be furnished to each stockholder briefly explaining the issues to be voted on at the meeting. These statements may vary in appearance and size, but each must include certain specified information under the rules of the SEC. That information is to be circulated to stockholders in advance of a meeting both to solicit their consent and to ensure that they have the facts at hand on which to base their decision to vote. A proxy statement must be filed with the SEC in preliminary form before it can be used. The process is roughly similar to the processing of a prospectus.

'Short Swing' Profits. The other requirement for companies registered under the Securities Exchange Act is that all directors, officers, and others who own 10% or more of the corporate stock must report monthly changes in their ownership of that stock. Moreover, they must also account to the issuer for any profits realized by them from any purchase and sale, or sale and purchase, of that stock within any period of less than six months.

The relevant portions of the Act are Sections 16 (a) and (b). They are very important and any company going public should be thoroughly familiar with them. Once it is incurred, there is no defense for liability for "short swing" profits. I urge you to have this fact in mind if and when you ever become subject to it.

Insider Information. My final point regarding what happens when you become public is even more of a general nature, and all I shall do is caution you to keep it in mind. That is liability for misuse of inside information at the expense of your outside stockholders, generally incurred under Rule 10 (b) (5) of the Securities Exchange Act.

The rule, if you read it, appears to be innocent enough. It states in general terms that you must not use any scheme to defraud in connection with the purchase or sale of a security. However, the way in which this rule has often been interpreted covers a multitude of things—and not only sins.

Generally speaking, it applies to the insiders in a company (a) who purchase stock from outsiders without disclosing valuable information that they alone know which might make the stock actually worth more than they are paying for it, or (b) who sell stock to outsiders at prices higher than they would be likely to get if the outsiders had access to that same information.

This has nothing to do with registration under the Securities Act. If you are an insider, and you have some inside information about your company of a material sort which might affect the judgment of either the buyer, if you are selling, or the seller, if you are buying, there can be a substantial risk of liability to you as a result.

In summary, I strongly recommend that you keep in mind Rule 10 (b) (5) regarding insider trading and Section 16 (b) regarding "short swing" profits as new risks when you are public. Remember also that you have the SEC filing requirements of Form 10-K annually, Form 9-K semiannually, and Form 8-K when occurring, and registration under the 1934 Act.

PR Opportunities and Requirements

Now that you have become a public company, you enter into a whole new world—one in which you acquire all kinds of obligations to make new disclosures that you never had to bother with before. If a Wall Street journalist happened to call you prior to your going public, I think you were privileged to talk and disclose information about your business to whatever degree you wanted to.

But since you are now a public company, the choice is not yours. You have to do a great number of things that were never a part of your life before.

From a public relations point of view, a number of very interesting things happen. You suddenly find yourself in a strangely different "public" world. You are now in a communications business, which is time-consuming and raises a number of management problems.

Increased Communications

As a new public company, you are competing with thousands of other public companies on the New York Stock Exchange, on the American Stock Exchange, and on over-the-counter, some of which are much better known than you and which have an active following. Therefore, you are going to have to start trying to attract the attention of the financial community, particularly the attention of the security analysts who follow your industry. And this is a vast problem.

You have to start planning for many kinds of stockholders' communications, among which is included a welcoming letter to the stockholder who bought your security in the offering. In this letter, you thank him, seek his loyalty, and express the hope that he will stay with you.

If you declare a dividend, you have to announce it promptly. You have to report your sales and earnings to your stockholders as well as to the financial community. You have to publish an annual report and a quarterly report to the stockholders. And you have to plan for an annual stockholder meeting.

You have to worry about your corporate identity. If your name as a private company was, let us say, the Icepick Manufacturing Company, which is not terribly exciting, you might wish to give a little thought to what you can do about your corporate name. For example, a company that we have been involved with was Howe Sound Company. Now, Howe Sound is a body of water in British Columbia where the company had a mine some 50-odd years ago; but a lot of people thought that this company was in the acoustic or hearing-aid industry.

So we had to change the name to Howmet because the word "Sound" was a problem.

You have heard of all kinds of name changes—Cities Service

became Citgo, U.S. Rubber became UniRoyal, Pittsburgh Plate Glass Company became PPG Industries, and so on. The name is important for you. It has something to do with your price/earnings ratio in the market, and the kind of identity you have.

Full Disclosure

Because you must make full disclosure, you have to decide on a corporate spokesman who, when phone calls start coming in and there is information to release, is prepared to be responsible for whatever statement is required.

You cannot get involved in unilateral disclosure. By that, I mean you cannot sit at your club and talk to a friend and tell him about a dividend increase or an acquisition that you are planning to make. Nor can you talk to a particularly good friend on Wall Street and tell him alone about what is going on. This is not the way it is done. You have to disclose fully and to everybody at the same time.

Again, to repeat, the kinds of things that must be disclosed fully and equally are sales and earnings. These are essential. You cannot just give them to *The Wall Street Journal.* This is not considered full disclosure.

If you are a listed company and the exchange determines, in its own judgment, that you have not fully disclosed a certain story which it feels is pertinent to the well-being of your stockholders, the exchange has the right to suspend trading in your stock pending full disclosure.

Full disclosure means coverage in *The Wall Street Journal* and the Dow-Jones, a broad listing in the trade and business magazines that have wide circulation in the financial community, and a reasonably wide distribution of the story to the security analysts of all the companies that participated in your underwriting group as well as perhaps 200 or 300 others.

287

You must reveal acquisitions. Even though the deal may not yet be firm, you have to reveal the fact when you have an agreement in principle.

You must talk about capital expansion, significant price changes in products, new products that will have an impact on the market, a new director or officers. All of these are typical things.

What happens when the analyst calls you? For the first 40 or 90 days, depending on your particular underwriting, you are restricted as to what you can say. You really cannot disclose very much, especially in terms of the future.

Telling Your Story

After you are out of the 40- or 90-day period following the underwriting, you have to be prepared to cope with questions from analysts who may call you as a result of what they have seen in your prospectus or have read about your company in the financial press. They will ask you all kinds of questions such as: How are you doing in your first quarter? How do you think you will do for the year? What about, say, your new weighing device? Are you going to make any money with it this year? Is such-and-such a division going to contribute to your corporate earnings this year?

These are the kinds of questions you have never had to answer before. They are somewhat competitive in nature in that, if you reveal some of this information, you may be telling your competitors things you have not told them before.

So you have to use pretty good judgment in what to say and in what not to say. You are not expected to make long-term projections and you should stay away from them. However, you should be candid and realistic in answering any questions. And you will have many of them.

Where to tell your story? To the business and financial press at large—*The New York Times, The Wall Street Journal,* the Chicago papers, the Boston papers, and so forth—and to a broad list of people who participated in your underwriting group. Perhaps you have had a big underwriting in which, say, 50 investment houses were in on the deal. Everyone should be called on and talked to, because they are all interested.

You have to begin to communicate with the institutional community, the mutual and growth fund groups, people who write market letters such as the *Dow Theory,* the *Value Line,* and so on. All these are news media that you have never had to be concerned with before.

If you become a company listed on the American Exchange or on the Big Board, you have even greater disclosure requirements than you do initially over-the-counter. When you get into the area of security analyst meetings, which means that perhaps you would arrange to visit a particular financial community and meet with a dozen or so people who participated in the underwriting, disclosure becomes critical. Usually, these would be meetings with security analysts who are specialists in your particular field, such as in the oil, the chemical, or the steel industry, or in whatever it may be.

You have to develop a rapport with these people so that they will begin to follow your particular security, because this —in combination with the support that your underwriters give you—is how you create an after-market for your new stock issue.

There are professional societies of security analysts in most of the major cities. If you are fortunate, you can obtain an invitation to appear before these professional groups. You will also proceed to have small informal meetings on your own with the proper individuals in New York, Boston, Chicago, San Francisco, and other metropolitan cities throughout the country. If you have an interesting technology that shows your production capabilities, you can invite these people to come in and take a tour of your plant.

The point is that you have to open up your front door of communications and make these people feel when they call you that they are going to get the answers they are looking for.

You, above all, should work in very close cooperation with your investment banker, because he is as concerned as you are about your after-market.

Building Your Reputation

It is also extremely important to start early to acquire a reputation for believability. If you make a prediction and go on record with something you think you are going to do, exceed your prediction. Never miss it, if you can help it. If you say that you think next quarter you will earn 25 cents, earn 25 cents or 27 cents; but do not earn 23 cents.

Never report things that you think are unlikely to happen, because once you do that you will lose this rapport. The people in the financial community have long memories. Some analysts are more likely to remember the things you did not do than the things you did well.

If you go on, exceed your predictions. Be candid. Disclose your good news as well as bad news. Be honest and avoid being what we call a "fair weather" discloser. If you have a bad quarter, or a strike in your plant, or a weather condition that will adversely affect your earnings, do not be afraid to talk about it.

News is not always wonderful. Sometimes if you handle bad news properly, it can be interpreted as a buying opportunity and turned around to a positive rather than a negative result. There is no need to feel that the absence of good news is a reason to stop disclosing.

In conclusion, as a public company, you will have many new demands on your time that you have never had before. But you will have, I think, even greater opportunities than you had before.

Investment Banking Services

Investment bankers are not legally obligated to provide any services following an offering. Therefore, the services they do provide vary widely among the various firms. Such services can be as important to the issuer as the underwriting itself. The issuer should therefore candidly discuss these areas with the investment banker at the outset, and review the firm's past performance of such services for other issuers.

Two of the most important services which some firms provide at no additional cost to the issuer are to make a good after-issue market in the stock (if it is traded over-the-counter), and to keep the financial community and investing public apprised of the company's progress.

The managing underwriter normally makes the primary market in the stock, if it is traded over-the-counter. A *good* primary market is one with a narrow spread between the bid and asked prices, and one in which the firm is prepared to buy or sell a reasonable number of shares at such prices. Following a small offering of say 100,000 shares at $10 per share, a good market would be 10 bid, 10¼ offered (i.e., a quarter point spread between the bid and asked prices), and one in which the firm would be prepared to buy or sell at least 300 shares at such prices, before raising or lowering the market. Following a larger offering of say 1,000,000 shares at $10 per share, the spread between the bid and asked prices might be as narrow as one-eighth of a point and the firm might be willing to buy or sell 1,000 or more shares at such prices, before raising or lowering the market.

The tendency of other firms is to spread the primary market. For example, if the managing underwriter makes the market 10 bid, offered at 10¼, other firms might make the market 9⅞ bid, offered at 10⅜. If the spread between the bid and asked prices is wide and only 100 shares can be bought or sold at such prices, it is very expensive for investors to buy or sell the shares and it inhibits trading in the stock. If the managing underwriter does not make a good market in the stock, the company does not receive one of the most important things it expected as a result of the offering—that is, *a readily marketable security.*

The managing underwriters should also keep the financial community and investing public currently informed of the company's progress through periodic research reports and bulletins. Such reports include projections and other investment considerations which are not included in the prospectus. Prospectuses can only describe the issuer's past, whereas investors are primarily interested in a company's future.

Other Services

In addition to the foregoing, there are a host of other services which some investment banking firms provide following an offering. As a result of his careful appraisal of your company in conjunction with the offering, your investment banker should be intimately familiar with your immediate and long-term financial objectives and requirements. Therefore, companies commonly consult their investment bankers concerning when to list their securities on a national exchange, their acquisition plans, bank and term loans, dividend policies, stock option plans, pension funds, profit sharing retirement trusts, etc. Most investment banking firms are pleased to provide informal advice concerning such matters at no cost to the issuer. If it is necessary for them to evolve or assist in the implementation of such programs, they are typically compensated accordingly.

Investment bankers are also often invited to serve on their client's boards of directors. However, few leading firms insist on board representation as a condition to underwriting an offering. It should be added that able directors are often a company's least expensive source of advice and assistance. Directors are conventionally paid modest fees, plus their expenses in attending meetings.

Index

295

Index

296